HISTORICAL DICTIONARIES OF RELIGIONS, PHILOSOPHIES, AND MOVEMENTS
Jon Woronoff, Series Editor

1. *Buddhism*, by Charles S. Prebish, 1993
2. *Mormonism*, by Davis Bitton, 1994. *Out of print. See no. 32.*
3. *Ecumenical Christianity*, by Ans Joachim van der Bent, 1994
4. *Terrorism*, by Sean Anderson and Stephen Sloan, 1995. *Out of print. See no. 41.*
5. *Sikhism*, by W. H. McLeod, 1995. *Out of print. See no. 59.*
6. *Feminism*, by Janet K. Boles and Diane Long Hoeveler, 1995. *Out of print. See no. 52.*
7. *Olympic Movement*, by Ian Buchanan and Bill Mallon, 1995. *Out of print. See no. 39.*
8. *Methodism*, by Charles Yrigoyen Jr. and Susan E. Warrick, 1996. *Out of print. See no. 57.*
9. *Orthodox Church*, by Michael Prokurat, Alexander Golitzin, and Michael D. Peterson, 1996
10. *Organized Labor*, by James C. Docherty, 1996. *Out of print. See no. 50.*
11. *Civil Rights Movement*, by Ralph E. Luker, 1997
12. *Catholicism*, by William J. Collinge, 1997
13. *Hinduism*, by Bruce M. Sullivan, 1997
14. *North American Environmentalism*, by Edward R. Wells and Alan M. Schwartz, 1997
15. *Welfare State*, by Bent Greve, 1998. *Out of print. See no. 63.*
16. *Socialism*, by James C. Docherty, 1997. *Out of print. See no. 73.*
17. *Bahá'í Faith*, by Hugh C. Adamson and Philip Hainsworth, 1998. *Out of print. See no. 71.*
18. *Taoism*, by Julian F. Pas in cooperation with Man Kam Leung, 1998
19. *Judaism*, by Norman Solomon, 1998. *Out of print. See no. 69.*
20. *Green Movement*, by Elim Papadakis, 1998. *Out of print. See no. 80.*
21. *Nietzscheanism*, by Carol Diethe, 1999. *Out of print. See no. 75.*
22. *Gay Liberation Movement*, by Ronald J. Hunt, 1999
23. *Islamic Fundamentalist Movements in the Arab World, Iran, and Turkey*, by Ahmad S. Moussalli, 1999
24. *Reformed Churches*, by Robert Benedetto, Darrell L. Guder, and Donald K. McKim, 1999

Historical Dictionary of Native American Movements

Todd Leahy and Raymond Wilson

Historical Dictionaries of Religions,
Philosophies, and Movements, No. 88

The Scarecrow Press, Inc.
Lanham, Maryland • Toronto • Plymouth, UK
2008

SCARECROW PRESS, INC.

Published in the United States of America
by Scarecrow Press, Inc.
A wholly owned subsidiary of
The Rowman & Littlefield Publishing Group, Inc.
4501 Forbes Boulevard, Suite 200, Lanham, Maryland 20706
www.scarecrowpress.com

Estover Road
Plymouth PL6 7PY
United Kingdom

British Library Cataloguing in Publication Information Available

Library of Congress Cataloging-in-Publication Data
Leahy, Todd.
  Historical dictionary of Native American movements / Todd Leahy and
Raymond Wilson.
    p. cm. — (Historical dictionaries of religions, philosophies, and movements ;
no. 88)
  Includes bibliographical references.
  ISBN-13: 978-0-8108-5773-5 (hardcover : alk. paper)
  ISBN-10: 0-8108-5773-1 (hardcover : alk. paper)
  e-ISBN-13: 978-0-8108-6262-3
  e-ISBN-10: 0-8108-6262-X
  1. Indians of North America—Government relations—Dictionaries. 2. Indians
of North America—Ethnic relations—Dictionaries. 3. Social movements—United
States—Dictionaries. I. Wilson, Raymond, 1945- II. Title.
  E93.L43 2008
  323.1197—dc22

                                                              2008011565

⊗™ The paper used in this publication meets the minimum requirements of
American National Standard for Information Sciences—Permanence of Paper
for Printed Library Materials, ANSI/NISO Z39.48-1992.
Manufactured in the United States of America.

To George and Zoey

Contents

Editor's Foreword

It has taken a very long time to address the discrimination and oppression in the history of the United States. And, although there is little merit in turning this into a contest, it is probably the Native Americans—previously known as Indians—who have fared worst. They were the original owners of the land and received newcomers with amazingly good grace given the circumstances, yet they were repeatedly uprooted from that land and sent even farther away from their homes, usually to land no one else wanted—at least at the time. Many of them were later relegated to reservations, which as intimated, were often not very hospitable places, while others preferred living elsewhere. Some Indians were successfully assimilated and others not, but terribly, few of them were able to preserve their own characteristics and traditions, let alone their pride. Admittedly, there were always some "Americans" who supported them and helped, at least as they understood it. But it was not until Native American movements emerged, fitfully and painfully, that more notable progress has been made. Yet, even in the 21st century, much remains to be done.

Historical Dictionary of Native American Movements deals with the story of the Native Americans, providing information that has until now been rather dispersed and hard to come by, which makes this book a particularly welcome addition to the series. The rather extensive introduction traces the history, which was hardly linear, and was complicated by the existence of so many disparate groups labeled as Indians and the various attempts to contain them, to disperse them, and then at long last to overcome some of the problems created by the earlier phases and find them a proper place in broader society. The major actors in the more recent phases were themselves Native Americans, and their movements were sorely needed. These movements—the more eminent leaders from the time of contact to the present day, the issues and causes—all have separate entries in the dictionary section. The chronology helps place the major events in broader U.S. history, while the list of acronyms should be kept handy when reading the literature. And there is a literature on these topics, one that is growing more rapidly now, although many blanks remain. Readers wishing to learn more about specific aspects should consult the bibliography.

The authors of this historical dictionary are among the more outstanding specialists. Both of them teach at Fort Hays State University in Kansas. Todd Leahy is assistant professor of history. He specializes in Colonial America and the Early National Period, emphasizing Indian history, and has written articles and is presently producing a book on the Canton Asylum for Insane Indians, which will soon appear in film as *Hiawatha Diary*. Raymond Wilson is chair and professor of history and teaches courses on Indian history and the American West, among other topics. He has written extensively, including many articles and several books, the most closely related to this volume being *Indian Lives: Essays on Nineteenth and Twentieth Century Native American Leaders*. This team has done a fine job researching a field and helping to fill a gap that should simply not exist.

Jon Woronoff
Series Editor

Preface

Native Americans in the United States, similar to other indigenous people, created political, economic, and social movements to meet and adjust to major changes that impacted their cultures. For centuries, Native Americans dealt with the onslaught of non-Indian land claims, the appropriation of their homelands, and the destruction of their ways of life. Through various movements, Native Americans accepted, rejected, or accommodated themselves to the nontraditional worldviews of the colonizers and their policies. *The Historical Dictionary of Native American Movements* is designed to provide a useful reference for students and scholars to consult on topics dealing with key movements, organizations, leadership strategies, and the major issues these groups confronted. We have tried to include major movements, but obviously, this study is not as comprehensive as we would like it to be. The focus is primarily on Indian-led movements; however, necessity dictates that several especially important Indian organizations founded by non-Indians must also be included.

Long before initial contact, Native Americans had already formed various movements to deal with other indigenous groups. These relationships continued and were obviously altered after the arrival of Europeans in the New World. Although contacts varied by circumstance, Native Americans generally welcomed and aided the newcomers in their attempts to settle in America. Many tribes believed that land was so plentiful that all could peacefully coexist. However, the European concept of land ownership brought these two distinct worldviews into conflict, often resulting in major warfare.

Native American movements provided various strategies for survival. Similar to other people, Indians constantly adapted to changes and made choices concerning their future. Strategies that worked for one nation did not necessarily guarantee success for others, resulting in major clashes in which Indian nations lost more than they gained. Indeed, re-gardless of popular misconceptions, Indians were active participants in their relationships with non-Indians—relationships that varied from In-dian nation to Indian nation. The wide-ranging nature of Native Amer-ican movements demonstrates that Indians did not speak with one voice, did not act as one group, and did not become silent in their at-tempts to preserve their way of life.

Acknowledgments

Any work of this nature owes a debt to the scholars who produced the monographs that make reference works possible. We must send a special note of thanks to the staff at Scarecrow Press, especially our editor, Jon Woronoff, for their understanding when this project took longer than originally planned. Special thanks to Lucinda Rowlands, production manager at *Indian Country Today*, for graciously supplying most of the photographs. We thank Amie Webb, former History Department student secretary, for her assistance. Thanks go to our families and friends, who suffered through our incessant talking about this book; they are the foundations upon which we build. This book is dedicated to George Moses, a valued friend and recognized scholar, and Zoey Frances Wilson, who is just beginning her life journey. As always, a special thanks to our wives, Janett and Sharon, who make everything we do possible.

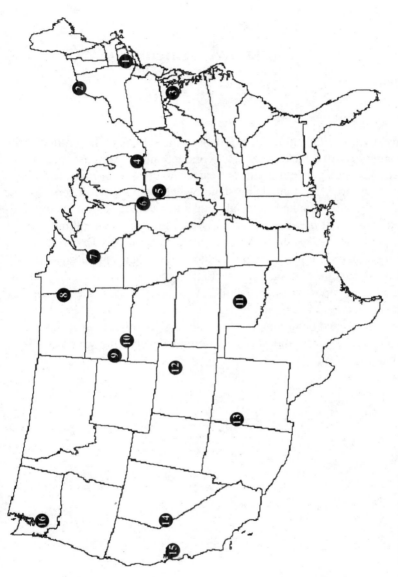

Native American Movements

MAP OF NATIVE AMERICAN MOVEMENTS

1. Ledyard, Connecticut. Pequot open Foxwoods Casino, 1992.
2. St. Regis, New York. International Bridge Blockade, 1968.
3. Washington, D.C. Trail of Broken Treaties, 1972.
3. Washington, D.C. The Longest Walk, 1978.
4. Detroit, Michigan. Pontiac's Rebellion, 1763.
5. Prophetstown, Indiana. Pan-Indian movement of Tecumseh and The Prophet, early 1800s.
6. Chicago, Illinois. American Indian Chicago Conference, 1961.
7. Minneapolis, Minnesota. AIM founded, 1968.
8. Fargo, North Dakota. Leonard Peltier convicted, 1977.
9. Rapid City, South Dakota. Women of All Red Nations founded, 1978.
10. Pine Ridge, South Dakota. Occupation of Wounded Knee, 1973.
11. Oklahoma City, Oklahoma. Red Earth Powwow.
12. Denver, Colorado. National Congress of American Indians founded, 1944.
13. Gallup, New Mexico. National Indian Youth Council founded, 1961.
14. Walker River, Nevada. Wovoka preaches ghost dance, 1880s.
15. Alcatraz Island, California. Occupation of Alcatraz, 1969–1971.
16. Washington State. Fish-ins, 1960s.

Acronyms and Abbreviations

AAIA	Association on American Indian Affairs
AFN	Alaska Federation of Natives
AFN	Assembly of First Nations
AIA	American Indian Association
AICH	American Indian Community House, Inc.
AICTM	American Indian Christian Tepee Mission
AID	American Indian Development, Inc.
AIDA	American Indian Defense Association
AIF	American Indian Federation
AIHEC	American Indian Higher Education Consortium
AIL	American Indian League
AIM	American Indian Movement
AIO	Americans for Indian Opportunity
AIPA	American Indian Progressive Association
AIPC	All Indian Pueblo Council
AMERIND	American Indian Movement for Equal Rights
ANB	Alaska Native Brotherhood
ANCSA	Alaska Native Claims Settlement Act
ANS	Alaska Native Sisterhood
BIA	Bureau of Indian Affairs
CERT	Council of Energy Resource Tribes
DRUMS	Determined Residents United for Mohawk Sovereignty
EAIA	Eastern Association on Indian Affairs
FBI	Federal Bureau of Investigation
FBIDA	Fort Berthold Indian Defense Association
GLITC	Great Lakes Inter-Tribal Council
IAA	Indian Actors Association
IAA	Indian Association of America

IACB	Indian Arts and Crafts Board
IAIA	Institute of American Indian Arts
ICA	Indian Confederation of America
ICI	Indian Centers, Inc.
IDLA	Indian Defense League of America
IRA	Indian Reorganization Act
IRA	Indian Rights Association
JOM	Johnson-O'Malley Act
LMC	Lake Mohonk Conference of Friends of the Indian
NAICJA	National American Indian Court Judges Association
NAIMA	National American Indian Memorial Association
NAGPRA	Native American Graves Protection and Repatriation Act
NARF	Native American Rights Fund
NCAI	National Congress of American Indians
NCAIED	National Center for American Indian Enterprise Development
NIDA	National Indian Defence Association
NIEA	National Indian Education Association
NIGA	National Indian Gaming Association
NIGC	National Indian Gaming Commission
NIYC	National Indian Youth Council
NLJAI	National League for Justice to American Indians
OSCRO	Oglala Sioux Civil Rights Organization
SAI	Society of American Indians
TOA	Teepee Order of America
UAAI	United Association of the American Indian
WARN	Women of All Red Nations

Chronology

c. 12,500 BCE Evidence points to human presence at Monte Verde in south-central Chile.

7000 BCE Earliest maize is cultivated in the Western Hemisphere in central Mexico.

c. 3400–3000 BCE A mound complex is built at Watson Brake in northern Louisiana.

c. 3500–1500 BCE Agriculture begins in the southwest.

c. 1000 BCE Poverty Point Mounds are built in northeastern Louisiana.

c. 800–100 BCE Great Serpent Mound is built in the Eastern Woodlands.

c. 100–300 Hopewell culture flourishes in the Eastern Woodlands.

c. 100–1400 Hohokam culture thrives in the southwest.

c. 700 The major cultural center Cahokia is established.

c. 700–1500 Mississippian Mound Builder cultures flourish in the southeast.

c. 900–1300 Anasazi culture reaches its zenith.

c. 1100 The cultural center Chaco Canyon in northwest New Mexico reaches its peak. Mesa Verde is built in Colorado.

c. 1200–1300 Severe drought disrupts Indian societies in the Midwest, Plains, and southwest.

c. 1300 Droughts and enemy raids prompt the Anasazi to abandon cliff towns.

c. 1400 The Iroquois Great League of Peace forms. The Huron Confederacy forms.

1492 Christopher Columbus sails to America.

c. 1500 The Apaches and Navajos arrive in the southwest.

1513 Juan Ponce de Leon establishes a relationship with Indians in Florida.

1519 Hernando Cortez defeats the Aztec Empire.

1520s Old World diseases become evident in America.

1523–1524 Giovanni de Verrazzano travels north along the Atlantic Coast.

1528–1534 Cabeza de Vaca and companions live among the Karankawas.

1539–1543 Hernando de Soto invades the southeast.

1543 Jacques Cartier abandons efforts to colonize along the St. Lawrence River.

1565 The Spanish found St. Augustine, Florida.

1580 The Indians begin trade with French along the St. Lawrence River.

1585–1586 The English attempt to settle Roanoke Island.

1598 Juan de Onate establishes the Spanish colony of New Mexico.

1607 The English establish Jamestown.

1609 New France allies with Huron and St. Lawrence Valley Indians against the Iroquois.

1614 The Dutch establish a trading post in Albany, New York.

1616–1619 The smallpox epidemic ravages New England Indians.

1620 The pilgrims establish the Plymouth Colony.

1622 The Powhatan Indians clash with the English in Virginia.

1633–1634 The smallpox epidemic ravages Eastern Indians.

1636–1637 The Pequot War occurs.

1643–1645 Kieft's War takes place in the New Amsterdam colony.

1644 The Second Powhatan War is fought.

1649 The Iroquois destroy Huron villages during the Beaver Wars.

1675–1676 King Philip's War takes place in New England.

1680 The Pueblo Revolt occurs in New Mexico.

c. 1680–1750 The Plains Indians acquire horses.

1689–1697 King William's War occurs.

1692–1698 Diego de Vargas reconquers New Mexico.

1700–1701 The Iroquois make peace with the British and French.

1702–1713 Queen Anne's War takes place.

1703–1704 English and Indian allies raid Spanish missions in Florida.

1704 French and Indian allies raid the British in Massachusetts.

1711–1713 The Tuscarora War takes place in North Carolina.

1712–1750 The Mesquakie Wars are fought with New France.

1715 The Yamassee War occurs in South Carolina.

1722 The Tuscaroras migrate north and join the Iroquois Confederacy.

1722–1727 The Anglo-Abenaki War is fought in northern New England.

1729 The Natchez uprising occurs against the French in Louisiana.

1734 "Walking Purchase" of Delaware lands in Pennsylvania takes place.

1742 The Dakota Sioux make peace with the French and establish trade in the northern Plains.

1744–1748 King George's War occurs.

1746–1750 The Choctaw Civil War takes place.

1750s Russian traders enter the Aleutian Islands and enslave Aleuts.

1754–1763 The French and Indian War, or the Seven Years War, occurs.

1759–1761 The Cherokee War takes place.

1763–1764 "Pontiac's War" occurs.

1768 The Treaty of Fort Stanwix is signed. The Iroquois cede Kentucky to the English.

1769 The Franciscans begin the California mission system.

1774 Lord Dunmore's War occurs.

1778 A treaty is signed between United States and the Delawares. The first treaty is signed between the Indian nation and the United States.

1790 The Northwest Confederacy is formed by Joseph Brant. Congress passes the first of the Trade and Intercourse Acts designed to regulate economic activity between United States and Indian tribes.

1790s The Western Cherokees begin to migrate to Arkansas and southern Missouri.

1791 Maj. Gen. Arthur St. Clair's is defeated in the largest military loss to the Indians in U.S. history.

1794 The Battle of Fallen Timbers takes place, where Anthony Wayne defeats the Western Confederacy.

1795 The Treaty of Greenville is signed, ceding much of Ohio to the United States.

1799 Handsome Lake's Longhouse Religion begins among the Senecas.

1803 The United States obtains the Louisiana Territory from France.

1804–1806 Lewis and Clark explore the Louisiana Territory.

1805–1811 Tecumseh and Tenskwatawa attempt to unite eastern tribes.

1807 Manuel Lisa establishes the American Fur Company at the mouth of the Big Horn River.

1813–1814 The Red Stick War occurs.

1817–1818 The first Seminole War takes place.

1819 The United States acquires Florida with the signing of the Adams-Onis Treaty.

1821 Sequoyah formulates the Cherokee syllabary. William Becknell starts Santa Fe trade

1824 The Bureau of Indian Affairs is created.

1825–1840 Rendezvous function as part of the fur trade in the Rocky Mountains. Anglo traders become established at Taos and Santa Fe.

1827 The Red Bird Uprising among Wisconsin Ho-Chunk takes place.

1830 The Indian Removal Act is passed.

1831 *Cherokee Nation v. Georgia* defines tribes as "domestic dependent nations."

1832 *Worcester v. Georgia* declares that state laws have no force in Indian Country. The Black Hawk War is fought in Illinois and Wisconsin.

1835–1842 The second Seminole War occurs.

1836 Creek removal to Indian Territory takes place.

1838 The Cherokee are removed from Georgia along the "Trail of Tears."

1845 Wildcat leads part of the Seminole nation to Mexico.

1846 The Treaty of Guadalupe-Hidalgo transfers the southwest from Mexico to the United States.

1847 The Pueblos attack Americans in the Taos Revolt.

1848 The California Gold Rush decimates the California Indian population.

1855 The Yakima and Rogue River Wars are fought in the Oregon Territory and Washington Territory.

1862 The "Great Sioux Uprising" takes place in Minnesota.

1863 The Mescalero Apaches are forced to the Bosque Redondo Reservation in New Mexico. Kit Carson wages campaigns against the Navajo.

1864 The Sand Creek Massacre takes place. The Navajo are removed to the Bosque Redondo Reservation in the Long Walk of the Navajo.

1865 Stand Watie becomes the last Confederate general to surrender.

1866–1867 Red Cloud's War takes place.

1867 The Treaty of Medicine Lodge is signed between the United States and Southern Plains Tribes.

1868 The Treaty of Fort Laramie is signed between the United States and Northern Plains Tribes.

1871 Congress terminates treaty-making with Indian tribes.

1872–1873 The Modoc War in California occurs.

1874–1875 The Red River War takes place.

1876–1877 The Great Sioux War is fought, where the Sioux and Cheyenne defeat Lt. Col. George A. Custer and the Seventh Cavalry at Little Big Horn.

1877 The Nez Perce War and Flight takes place. Crazy Horse is murdered. Government lawyers force the Sioux to accept a treaty ceding the Black Hills.

1878 The Paiute, Bannock, and Sheepeater wars take place in Oregon and Idaho.

1878–1879 The Cheyenne flee Indian Territory to return to the Northern Plains.

1882 The Indian Rights Association is established in Philadelphia, Pennsylvania.

1883 The Lake Mohonk Conference of Friends of the Indian is established in Lake Mohonk, New York.

1886 The Apaches end their military resistance.

1887 The Dawes Severalty Act is passed.

1890   Sitting Bull is assassinated. The Wounded Knee Massacre occurs in South Dakota. The Indian population in the United States reaches an all-time low.

1903   *Lone Wolf v. Hitchcock* states that Congress has "plenary power" over Indians.

1911   The Society of American Indians is formed.

1912   The Alaskan Native Brotherhood is formed. Jim Thorpe wins gold medals in the decathlon and pentathlon at the Stockholm Olympics.

1916   Charles Eastman publishes his autobiography *From Deep Woods to Civilization.*

1918   The Native American Church is incorporated.

1922   The All Indian Pueblo Council and Eastern Association on Indian Affairs were formed to resist the Bursum Bill.

1923   The American Indian Defense Association is formed.

1924   Congress grants citizenship to all Indians not enfranchised by other legislation.

1928   The Meriam Report on conditions on Indian reservations is published.

1934   The Johnson-O'Malley Act and Indian Reorganization Act are passed.

1935   The Indian Arts and Crafts Board is established.

1942   The U.S. Marine Corps establishes the "code talker" unit using bilingual Navajos.

1944   The National Congress of American Indians is established.

1945   Ira Hayes returns home a war hero after participating in the "raising of the flag" at Iwo Jima.

1946   The Indian Claims Commission is established.

1950   The commissioner of Indian affairs, Dillon Myer, announces the termination policy.

1953 Public Law 280 extending state jurisdiction to Indian reservations passes in Congress. House Concurrent Resolution 108 supports termination policy.

1961 The American Indian Chicago Conference is held. The National Indian Youth Council is formed. The Menominee Tribe is terminated.

1962 Tribal leaders present the "Declaration of Purpose" to President John F. Kennedy.

1964 *People v. Woody* strengthens Native American Church use of peyote by Indian members.

1968 The American Indian Movement is founded. Congress approves the American Indian Civil Rights Act.

1969 Kiowa author N. Scott Momaday wins the Pulitzer Prize for *House Made of Dawn*. Vine Deloria Jr. publishes *Custer Died for Your Sins: An Indian Manifesto*. Activists take control of Alcatraz Island.

1970 The Richard M. Nixon Administration announces the end of termination as national policy.

1971 The Alaska Native Claims Settlement Act is passed. The Native American Rights Fund is created. Indians create the National Tribal Chairmen's Association.

1972 The Trail of Broken Treaties march to Washington, D.C., ends with the occupation of the Bureau of Indian Affairs.

1973 The Siege at Wounded Knee, South Dakota, occurs. The restoration of the Menominee takes place.

1974 Women of All Red Nations is founded. The Indian Finance Act is passed.

1975 The Council of Energy Resource Tribes is formed. Leonard Peltier is convicted of shooting two FBI agents on the Pine Ridge Reservation. The Indian Self-Determination and Education Assistance Act is passed.

1977 The American Indian Policy Review Commission Report is submitted to Congress.

1978   The "Longest Walk" from Alcatraz Island to Washington, D.C., takes place. Congress approves the American Indian Religious Freedom Act. The Indian Child Welfare Act is passed. *Oliphant v. Suquamish Indian Tribe* weakens tribal jurisdiction over non-Indians on reservations.

1980   The Supreme Court sides with the Sioux, upholding the $122 million judgment against the United States for illegally taking the Black Hills.

1982   The Indian Mineral Development Act is approved.

1985   Wilma Mankiller becomes the principal chief of the Cherokee Nation.

1986   The restoration of the Klamath occurs.

1988   The Indian Gaming Regulatory Act is approved.

1990   The Native American Graves Protection and Repatriation Act is passed.

1992   The Mashantucket Pequots open the Foxwoods Casino in Connecticut.

1994   Representatives of all federally recognized tribes meet with President Bill Clinton.

1996   The Cobell case is filed. Winona LaDuke runs as vice presidential candidate of the Green Party. The Mohegan Sun Casino opens in Connecticut.

1998   The Mashantucket Pequot Museum and Research Center opens.

1999   Makah hunters kill a whale under authorization from the International Whaling Commission.

2000   Assistant Secretary Kevin Gover apologizes to the Indian people of the United States for the Bureau of Indian Affairs past record of "racism and inhumanity." Winona LaDuke runs for a second time as vice presidential candidate of the Green Party.

2004   In *United States v. Lara*, the Supreme Court upholds the right of Indian Nations to arrest and prosecute non-Indians for crimes committed on Indian land and that said crime is also grounds for prosecution under federal statutes without violating double jeopardy.

2007   The Cherokee Nation expels Cherokee freedmen from tribal rolls.

Introduction

"In 1492, Columbus sailed the ocean blue." This simple childhood rhyme was designed to help school children remember when and by whom the New World was discovered. However, when Christopher Columbus landed on the island of Hispaniola in October 1492, the people he met had already lived there for thousands of years. Far from a discovery, far from a New World, Columbus sailed into an old world full of diverse peoples with a myriad of cultures.

The Admiral of the Ocean Sea looked upon his hosts, and believing he had landed on an island off the coast of China or Japan (known as the Indies), Columbus called them "una hente Indios," or people of the Indies. In short, Columbus named these new people "Indians"—a mistake made by an Italian sea captain, sailing for Spain, that has stuck for more than 500 years.

After years of exploration, Europeans came to realize that they had not found a westerly route to Asia, but rather a world previously unknown to European cartographers. New questions swirled in the European mind as they began to consider the people Columbus named Indians. Who were these "Indians?" Where did they come from? And in Puritan, Massachusetts, "If God gave us this land for a New Jerusalem, why are they here?" Hundreds of years of study have allowed modern historians, anthropologists, and archaeologists to answer some of these ancient questions, speculate on others, and disregard still others. The history of American Indian peoples does not begin on that fateful day in October when Columbus waded the surf and christened San Salvador. The history of the various people who came to be known collectively as "Indians"; who greeted numerous explorers after the adventurous Spaniards kicked off a quest for empire; who lived with each other, fought with each other, and first "discovered" the "New World," actually predated the admiral of the ocean sea by some 40,000 years.

American Indian people have constructed elaborate stories about the creation of different worlds and their journeys through them. The Europeans who encountered these native peoples told their own fanciful creation story, but it was a 16th-century Jesuit, Jose de Acosta, who first postulated that American Indians migrated across the Bering Sea from Asia. Non-Indian scholars have come to regard this crossing as the final stage in human dispersal around the globe, and the Beringia migration has come to be seen as the "most likely" solution to the question of the first inhabitants of the Americas. The Beringia Migration is by no means the only accepted theory, but it remains as it has for many years, the most likely and thus, we begin our story there.

More than 1,000,000 years ago, the Earth's climate grew colder. As temperatures fell, water levels diminished and the seas parted to reveal previously unknown land. Years of submersion made these newly exposed territories lush and fertile. One of these lush landscapes was found where the Bering Sea had once been. As North American continental glaciers retreated, an "ice-free corridor" developed between two massive ice formations. This corridor opened a passageway through the Alaskan interior and into the middle sections of the North American continent. According to the most likely scenario, people followed game and vegetation through this "ice-free corridor" from Asia and thus became the "discovers" of the New World.

AMERICA BEFORE COLUMBUS

Although many Indian people believe otherwise, archaeological, dental, biological, floral, and faunal evidence supports the idea of a link between Asia and America. If people inhabited North America all along, then certainly they would have left some evidence that predated the retreat at the Last Glacial Maxim. A reading of recent and historical anthropological literature simply does not reveal any evidence of a human presence in North America prior to the Last Glacial Maxim. Thus, the most likely theory of human arrival in the New World, the Beringia Migration, continues to offer the best starting point for a discussion of American Indian history, culture, and movements.

The first evidence of Paleo-Indians living in North America came from Folsom, New Mexico, in 1927. Archaeologists found man-made artifacts mixed with the bones of a species of bison extinct for thousands of years. A few years later in Clovis, New Mexico, archaeologists uncovered the fluted-point spear and arrow tips that now bear the name of the site, Clovis points. The dissemination of the Clovis points offered the best understanding of the diffusion of peoples across the North American continent. As early as 11,500 years ago, people sharing a similar culture had a distinct impact on the environment of the continent. Despite evidence to the contrary and a verdict that is still out, many scholars see the Clovis, Paleo-Indian cultures as the first inhabitants of North America.

Paleo-Indians depended on their Clovis points for survival. Searching for the best flora and fauna, Paleo-Indians developed economies based on hunting and gathering. As skilled hunters, they decimated a number of animal species, including mammoths, mastodons, saber-toothed cats, giant camels, and other species all fell, before the spear of the Clovis hunter. The relationship between these Paleo-Indian hunters and the megafauna they followed led some scholars to conclude that these two-legged predators pushed their prey to extinction. A more likely scenario is that with the help of drastic climate warming and hunting, the megafauna became extinct. Smaller animals may have been able to adapt to the changing climate and hunting situations, but those of a larger, slower-moving, lower reproductive rate variety quickly became extinct.

New hunting, gathering, and technological situations gave rise to distinctly new cultures. In some areas of North America, people began moving away from the nomadic lifestyle of their forebears. Relying on human intervention in natural, environmental processes, these people relinquished the life of following the herd for a life that depended on the domestication of plants. The change in food source and production brought together larger groups of people who remained in a given area for a much longer duration. These semisedentary horticulturalists have been termed *Archaic peoples* by scholars.

Although new food gathering methods were in use, the hunt was not totally abandoned. A number of American megafauna were extinct; however, one species, the American bison, or buffalo, not only survived but flourished. The buffalo ranged from the Southeast to as far west as the Northwest Coast, from the Rio Grande Valley to Lake Erie and points beyond. The herds were the most plentiful on the Great Plains, but such a range made the buffalo hunt a common event in the lives of Archaic Indians. Hunters, on foot and using spears and arrows hunted the great beasts in arroyos, ponds, traps, and corrals. Perhaps the most common form of communal hunting was the "buffalo jump." Gathered in large herds, the buffalo were easily stampeded by hunters. As the massive animals broke into a terrorized stampede, hunters would guide them toward a cliff or ledge. Too huge to stop, the buffalo stampeded over the cliff providing waiting hunters at the bottom with an opportunity to harvest great amounts of meat. Pictographs dated to this time demonstrate that hunting was a communal exercise of great importance. In addition to providing meat for a newly settled community, the hunt began to take on religious connotations.

More secure in their existence, Archaic Indians developed semicomplex living arrangements based on the availability of food stuffs in a given area. Poverty Point, Louisiana, was the largest Archaic town. Settled more than 30,000 years ago, the six C-shaped earthworks that formed the basis of the town surrounded an enclosed plaza area. At its zenith, Poverty Point may have been home to nearly 1,000 people who lacked agricultural developments. The population was sustained by hunting, fishing, and gathering wild foods—feats scholars once believed impossible. Poverty Point became the headquarters for trade in North America. Archaeologists have discovered raw materials and finished goods from nearby Florida and the Ouachita Mountains and from far more distant points, like the Ohio River Valley, the Great Lakes region, and the Missouri Valley. Poverty Point demonstrated that nonagricultural people living seasonally mobile lifestyles possessed the means to develop impressive communities.

For more than 10,000 years, hunters and gatherers developed techniques and strategies for living with their environment. These hearty first pioneers had no reason to change their lifestyle until some outside force acted upon them. This time however, the outside force that caused North American Archaic Indians to change their lifestyle was not a change in the climate or the extinction of a number of animal species. Rather, the next change in Indian culture in North America would come from a tiny plant grown in the fertile central valley of Mexico. When corn (maize) arrived north of the Rio Grande, the world of Archaic Indian peoples was shaken to its core.

The earliest known agricultural production in world history occurred 10,000 years ago in the valley between the Tigris and Euphrates Rivers. In North America, humans turned to domestication much later, making them independent from development around the world. In North America, the change from horticulturalist to agriculturalist occurred over thousands of years and offered both positive and negative consequences to the people now entirely dependent on plants for their food. Agricultural production provides a predictable food source, allows for easy storage of surplus, and is susceptible to human manipulation, all making life easier. However, agricultural production also increased the sedentary nature of life. As sedentism increased, disease became more pronounced and warfare rose dramatically.

Despite the negative consequences of agricultural production, Indian people began to develop highly complex agricultural societies. The most important crops in early North American agriculture were corn, beans, and squash. So important were these three crops that scholars referred to them collectively as the "North American Triad." Scholars have determined that agriculture developed in the central valley of Mexico and moved north along the complex network of trade routes that connected all corners of Indian America.

The importance of new crops changed the cultures of the Archaic peoples who first undertook agricultural production. By the year one of the Common Era, archaeological evidence demonstrates that Indians were increasingly reliant on plant material for food. The use of stone hoes, seed storage pits, and an increased thermoconductivity of ceramics demonstrates that more and more time was being spent in the cultivation of food sources. As humans moved toward a more stable and secure food source, cultural patterns began to change. No longer did sites like Poverty Point dominate trade; in fact, the site was almost entirely abandoned. New centers of trade and agricultural production rose to take the place of the Archaic sites, turning the area east of the Mississippi River over to a cultural form scholars have termed "Woodlands" and turning the southwest over to the Anasazi.

In the eastern part of the country, groups remained spread out across the territory, especially in floodplains, but they remained close enough together to rely on one another. In the Ohio River Valley, the Adena culture flourished producing large earthworks and engaging in trade with people from across the continent. Although few habitation sites have been found, scholars know the Adena people through their burial mounds. These large complex structures tend to be located on high ground and can be seen from miles away. Although towns are not found nearby, scholars postulate that the mounds served as both burial complexes and territorial markers. Although people remained spread out during the Adena period, archaeologists believe that the increased reliance on plant matter for food demonstrated that people were increasingly moving into closer proximity to one another.

By the first year of the Common Era and lasting until the year 500, the "Mound Builder" culture of the east developed. The geometric-shaped mounds built during the period often referred to as the Hopewell culture have prompted wild speculation. Theories abound as to how, why, and who built mounds larger than the Adena culture in complex, geometric forms. The Hopewell period was marked by a continued increase in agricultural production. For the first time in North American history, a true food producing society existed as humans began to use the hunt as a supplement to readily available plant matter. As the reliance on agriculture increased, people formed sedentary villages. Hopewell houses tended to be substantial works with storage coffers for seeds nearby. In the center of a village was a large earth oven designed for steaming food. Many Hopewell sites denote long-term occupation as huge midden piles have been found associated with numerous sites. Near the year 500, the Hopewell culture went into decline. Only in the southeast, where the Mississippian culture developed, did the Woodland period come to an end. When Europeans landed on the shores of Virginia and New England, they met Indian peoples living in the Woodland traditions.

In the American southwest, at the same time that the Hopewell and Adena people were building their complex mound structures, the Anasazi people were engaged in their own building patterns. Agriculture in the arid southwest was difficult at best. The need to irrigate large sections of land and then protect that land from those looking to secure their own food supply made life in the region tenuous. However, the Anasazi people built elaborate irrigation systems, planted fields of corn, and developed a culture based on agricultural production. Commonly called "cliff dwellers," the Anasazi and other southwestern peoples, like the Fremont, built huge cities into the sides of the exposed cliffs. From this vantage point high above the ground, the inhabitants watched over their fields, protecting them from nomadic people. At some point around the year 1,000, the Anasazi seem to have abandoned their cliff towns for life on the arid landscape. Why the "cliff dwellers" abandoned their homes remains the subject of scholarly investigation and wild speculation.

Back across the Mississippi River in the floodplains of major rivers, a complex, highly organized society developed. Known as the Mississippian culture, archaeologists have discovered sites as far west as Sprio, Oklahoma, and as far north as Cahokia, Illinois. The Mississippian culture produced the most complex Indian societies north of Mexico. Subsistence was based almost entirely on agricultural products, with only small amounts of hunting and fishing being carried out to supplement an otherwise vegetarian diet. During the Mississippian period, Indians were as dependent on agriculture as any North American society ever became. So secure was the food source that social and political organization grew to its most complex levels. Ranked social groups and fixed hereditary offices with "divine" chiefs define the Mississippian culture. People owed allegiance to high-ranking chiefs, and all people in the village were linked together through economic obligations. All surplus—both food and labor—were used by the chief, and as such, large mounds, like Monk's Mound at Cahokia, were developed. Though large, the distribution of these societies across the region is spotty at best. A large no-man's-land between major urban centers with arable land like the Savannah River Valley was left entirely vacant. Empty expanses of good land denote an increase in warfare during the period. Archaeologists have uncovered intercomplex rivalries and palisades around major sites. The lack of communication and increased warfare between sites played into the hands of a new group of people in North America.

INDIANS AND EUROPEANS MEET

When the Spanish conquistadores landed on what they christened "La Florida" and launched their entradas northward, they heard rumors of major cities filled with people, food, and valuables. Hernando De Soto and his expedition were the guests of many Mississippian chiefs and the conquerors of many others. The arrival of Europeans came at the same time that the Mississippian culture had begun to decline. However, the decline of the great Mississippian culture did not prompt the newcomers to leave the area. Rather, the Spaniards, followed by the French and later the British, landed in this "New World" and sought to make claims based on the discovery of land already occupied for thousands of years.

Despite the centuries old diversity among Indian peoples in North America, Europeans refused to see diversity in Indian America. Rather, they chose to view all Indians as "savages" and saw their distinct cultures as parts of a monolithic "Indian" culture. Inevitably, Europeans judged Indians by European values. The first explorers and others who followed judged Indian peoples not by what they had achieved, but rather by what they believed these American civilizations lacked. Europeans quickly decided that despite the advances made by Indians over the millennia, these "savages" needed "civilization." By "civilization," Europeans usually meant Christianization, the adoption of European clothing and gender norms, and settling down to a life of agricultural production. The diversity of Indian life in these heady days of European "discovery" was so complex that any attempt at "civilization" without a resort to violence was doomed to failure.

Indian peoples, as has been demonstrated, had long practiced settled agriculture. However, in the "Spanish" territories and the vast interior of the continent, nomadic hunters and gatherers continued to roam freely. Even among the agricultural peoples, traditions, values, and crops varied from region to region and tribe to tribe. If there was one characteristic that all tribes shared it was the use of corn. However, the degree to which one group utilized this specific crop varied from the usage found among other people. In agricultural terms, the Europeans encountered a situation unlike anything they had ever seen before—thousands if not millions of diverse peoples using the land in different and unique ways. Despite the complexity of Indian agriculture, Europeans only saw that Indians did not pursue agriculture in the European manner. Thus, Europeans immediately labeled Indian agriculture "savage."

Complicating matters further for the new arrivals was the social and political complexity of Indian life. From matrilineal, clan-based societies to religious-based societies led by priests to hereditary chieftainships ruled by a dynastic family, Europeans confronted them all. Rather than seeking to understand Indian peoples on their own social and political terms, Europeans chose instead to attempt to enforce their will upon all Indians. The European habit of "chief-making," in which Europeans chose an Indian leader by his willingness to work with the newcomers, undermined the political structure of the Indian community. European gift-giving habits created allies in a hostile environment but also plunged Indians into a cycle of dependency from which some would never recover. No matter what type of political unit Europeans encountered, it lacked the "enlightened" understanding that their monarchies provided a civilized people.

Language was yet another stumbling block for the newcomers. Hundreds, if not thousands of dialects and languages were spoken by the more than 500 distinct peoples Europeans encountered. Even when agricultural production or political organization was familiar to the Europeans, the languages spoken by Indian peoples bore no resemblance to the languages of Europe. The Latin, German, and Slavic mother tongues had no function in America. For both Indians and Europeans, communication hampered each dealing, whether friendly or combative.

One aspect of Indian life that so confounded the European arrivals that they made a special mission of eradicating it from their midst was Indian religious practices. Indian religion found a special place in the European mindset—pagan and unknowing at best, devil worship at worst. The only unifying principle among native people, in religious terms, was the belief in a universal spirit and the development of animistic religious traditions. In an environment where everything was alien, Europeans sought to recreate the traditions and cultures they knew back home. With aliens in their midst, Indians sought to adapt these newcomers to a worldview that had developed over thousands of years. What happened as each group attempted to fit the other into their respective worldview was inevitable; the way it happened was unconscionable.

THE 18TH CENTURY

As colonization projects continued, others began to flourish and take on the trappings of permanency. Indian people of the 18th century were forced to live with their European neighbors or head off into an ever shrinking "West," hemmed in by the Spanish on one side, the British on the other, and the French to the snowy north.

Power struggles on the European continent often had a deleterious effect on the "New World" colonies. Each colonial power sought to use its plantations to spread its influence and outdistance its rivals, bringing as many Indian peoples under its sway as possible. In this battle for control of trade and world domination, the very people caught in the middle—the Indians—would suffer the most disastrous effects to their cultures and livelihoods. In the English colonies, there was the constant threat of land dispossession. Among the Spanish, the goal was to reduce the Indians to a form of slavery on the land. For the French, the goal was to merge the two groups of people and thereby create a new culture—one neither uniquely French nor Indian but dominated by the former. Regardless of European goals, they all recognized that Indians were an important part of their colonial ventures.

Europeans of all nationalities attempted to create divisions within the tribes and in doing so create a group subservient to European interests. Europeans commonly used trade to secure the friendship of various people within tribes. After giving vast quantities of trade goods to an individual or family, they would often withhold those items from other tribal members. In effect, those who sided with the European invaders received benefits from their alliance in which their tribal kinsmen could not partake. This process of "chief-making" undermined the existing tribal structure and elevated some in the tribe over others more deserving of the title. As Indians vied for access to trade items—especially guns and ammunition—they were increasingly drawn into an ever-expanding global economic system.

Driving the global economy was the collection of animal pelts and hides and their shipment back to Europe. The first exchange of beaver pelts for European trade items was recorded among the Micmacs near present-day New Brunswick. Beaver pelts harvested in the Northern colonies were very fashionable in Europe, where fur was a mark of social status. In the Southern colonies, the trade of deerskins was equally important for the production of more durable leather products. The metal tools, weapons, and utensils and the woven cloths traded to the Indians in exchange were equally sought after by the Indians and increased their involvement in the Atlantic economy. Americans, Britons, Dutch, French, Russians, Swedes, and Spaniards all participated in the hide trade at various times in their colonial histories in such cities as Albany, New York, Charleston, South Carolina, Detroit, Michigan, and

Montreal, Canada, which began as trading posts. The search for furs contributed mightily to further European expansion into Indian territories. Even in the emerging global economy, Indians were fulfilling a role that ultimately played into the preconceived notions Europeans held about them.

Europeans provided capital, organization, and equipment for the fur trade. Indians provided the labor force. The focus on hunting animals for hides rather than food undermined traditional hunting patterns and led to overhunting, in some areas to the point of extinction. Contagious diseases spread among tribes as increased European contact brought them in closer proximity to deadly microbes. New tools made Indian life easier but undercut traditional craftsmen in the villages. The development of an arms race made warfare in Indian Country far more dangerous and deadly. Even Indian agriculture was undermined as entire communities shifted their focus to the gathering and preparing of hides. But the most drastic impact came by way of the fur trade commodity, alcohol. Alcohol unleashed its ravages across Indian Country in a process that continues today. The increased involvement of Indian peoples in the fur trade brought them into closer relationships with the European powers and forced them to negotiate a diplomatic position among nations vying for control of ever more territory.

In 1689, Britain and France embarked on a series of wars that culminated in the 1815 defeat of Napoleon Bonaparte at Waterloo. In all of those that saw an American theater, Indians allied with the rival powers and fought to the death in the name of a king that barely recognized them as people. The conflicts that culminated in America with the Seven Years War but included the precursors King William's War, Queen Anne's War, and King George's War, and the French and Indian War, were often the result of European intrigues and dynastic successions that, however, did not limit the violence and bloodshed in which Indians were actively participating. Such Algonquian people as the Abenakis, Delawares, and Shawnees took the field of battle in support of their French allies, while Mohegans and Mohicans sided with the British.

The nations that found themselves occupying the lands between those claimed by France and those claimed by Britain were in the most precarious situations. Forced to play the two powers against one another, the Abenakis of northern Maine and the Iroquois of upstate New York were forced to balance their desires with those of the European colonizers. As war became an everyday occurrence during the 18th century, Indian nations sought the aid of Europeans in their battles with other Indians. As a result of these shifting alliances and nearly endemic warfare, Indian Country was left broken and battered—the scene of some of the most intense fighting of all of the colonial wars. Warfare became a fact of life in Indian communities. Ceremonial and social obligations were left unperformed, food gathering cycles were disrupted, and the burden placed on women increased as the men of the village took to the battlefield. Through the years of warfare, Indians were forced into a cycle of dependency on Europeans. As native crops were destroyed and family members dispersed, the role and presence of Europeans in the villages increased. The lack of food made Indians even more vulnerable to European-introduced diseases and unleashed a flood of Indian migrants to new lands.

When the native peoples of New England were forced from their homes after King Philip's War in the 1670s, many moved north and found security among the Abenakis. As pressure increased in Abenaki territory, many of the recent migrants were forced from their homes a second time, seeking refuge in land farther north. In 1722, the Tuscaroras, fleeing a war that bears their name, left North Carolina and were adopted as the sixth nation of the Iroquois Confederacy. Perhaps the most disastrous story, however, is that of the Shawnees. Many Shawnees migrated from their Ohio lands in the 1690s, the result of increased warfare by the Iroquois. The Shawnees moved to the southeast, especially Kentucky, and developed a close relationship with the Creeks. The Shawnees' relationship with the Creeks brought them into close contact with British traders. With a new trading partner, the Shawnees felt prepared to regain their vacated Ohio River Valley homelands. However, by the middle of the 18th century, the Ohio Country had become a virtual battleground and the home to displaced Delawares, Mingoes, and other groups seeking a reprieve from European wars of supremacy.

Some tribes split over European alliances. New communities formed as militants from various tribes joined forces to form multitribal groups, and others still sprang up as the dispossessed sought the safety that came with increased numbers. These years of systematic warfare and destruction left a mark on Indian societies. Europeans were led to construct the stereotype of the warlike and savage Indian. Indians were left to pickup the pieces of their broken communities and seek peace and security in new areas—one of those new areas being the Ohio Country.

Security in the Ohio River Valley was short-lived, as the colonial rivalries spilled over into that region in what became known as the French and Indian War, later called the Seven Years War. The battle for the Ohio Valley started as early as 1753, when the French began a building program that would end with a string of forts across the valley. Britain sent troops and colonial militiamen to drive the French out of their western backyards. Under the command of General Edward Braddock, the British moved to destroy the newly built French outposts. In 1755, as Braddock's troops and the Virginia militia, with Lieutenant Colonel George Washington at its head, moved toward Fort Duquesne at the forks of the Ohio, they were routed by a small French battalion and a score of Indian allies. Unable to stop the building of the French forts, the British embarked on a global campaign, taking the fight to France wherever it held colonies.

As early as 1758, British peace commissioners met with Ohio Valley Indians. The results were often less than the full peace the British hoped to secure. The Ohio Indians were not immune to British peace overtures. In their negotiations with Indians, British agents routinely promised that should the Indians ally with Britain, King George would protect Indian territories. The promise of a secure homeland was one that Ohio Indians could not ignore, and in 1759 peace was established. Although Britain and France remained at war, the Franco-Indian alliance in the Ohio Valley began to unravel. Britain quickly captured Fort Niagara, laid siege and took Quebec, and gained control of the American coastline. Therefore, France was unable to supply its remaining Western Indian allies, and Indians of the Ohio Valley sought out the British and made peace. The strategy of Indian people throughout the half-century of conflict was to fight to maintain their independence. As long as Britain and France remained rival powers, Indians could diplomatically negotiate a secure homeland for themselves. As 1763 drew to a close, Indian peoples lived in a new world. France, the great counterbalance to England, was gone from America.

The most damaging result of the years of perpetual war was the taking of captives, both Indian and European. Indians, in carrying out their traditional "mourning wars," carried away captives and adopted them into their societies, made them slaves, or murdered them in retribution for tribal losses. As warfare continued, a growing Indian slave trade developed. Tribes raided their neighbors seeking captives whom they sold to the British. The slaves were marched east, usually to Charleston, where they were sold to southern gentry or shipped off to work on Caribbean plantations. The most dramatic captivity was the taking of white captives by Indian raiders. Stories of Indian captivity like that of Mary Jemison or the Williams family have been recorded by historians and remain in print to this day. Among the captives, fates were varied. Women and children were more likely to remain with their captors, while men were frequently killed or bartered, and some—both male and female—were returned to Anglo society. Those who returned to colonial society did not always do so happily.

When Colonel Henri Bouquet defeated a force of Ohio Valley Indians in 1763, he demanded that all white captives be turned over to his force. Although many of the tribes relented, they reminded Bouquet that the captives now turned over, although white, were bound to their Indian families. Many of the captives grudgingly accompanied the Swiss mercenary back across the Appalachian Mountains. Those captives who returned with Bouquet either successfully escaped or suffered the harsh reality that the life they once knew was forever gone.

After more than 50 years of incessant warfare, peace was restored to the British colonies after 1763. Indian nations once allied with the French were forced to come to new trade terms with the House of Hanover, and further to the West, in Spanish held territories, Indian life changed as the Bourbon Dynasty ascended to the Spanish throne and brought Enlightenment ideas to the bureaucracy of Spanish imperial politics. The British treated all Indians as defeated people and saw little reason to empty the colonial treasuries to ensure goodwill. Indians were no longer able to play rival powers against one another and, with their supremacy secure, English settlers flooded Indian land. Conflict between Anglo settlers and Indians was nearly inevitable.

Seeking to avoid conflict with the Indians, the King of England proclaimed in 1763 that the summits of the Appalachian Mountains would form the western end of British settlement. Colonial land speculators, like Washington, launched a series of protests claiming the king had overstepped his authority and that the lands of the Ohio Valley belonged to the colonies by right of conquest. Unable to control the colonials,

British settlement spilled into the valley. The Proclamation of 1763 proved to be the first of many attempts by the British Crown to control the colonies, which the colonists ultimately answered with revolution.

British Royal authorities had no intention of keeping their colonial countrymen out of the Ohio Country; rather, British agents like Sir William Johnson attempted to negotiate land sales from the Indians to gain clear title to the lands. The violence that British negotiators were supposed to avoid erupted in 1763, when Ottawa leader Pontiac launched a surprise attack on Fort Detroit. Pontiac's attack on the British outpost signaled a larger action, and Indians across the Great Lakes and Ohio Valley united against the British. Although historians have given Pontiac credit for starting a general uprising among Ohio Indians, the fact remains that Pontiac's actions were decidedly local—his focus remained the besieged Fort Detroit. However, a generalized Indian uprising was underway. United Indian forces drove British settlers back across the Appalachian Mountains as far east as Carlisle, Pennsylvania. The Indian warriors destroyed numerous forts and countless settlements in what has become one of the most famous Indian movements in American history. To halt the warfare that raged on the frontier, British general Sir Jeffery Amherst ordered Bouquet to distribute smallpox-infested blankets to those Indians who sought peace. When the tribes of the Ohio Valley were subdued and Pontiac's siege proved unsuccessful, the British attempted to return to their policy of negotiated land sales.

In 1768, Sir William Johnson met with a delegation from the Iroquois Confederacy at Fort Stanwix. Through diplomatic cunning, the Iroquois sold huge tracts of land south of the Ohio River—modern Kentucky and Tennessee—to the British, despite the fact that the Shawnees and Cherokees both claimed the territory. Iroquois diplomats once again diverted the attention of a European power from their territory in New York to other "less attractive" territories. The effects of the land sale were disastrous in Indian Country. With the sale of Kentucky, a huge hole was torn in the Indian lands of the Ohio Valley, and numerous settlers poured into the region. Sure that the British possessed title to the new lands, settlers paid no attention to the claims of the Shawnees and Cherokees. As more settlers entered into the region, new conflicts developed.

The rush of settlers into Kentucky turned the region into a "dark and bloody ground." In 1774, Lord Dunmore's War, named after the governor of Virginia, erupted as the Shawnees attempted to stop English migration into their territory. Despite the protests of Shawnee chief Cornstalk, warriors met British and colonial forces at Point Pleasant, in modern West Virginia. The Shawnees were forced to accept the English in Kentucky and the Ohio River as the southern boundary of their lands. Before another Indian land sale could be transacted, the American Revolution ended British negotiations but not the struggle of Indian peoples to retain their lands.

THE AMERICAN REVOLUTION AND ITS AFTERMATH

The American Revolution split Indian nations the same way the war split Britain from its colonies. In Indian Country, both Americans and Britons sought allies. For most Indian peoples, the events surrounding the revolution were comparable to a family struggle—one in which Indians should play no part. Eventually, economic and diplomatic pressures forced Indians to choose sides. Left with little choice, most Indian peoples fought alongside the British. Indians recognized that should the colonies prevail, their lands were at risk of being taken from them. Thus, the best hope of retaining Indian independence was to side with the Crown.

The American Revolution brought civil wars and destruction to Indian nations. Ignoring the teaching of Deganawida, the Iroquois Confederacy split; the Oneidas and Tuscaroras sided with the Americans, and the Mohawks, Onondagas, Cayugas, and Senecas supported the British. At the Battle of Oriskany, for the first time in nearly 1,000 years, Iroquois warriors killed each other in battle. In response to Iroquois raids on the frontier, now General George Washington sent his subordinate, General John Sullivan, on a campaign to destroy Iroquois villages and burn their fields. Sullivan's army marched into the heart of Iroquois territories and laid waste to as much as possible. Washington's orders gave no quarter to the Iroquois nations, even those who sided with the Continental Army, and Sullivan fully carried out his orders. Deprived of food and shelter in the middle of winter, Iroquois refugees sought help from Fort Niagara. American soldiers marching with Sullivan wrote accounts of the fertile lands available in upstate New York. Land speculators prepared for the end of the war.

Among the Cherokees, warriors ignored tribal elders and attempted to use the American Revolution to expel Americans from their territory. In retaliation, American troops burned entire Cherokee towns and forced numerous land-ceding treaties upon the defeated Indians. In the Ohio Valley, Indians found themselves pulled by the competing sides— the British at Fort Detroit and the Americans at Fort Pitt. Shawnee and Delaware chiefs attempted to keep their nations' neutral, but efforts proved futile as the war spilled into the Ohio Valley once again. The Delawares signed a treaty with the Americans in 1787, but a massacre of a peaceful assembly at Gnadenhutten led the nation into British arms. The Shawnees tried to remain neutral until Chief Cornstalk was killed under a flag of truce in 1777. By 1782, Shawnee warriors alongside British regulars attacked Kentucky militiamen like Daniel Boone. Only in New England, where relationships with the Americans were the most secure, did the colonials find willing and able Indian allies.

In 1783, Britain recognized American independence in the Treaty of Paris. In accordance with the treaty, Britain ceded all territory north of Florida, south of the Great Lakes, and east of the Mississippi River to the new nation. Despite promises to the contrary, the Crown abandoned its Indian allies, who were not involved in treaty negotiations, to the Americans. For their part, the Americans viewed all Indians as defeated people and began the process of securing title to Indian lands by right of conquest. Just one year later, an Indian delegation visited the Spanish governor of St. Louis and complained that American sovereignty meant continued death and destruction for Indians. In a series of treaties, Fort Stanwix (1784), Fort McIntosh (1785), and Fort Finney (1786), Indians recognized the American nation and ceded huge parcels of land in exchange for peace with the newly born United States.

No longer able to play competing powers against one another, Indians were forced to negotiate with the new nation. The new nation regarded its existence and expansion as inevitable and divinely ordained and, as a result, war and treaty-making endeavors came to define the relations between the United States and the various Indian nations. Indian nations stood in opposition to the stated policy of the United States. Indians refused to give up their lands, for doing so would diminish the tribal land base, limit traditional activities, and reduce available resources. Also at the end of the American Revolution, a smallpox epidemic ravaged the Western frontier of the United States. The epidemic

killed millions of Indians. As the new nation expanded, it found a territory thinly populated. Like their Puritan forefathers, Americans believed that God had cleared the way for them by removing Indians from
the land—fortuitous yes, but Americans believed that they had to speed
the policy along.

The United States followed the example of the British when establishing Indian policy. The Constitution dictated that only the federal
government had authority over Indian affairs and that Congress possessed the power to buy and appropriate Indian lands. The Department
of War took responsibility for all Indian affairs, and the first secretary,
Henry Knox, was charged with developing policy. The United States
feared the use of Indians by European powers that still had designs on
the American interior. The British in Canada and the Spanish in Florida
encouraged Indians to violently resist efforts by the United States to secure more territory. Although Indian policy grew more complex over
time, the basic goal in the early years of the new republic was to secure
the territory between the Appalachians and Mississippi for American
settlers.

All out war against Indian nations was not a basis for Indian policy.
Secretary Knox and now President Washington were both men experienced with Indian affairs. The policy developed by these two men was
to negotiate with the Indians, demonstrate that the United States would
act as a protector by securing specific boundaries, and establish liberal
trade. Despite the best intentions of the new nation, simply dealing with
Indians was not enough as land speculators and unscrupulous traders violated U.S. promises with impunity.

In an attempt to regulate the frontier and reaffirm the authority of the
federal government, Congress passed a series of trade and intercourse
laws designed to implement treaties and enforce their provisions against
scheming whites. Through the acts, Congress declared that only li-
censed traders could operate in Indian Country and that no sales of Indian lands were valid without congressional approval. The acts were the
direct result of claims that the treaties made by the United States were
not respected by that government. However, the federal government
was unable to stop settlers on a distant frontier from violating Indian
rights. In fact, states argued that the federal government was guilty of
overstepping its authority, as the King of England had done in 1763
when striking the Proclamation Line.

In 1787, Congress passed the Northwest Ordinance, which stated that the United States would observe the "utmost good faith" when dealing with Indians and that only "just and lawful war" was grounds for an invasion of Indian lands. However, the same document outlined a plan for national expansion by dividing the territories into districts that would pass through a territorial period before becoming states. Indian nations inside the new territories quickly found themselves engaged in a "just and lawful war."

In the 1780s, Mohawk leader Joseph Brant emerged as the most outspoken critic of American Indian policy. Brant initiated a movement to gather tribes against the United States that posed a united front against further expansion of the young nation. Known as the Western Confederacy, Brant and his followers rejected all treaties signed by individual tribes and blocked American settlement west of the Ohio River. Meeting on the banks of the Detroit River in 1786, the confederacy sent a message to Congress expressing their desire for peace but stating that should Americans continue to violate Indian treaties, the confederacy would resist by force.

Efforts by the United States to break up the Western Confederacy met with little success. In 1790, President Washington sent General Josiah Harmar and 1,500 soldiers into the Ohio Valley. Under the military leadership of Little Turtle, a Miami, and Blue Jacket, a Shawnee, the united Indians routed the expedition and forced Harmar to retreat. One year later, General Arthur St. Clair was sent to the Ohio Valley to crush the confederacy. Little Turtle's victory over St. Clair's force was the greatest defeat Indians ever inflicted on the U.S. army. St. Clair suffered 600 dead and 300 wounded at a time when the military power of the nation was at its lowest. For a short time, it seemed as though Little Turtle had successfully defended Indian lands in the valley.

While the United States attempted to regroup from such a resounding defeat, divisions tore apart the Western Confederacy. After St. Clair's defeat, Brant argued for a peaceful settlement with the United States. Western leaders, particularly Little Turtle, rejected Brant's calls for peace and viewed the Mohawk leader with increasing suspicion. Little Turtle believed that after defeating two armies from the new nation, the United States would not venture into the Ohio Country a third time. The Miami war leader could not have been more wrong.

While divisiveness raged in the Western Confederacy, the United States Congress was appropriating $1,000,000 to raise and train a new army under the command of General Anthony Wayne. General Wayne's mission was straightforward: Defeat the Western Confederacy. Wayne and the new American army entered the Ohio Valley in 1794; the Confederacy was in shambles. A small Indian force met Wayne's troops and was summarily defeated. The Indians were forced to flee to a nearby British outpost. Although the British had been comfortable igniting Indian hostilities, they were unwilling to enter into another war with the Americans. The following year, 1795, Wayne dictated the Treaty of Greenville to an assembled group of Indians in the Ohio Valley. Indian land cessions amounted to two-thirds of present-day Ohio and parts of Indiana. In return, the Indians were promised, once again, a permanent boundary between their lands and the American holdings.

Despite military engagements in the Old Northwest, force was not the only method the United States used to confront Indians. Missionaries and other reform organizations believed it was their duty to "civilize" the Indians. "Civilization" often involved a total annihilation of Indian traditions and values and the forced acceptance of Christianity. Others like Creek agent Benjamin Hawkins attempted to undermine traditional Indian lives. Hawkins tried to revolutionize Creek life by redefining economic life around Anglo-style agriculture and restructuring Indian gender roles. Hawkins's program demonstrated the lack of understanding about Indian culture that existed in the early years of the American republic.

During a time of intense pressure, Indians sought any refuge. Some turned to religious movements, others attempted to accommodate their new neighbors, and others still armed themselves for further military confrontations. As the 19th century dawned, Indians attempted to negotiate another new world. Gone were the colonial powers that could be played against one another. Indian people were left to deal with one power, a power that held as its national mission the perpetual expansion of its people.

THE 19TH CENTURY

As a new century began, conflicts among Indian peoples and white settlers continued unabated. These struggles would now take on a decid-

edly legal cast as the new nation passed the Indian Trade and Intercourse Acts, a series of laws enacted incrementally between 1790 and
1834. Designed to regulate trade, establish law and order, and promote
civilization programs in Indian Country, the laws echoed the British
colonial policies that would form the basis of so much legislative action
in the early years of the United States. Eager to end the influence of
Spanish and British traders in the interior, President Washington, using
his new executive powers, called for the building of a number of gov-
ernment-sponsored trading posts in the West designed to wean Indians
off of European goods, make the Indian peoples some profit, and endear
the Indians to the United States.

Between 1800 and 1820, the government trading posts grew, but they
never flourished to the extent that Washington had hoped. While Americans offered their Indian neighbors all of the goods they needed, the
new factories failed to offer all of the goods Indians wanted. Many government trading posts stopped short of trading guns and ammunition for
hides, much to the chagrin of the Indians. However, the American Fur
Company, established in 1807, was more than willing to trade for
weapons. Rather than seek trading partnerships with the U.S. government, Indian peoples shrewdly made their own way and established relations with private traders and companies—for better or worse.

Attempting to regulate disputes between Indians and white settlers offered the federal government the opportunity to launch a series of "civilization programs." In a 1791 message to Congress, President Washington
paved the way for efforts to bring Indians into mainstream American culture by calling for a number of experiments designed to show Indians the
"blessings of civilization." Although outlined under Washington, the civilization programs did not reach their maturity until the presidency of
Thomas Jefferson. An adherent to the tenets of Enlightenment rationalism,
Jefferson believed that Indians were at a lower stage of civilization than
Europeans—a result of the isolation of the New World. With a little help,
Jefferson argued, Indian peoples would quickly advance up the civilization
ladder until they reached a place equal to that of Americans. Jefferson's
policy, despite its apparent egalitarianism, had more sinister applications,
for although Jefferson saw an America with Indian inhabitants, he believed
that first Indians had to give up being Indians. Indian peoples had to cast
off all remaining aspects of their traditional cultures, sell their homelands,
become yeoman farmers, and move west as quickly as possible, Jefferson
argued, if they wished to assimilate into American society.

Jefferson would not use federal officials to push his civilization projects; rather, he chose to turn the responsibility for Indian affairs over to various missionary groups. The missionary groups readily accepted their new position with the federal government and saw their role as the harbinger of civilization as part of God's plan. Moravians below the Ohio River Valley and Quakers in the North responded to the government's call and took up positions in Indian villages west of the Appalachian Mountains. Initially, the missionaries reported success. In the South, Creek and Cherokee men gave up the traditional methods of gaining status and sought to plant, raise animals, and otherwise become southern plantation owners. In the North, Shawnees, Delawares, and Miamis built log homes and cleared land, settling down to become the independent farmers Jefferson dreamed they would.

Growing inside of the American civilization programs were the seeds of their own destruction. Many of the missionaries were ethnocentric and demanded that Indians immediately adopt all Euro-American norms. Few of the missionaries learned the Indian languages or customs they encountered, and others chose to deride their charges rather than carry out their jobs. The most conspicuous example of the missionaries' inflexibility was the mission school that subjected Indian students to the strict, regimented education prevalent in Anglo-America at the time. Discouraged that most Indian people seemed to reject American efforts at civilization, the federal government sought alternatives, and so did Indian peoples.

In the Trans-Appalachian region, Indians faced further encroachment on their lands from hunters and squatters, despite the Treaty of Greenville. In the Indians' minds, the United States could not control their own citizens. Upset by the destruction of their old ways of life, frustrated by the failures of federal policy, and angered over the increased use of alcohol among their people, some Indian leaders sought solace in religious movements. The Senecas of New York and Shawnees of the Ohio Valley were among the first to feel the effects of such movements.

The Seneca known as Handsome Lake, half-brother of Cornplanter, led a religious movement designed to return the Senecas to their position of prominence in New York. In a number of visions, Handsome Lake claimed he received divine inspiration. He ordered the Senecas to renounce alcohol, return to their seasonal rituals, and quit sexual promiscuity, gambling, and spousal abuse. In short, he said that the

Senecas must revive their traditional ways, even while adopting some aspects of white culture, like small households, schools for children, and farming. The Longhouse Religion, as Handsome Lake's movement became known, attracted a large number of converts and provided a viable alternative to the total assimilation being pushed by the United States. Further west, an even larger movement was emerging.

Among the Shawnees, a religious revitalization movement came in the person of Tenskwatawa. Known to Americans as the "Shawnee Prophet," the younger brother of Tecumseh developed a religion that sought no cooperation with whites and demanded that Indians return to their traditional ways of life. The Shawnee Prophet was challenged by traditional Indian leaders, and even William Henry Harrison, then governor of Indiana Territory, but in each instance, Tenskwatawa and his brother used the challenges to assert the power of the Shawnee Prophet's vision. In 1809, when Harrison purchased more Indian land from friendly chiefs, Tecumseh used his brother's influence to strengthen ties with the British and seek allies among the southern Indians. Unfortunately for Tecumseh, while he was away, Tenskwatawa's village, Prophetstown, was attacked by Harrison. The Shawnee Prophet survived the battle, but his power to rally large numbers of supporters was gone forever. Tecumseh, however, sided with the British during the War of 1812, and he met his demise at the Battle of the Thames in 1813. Although killed in battle, Tecumseh and the Shawnee Prophet's message resonated in the South among the Creeks.

Tecumseh's time among the Creeks accelerated a growing rift in the tribe that would result in a Creek civil war known as the Red Stick War, which spiraled out of control when the Americans became involved. Assisted by Creeks, Choctaws, and Cherokees, the Americans attacked the Red Sticks at every opportunity. The war came to end in March 1814, when General Andrew Jackson led a well-armed force against the Red Sticks at Horseshoe Bend.

While Indians along the Missouri River and in the interior of the American West met their first Americans, Indians in the East struggled to make sense of a world where they were increasingly surrounded by whites. In the years between 1815 and 1840, five states west of the Appalachians entered the Union. The tribes of the Mississippi River were forced to adapt to a dynamic new world in which they were now minorities acculturating into the more dominant Anglo society.

Nowhere was this acculturation more evident than in the American southeast. Cultural conflicts that began during the American Revolution sped up during the War of 1812 and broke into a full sprint during the period known as the Early Republic. Changes among the southeastern Indians produced cultures that were no longer Creek, Cherokee, or Choctaw, but neither were they white, Anglo, and Protestant. Rather, the acculturation of the Indians produced a culture that was wholly unique. As the deer hide trade faded away into the forest, mixed heritage planters built lavish plantation homes complete with cotton agriculture and slaves. Protestant missionaries served as the harbingers of change, but the fluid nature of Indian cultures allowed for the ready acceptance of some white traits, while others were left to the fringes of Indian culture.

Perhaps the best example of this acculturation can be found among the Cherokees. Cherokee parents sent their children to school to learn math, reading, and geography, as well as to read the classics, just like their white counterparts. Slaves worked on Cherokee plantations cultivating cotton for sale at markets; grist and saw mills were opened; and other Cherokees became real estate capitalists and operated inns and ferries. Public roads spread across the Cherokee homeland. More significant was the newly formed Cherokee syllabary, which allowed for the creation of a national newspaper, *The Cherokee Phoenix*, as well as a national constitution modeled after that of the United States. Ironically, the more Indian peoples, both in the southeast and northern areas east of the Mississippi, changed and adopted white practices, the more their Anglo neighbors demanded.

The Indian Removal Act of 1830 was passed by Congress and quickly signed by now President Andrew Jackson. The Removal Act formed the foundation of Jacksonian Indian policy and declared that in exchange for lands in the East, the United States would set aside lands in the West as a future home for as long as the grass grew and rivers flowed. Further, the government would pay the cost of removal and support the tribes for one year after the Indians arrived in the West. With the passage of the Removal Act, white planters eager to acquire more cotton land used the passage to extend state jurisdiction over Indian lands. Even if Indians stayed in the East, Southerners argued, they were now subject to state laws.

Rather than allow states to take responsibility for Indian affairs, the federal government moved quickly to secure Indians' Eastern homelands in exchange for Western lands. The story of the removal of Indians to lands in the West is one of devastation, death, and starvation. The Cherokee "Trail of Tears" is the most often discussed, but every tribe in the southeast experienced destruction on its forced marches to the newly formed Indian Territory.

Almost all of the tribes that experienced forced removal sought to ward off the inevitable. Most of the opposition was more moderate, refusing to assemble at government camps or escaping into wooded areas of their homeland. Such legal challenges as the two famous Cherokee Cases resulted in the U.S. Supreme Court sympathizing with the Cherokees in the first instance and finding in their favor in the second. Removal continued unabated regardless of the Supreme Court decisions. However, some tribes resisted militarily. The Black Hawk War in the Old Northwest and the Seminole Wars in Florida were desperate attempts by Indian holdouts to maintain their traditional homelands and stave off the onrushing juggernaut of white America. Armed resistance movements proved unsuccessful, and numerous tribes were ultimately removed to Indian Territory.

By 1850, the United States had removed almost all Indian communities east of the Mississippi River, taking them either by force or acquiescence to lands in the West. Significant numbers of Indians were able to remain in the East, but their once huge land base was reduced to a few scattered reservations of minimal lands. The tribes removed to the West faced new challenges and were forced to rebuild their lives and societies in new territories. With the end of the Mexican War, the United States secured territory from Mexico and created a vast inland empire that stretched from the Atlantic Ocean to the Pacific Ocean.

In these new lands, the United States was determined to protect the settlers moving west. Seeking to create a safe haven for white emigrants, U.S. negotiators met with the various tribes of the Northern Plains at Fort Laramie in 1851. The Americans hoped to confine the tribes to specifically defined areas; this was a plan to not only protect settlers but also reduce intertribal conflict. However, by 1854, all hopes to avoid conflict were dashed when Lieutenant John Grattan overreacted to members of the Brule Lakota killing a settler's cow and led his command against the Indians. When the smoke cleared, Grattan and his entire command lay dead. The hopes of peaceful coexistence between Indians and whites in the West died that day with Grattan.

The American Civil War, in which numerous Indians took part, slowed the pace of westward expansion, and most federal troops were recalled from the West for service in the East. Despite the lack of troops in the West, conflict between Indians and Americans continued. In Minnesota, the Dakota, led by Little Crow, went to war in 1862 over the failure of the United States to live up to treaty obligations. "The Great Sioux Uprising" ended with the trial of 400 Indians, 38 of whom were executed in the largest public hanging in U.S. history.

Across the nation, violence between whites and Indians was at an all-time high. In Colorado, the discovery of gold brought settlers into conflict with the Cheyennes. Thousands of settlers poured into the new territory and forever changed the Cheyennes' way of life. A group of Cheyennes under Black Kettle were told to make camp at Fort Lyon on Sand Creek. As tensions rose, Black Kettle's band became an easy target for the Third Colorado Cavalry under the command of Colonel John M. Chivington. Black Kettle raised both an American flag and a white flag, but the soldiers attacked anyway and massacred almost 300 Indians, mostly women and children.

In the southwest, Kit Carson led an American command under General James Carleton against the Navajos. The campaign was merciless, and the Navajos were forced to surrender. In 1864, the Navajos were removed to the Bosque Redondo Reservation, near Fort Sumner in New Mexico. The nearly 400-mile trek killed numerous Navajos and is remembered among them as the "Long Walk." Confined to barren territory, the Navajos suffered malnutrition and disease; alkaline water and a grasshopper invasion seemed to seal their fate. After four years in the New Mexico desert, the Navajos signed a treaty with the Indian Peace Commission that allowed them to return to their homeland and reestablish their traditional sheep and goat herds. For their part, the Navajos promised to stay on their reservation, stop raiding, and remain at peace. The "Long Walk" is remembered among the Navajos as one of their defining moments—the same way that the Cherokees remember the "Trail of Tears."

Securing the West was a national priority, and the national consensus seemed to argue that the West would be the salve to heal the wounds of the Civil War. In the years following 1865 and lasting until 1890, the West was constantly aflame with battles between Indians fighting to protect their way of life and Americans fighting to expand theirs. The

U.S. army and its battles with the various Indian nations of the West and southwest was only the birth pangs of conflict. Despite Hollywood myth-making, more than military bullets went into confining Indian peoples to reservations across the Trans-Mississippi West. The transcontinental railroad was completed in 1869; spur lines began to crisscross the region the following year. Buffalo herds were systematically destroyed by order of General Philip Sheridan between 1867 and 1883. Drought brought further suffering to the Plains Indians. In the Far West, Chief Joseph led the Nez Perce on a flight over the Rocky Mountains in an effort to escape troops under the command of General O. O. Howard and reach safety in Canada; they were unsuccessful. Geronimo led his Apache band off the reservation and into the mountains between the United States and Mexico, only to be captured and shipped to Fort Marion in Florida, then ultimately to Fort Sill in Oklahoma. Across the West, the Indian people found themselves surrounded by whites and confined to an increasingly shrinking land base. Confinement to reservations was now a fact of life, but as usual, Indian peoples did not go quietly into extinction.

Militarily defeated, their subsistence destroyed, and their lands gone, many of the once-powerful western tribes found themselves in desperate situations. Many Indians, confined to reservations, succumbed to the ravages of alcohol. Others, however, sought to restore their power by turning to the teachings of men whose history stretched back to the first arrival of Europeans—men preaching a message of renewal and restoration. The most famous revitalization movement of late 19th century was born on the Walker River Paiute Reservation in Nevada. Known as the Ghost Dance, its prophet, Wovoka, preached a message of hope offering a proposition that should Indian peoples perform certain rituals, the Earth would turn over, whites would fall off, the buffalo would return, and Indians would be returned to their former way of life.

Among the Lakota, the Ghost Dance came to represent the fate of the nation. Those who practiced the ritual believed they were seeking to restore their people to their rightful place of dominance on the Northern Plains. To the Indian agent assigned to keep control of the Lakota and force them to assimilate to white ways, the Ghost Dance posed a major threat. One important Ghost Dance leader, Sitting Bull, always regarded as an instigator, was killed in an arrest attempt at his home on the Standing Rock Reservation. Two weeks later, on the banks of Wounded Knee

Creek, the way of life Indian people once knew was totally demolished when the Seventh Cavalry opened fire and massacred more than 200 men, women, and children of Big Foot's band of Miniconjou Lakota. Many band members were wounded, but they were left lying in the field as a blizzard moved into the area. The fate of Indian peoples across the nation was sealed on that ominous day; now, Indians would be forced to conform to the norms of white civilization. The reservation would become a new form of school—one built to control its captive audience and teach Indians why their culture was "wrong" and white culture was "right."

With warfare at a minimum or nonexistent, the federal government revised its Indian policy. Now, the government's focus was breaking-up tribal entities, offering a program of detribalization, and bringing Indians into the dominant culture. The new policies were championed by white reforms who styled themselves "Friends of the Indian." The policy was multifaceted, but breaking-up of the tribal land base and educating individual Indians formed the twin pillars of the new direction in Indian affairs. The Indian Rights Association, established in 1882, and the Lake Mohonk Conference of Friends of the Indian, created in 1883, supported these new policies.

In 1887, Congress passed the Dawes Severalty Act, which was designed to abolish reservations and disperse lands to individual Indians as private property. Reformers saw the plan as a way to integrate Indians into mainstream culture; Indians saw it as another way to divest them of their traditions. The act had five major provisions: 1) Each head of household would receive 160 acres, with lesser amounts for other tribal members; 2) Indians would select their own plots, but should they fail to do so, lands would be selected for them; 3) the federal government would hold the title for allotted lands in trust for 25 years; 4) all allottees were granted citizenship; and 5) all "surplus" land was available for purchase. The policy of allotment remained the cornerstone of federal–Indian relations until the 20th century, costing Indians tens of millions of acres of land. But the policy has had lasting effects on Indian Country; stripped of their tribal land base and seeing their customs and traditions under continued assault, Indian peoples were able to resist in only small, day-to-day ways, like hiding their traditional practices. Indians were now, as the title of Indian author D'Arcy McNickle's novel suggests, *The Surrounded*.

The other major federal program designed to bring Indians into mainstream America was education. Reservations, reformers argued, were obstacles to "progress"; they believed education was the key to making Indians into darker-hued copies of their white counterparts. Colonel Richard Henry Pratt, in Carlisle, Pennsylvania, founded the school that served as the exemplar of Indian education. Pratt first came to the model he would use for Carlisle when he began his "civilization program" among Indian prisoners of war at Fort Marion Florida. The superintendent of Rainy Mountain School in Oklahoma best described Pratt's model when he said that the goal was "to change them [Indians] forever." Indian children were forcibly removed from their homes, packed on trains, and shipped to parts of the nation that were entirely alien to them. Once they arrived at their destinations, whether in Carlisle or other Indian schools like it, Indians were stripped of their traditional clothes, shorn of their hair, and deprived of the camaraderie of fellow tribal members. Students were dressed in new military-style clothing, given new names, forbidden to speak their native languages, and told that the biggest obstacle facing their incorporation into American society was the fact that they were Indians. These federally managed boarding schools were designed not only to educate Indian students, but they were also established to eradicate any and all traces of Indian culture.

War and violence were now relegated to the past. Never again would Indians engage in military movements against the U.S. army. Indian peoples continued to lose large amounts of territory as the allotment process continued to sweep across the nation like wildfire. Reformers, however, had cause for hope. Those who termed themselves "Friends of the Indian" now looked forward to the day when Indians would vanish from the national landscape, becoming part of the dominant culture. Few reformers bothered to ask Indians their thoughts and feelings; if they had, reformers would not have liked what they would hear.

THE 20TH CENTURY

At the beginning of the 20th century, many people viewed Native Americans as the "vanishing race." Indeed, the 1900 federal census revealed only 250,000 Indians living in the United States out of a total population of 12,866,020. Although this count of Indians was extremely inaccurate, the perception remained that the Native American population was drastically declining and would eventually disappear. Indians, however, endured and persevered despite alarming losses in population and in lands held as a result of wars, diseases, reservation conditions, and the devastating land allotment policy of the Dawes Severalty Act that would continue for three more decades.

As the United States entered the new century, a major reform movement known as Progressivism swept the nation. At the same time, a white-educated generation of Indians like Dr. Charles A. Eastman, Sioux; Dr. Carlos Montezuma, Yavapai; the Reverend Sherman Coolidge, Arapaho; and Gertrude Bonnin, Sioux, appeared and demanded that the ideals of the Progressive Movement, calling for political, economic, and social improvement, be extended to Native Americans as well. These Indians, known as Red Progressives, founded the Society of American Indians (SAI) in 1911, the first major pan-Indian organization that was run by Indians, unlike other reform movements like the Indian Rights Association and the Lake Mohonk Conference of Friends of the Indian, which were directed by eastern white reformers.

Among the reforms the SAI leadership advocated were improved health and medical services on reservations, more educational opportunities for Indian students, abolition or restructuring of the Bureau of Indian Affairs (BIA), a thorough study of peyote use, and the granting of U.S. citizenship to all Native Americans. The citizenship issue was strongly argued, and the more than 10,000 Indians who served in World War I were often cited in the arguments as a major reason for extending citizenship because of Indian patriotism in the war effort. The passage of the Snyder Act in 1924 extended U.S. citizenship to those Indians who had not been granted citizenship status by way of treaty provisions or other legislation. However, citizenship did not guarantee improvements in Indian political, economic, or social rights. For example, Indians could not vote in New Mexico or Arizona until after World War II. Such issues as peyote use and the effectiveness of the BIA were controversial subjects that weakened and divided the SAI and ultimately led to the demise of the organization. At the same time the SAI movement was advocating reforms, elsewhere, native people in Alaska organized the Alaska Native Brotherhood in 1912 to demand protection of their rights and resources.

During the 1920s, most of mainstream America enjoyed a better way of life, but Native Americans continued to face many hardships. Land allotments continued to break up reservation lands, and in Oklahoma, unscrupulous whites cheated and in some cases murdered members of the Five Tribes, the Osage, and other tribes for their oil lands. In addition, the Bursum Bill, introduced in 1921 and again in 1922, threatened the lands owned by Pueblo Indians in New Mexico. Had the Bursum Bill been enacted, it would have placed the burden of proof of land ownership on the Pueblo Indians instead of on the squatters and others on the disputed lands. A chorus of protest came from many organizations, including the General Federation of Women's Clubs, the Indian Rights Association, and the SAI.

John Collier, a social worker and future commissioner of Indian affairs, organized the American Indian Defense Association (AIDA) to combat the bill. The AIDA supported such needed Indian reforms as the ending of land allotments, improving education and health services on Indian reservations, and allowing Indians to have more participation in issues affecting them. After the failure of the Bursum Bill, Congress established the Pueblo Lands Board to determine land ownership and compensate claimants.

Pressure to reform federal Indian policies remained, and in 1922, the secretary of the interior established the Committee of One Hundred to review Indian policies and make recommendations. Well-know Indian and white reformers served on the committee, and their findings were published as *The Indian Problem* in 1924. Included in their recommendations were improvements in Native American education by way of curriculum revisions and government scholarships, a thorough study of peyote use, recognition of Pueblo land rights, and increased scrutiny in granting Indians ownership of their land allotments.

In 1926, Secretary of the Interior Hubert Work called upon the Institute for Government Research, a private research group later referred to as the Brookings Institution, to launch a more comprehensive study of Indian affairs. Dr. Lewis Meriam headed the group, which traveled to reservations throughout the United States and issued their findings that were published as *The Problem of Indian Administration*, often called the Meriam Report, in 1928. The 872-page report offered shocking and deplorable details on reservation conditions. For example, Indian mortality rates and infant mortality rates were among the highest of any ethnic group living in the United States, which was largely due to ill-equipped and understaffed hospitals and health facilities on or near reservations and also because of poor eating habits. The Meriam Report recommended more congressional funding for Native American health and educational needs and a restructuring of the BIA. Moreover, the issuing of land allotments on reservations was blamed as one of the major causes of Native American poverty.

With the election of Herbert Hoover as president of the United States in 1928, more attention was given to implementing the recommendations of the Meriam Report. Under President Hoover, attempts were made to improve the standard of living of Native Americans by providing more hygiene and disease prevention programs; coordinating better state, local, and BIA health care services; offering programs on nutrition; initiating educational changes, like hiring better teachers; relaxing the disciplined and regimented military system of instruction in Indian schools; revamping curriculum to place more stress on Indian culture; establishing more government day schools and decreasing the number of boarding schools; and helping Indian graduates find employment. In addition, the BIA was reorganized into five divisions—health, education, agricultural extension, forestry, and irrigation—to better meet Native American needs. Finally, although land allotments continued, more efforts were attempted to better protect Indians' title to the allotted lands.

With the coming of the Great Depression and the discrediting of the Hoover administration in 1929, congressional appropriations dwindled, and Indian reform programs faltered. The nation demanded new leadership and policies, and Franklin D. Roosevelt, proclaiming a New Deal for America, won the presidential election in 1932. His appointee as commissioner of Indian affairs, John Collier, promised an Indian New Deal as well.

Commissioner Collier had been an active Indian reformer since the 1920s, but unlike most reformers, he was not an advocate of land allotments and forced assimilation policies that tried to eradicate all aspects of Indian cultures. His approach was more of an acculturated one in which Indians could retain their Indianess and still operate successfully in mainstream America. His cultural pluralism beliefs are apparent in Indian New Deal legislation: the Johnson O'Malley Act of 1934, the Indian Reorganization Act of 1934, and the creation of an Indian Arts and Crafts Board in 1935.

The Johnson O'Malley Act attempted to help poverty-stricken rural Indian communities by authorizing the secretary of the interior to contract with states for relief funds to improve Indian education, which received the most attention, as well as agricultural, medical, and welfare services. However, monies appropriated to public schools with Indian students in attendance encountered such difficulties as school districts not providing special programs for their Indian students and placing the funds in their general operating budgets. As the years passed, these problems were rectified, in most cases, and by the 1970s, real curriculum changes and bilingual programs were in place to improve Indian education in public schools, although problems of discrimination remained.

The centerpiece of the Indian New Deal was the Indian Reorganization Act, introduced as the Wheeler-Howard Bill, which contained several significant provisions, one of the most important being the ending of land allotments on reservations that had been going on since 1887. In addition, tribes could vote to establish tribal governments and then tribal corporations; some of the other provisions were allocating funds so Indians could purchase additional lands, giving Indians preferential treatment in securing employment in the BIA, and creating scholarship funds to help Native American students. Provisions of the Indian Reorganization Act were later extended to native peoples in Oklahoma and Alaska with special legislation because tribes there were ineligible because of previous federal legislation. Many non-Indian congressmen and reformers still believed in assimilation policies and criticized Collier for allowing Indians to remain "outside" of mainstream America. Some Indians, too, complained that the new political and economic opportunities failed to recognize past Indian traditions and that white authorities still had final approval in the entire process.

The third piece of Indian New Deal legislation that expressed Collier's Indian reform movement views was the creation of the Indian Arts and Crafts Board, which attempted to improve and protect Indian-made products. A special government trademark on the products guaranteed that they were handmade by Indians. Special courses were offered to help aspiring Indian artists. In addition to aiding Indian economic development, the board also demonstrated Collier's views of allowing Indians to keep and practice their traditions.

When the United States entered World War II, the nation's attention was directed toward defeating the Axis powers. Approximately 25,000 Indians served in the war, many of whom distinguished themselves in battle and some as Indian code talkers who developed a code that the enemy could not break. At war's end, Collier had resigned in disgust because of the lack of congressional support for his programs and a new wave of forced assimilation policies that threatened Indians and their tribal existence. A more conservative nation that feared communism and stressed an American way of life believed Indians needed to be "liberated" from their special status and become part of mainstream America so they could fit in and become part of the majority.

Ways to achieve this goal were to settle all land claims that Native American tribes had against the federal government, terminate the special relationship between the federal government and Indian tribes and allow state jurisdiction over Indians, and relocate reservation Indians to major cities, primarily to provide more economic opportunities.

The Indian Claims Commission was established in 1946 to achieve the first objective by allowing Indians to file suits to settle treaty violations regarding mainly loss of tribal lands and mismanagement of tribal resources. Most land issue cases were settled by cash payments to Indians instead of returning the land to them. The Indian Claims Commission did not finish its work until 1978. With all Indian claims settled, Native Americans would be ready for termination.

New commissioners of Indian affairs who succeeded Collier, as well as members of Congress—especially from Western states—supported the termination policy to end federal government services and responsibilities to Indian tribes. In 1953, House Concurrent Resolution 108 was passed that identified tribes that were "qualified" to be terminated. Shortly afterward, Public Law 280 was enacted that transferred federal jurisdiction over Indian tribes living in California, Minnesota, Nebraska, Oregon, and Wisconsin to these states. More than 60 Indian groups had federal services terminated, including the Menominee in Wisconsin and Klamath in Oregon, whose termination laws were passed in 1954, but both tribes were able to delay its application to them until 1961.

The Menominee and Klamath engaged in lumbering operations and had valuable timber resources; both tribes had been awarded settlement monies from the Indian Claims Commission. As a precondition to receiving the millions of dollars owed to them, the tribes had to agree to termination, which they did without realizing the major repercussions of such a decision. Both tribes lost their special status and suffered tremendous health and economic disasters. Some Indians had to sell their lands to survive. Fortunately, after years of fighting against termination, the Menominee were restored to tribal status in 1973, and the Klamath regained tribal status in 1986.

The third program of post–World War II assimilation was relocation, which also caused undue suffering. Between 1952 and 1973, more than 100,000 Indians were relocated to such major urban areas as Los Angeles, California, Cleveland, Ohio, Minneapolis, Minnesota, Chicago, Illinois, and Denver, Colorado, to provide better job opportunities than reservation life could offer. Many Indians were sent far from their homelands to deter and make more difficult their returning to their reservations. The BIA was often negligent in providing decent lodging and jobs to relocated Indians. Moreover, rural Indians frequently had major difficulties adjusting to urban life in big cities. Unaccustomed to such conditions, approximately one-third of the relocated Indians went back to their reservations.

Denouncing this new assault on Indian tribalism was the National Congress of American Indians (NCAI) that was founded in 1944 as a Pan-Indian movement and supported many of the Indian New Deal programs. The NCAI became the major organization representing Native American interests during the 1940s and 1950s, and it continues its efforts into the 21st century. However, because of the new assimilation policies and other Indian issues that needed addressing, Native Americans engaged in activist movements in the 1960s and 1970s similar to other groups, like African Americans, women, college students, and anti-Vietnam protesters who demanded a better America and political, economic, and social reforms.

Urban Indians were among the leaders of the new Indian activism. They had established Indian centers in the cities and became more aware of the issues affecting Indians both on and off the reservation. Native American Red Power movements and leaders in the scores of demonstrations in the 1960s and 1970s focused on improving reservation conditions, correcting treaty violations, demanding Indian self-determination, and recognizing Indian sovereignty. Two important movements—one in 1961 and the other in 1968—were significant events in Indian activism. In 1961, hundreds of Indian activists gathered at the American Indian Chicago Conference, a meeting that is considered by many as the beginning of Indian reform movements, and at the conference, the many long-standing issues were presented to the newly elected U.S. president, John F. Kennedy. Shortly thereafter, many of these same Indians founded the National Indian Youth Council (NIYC), whose members looked upon its organization as a more aggressive movement than the NCAI. In 1968, the American Indian Movement (AIM) was founded by Indians in Minneapolis, Minnesota, to protect Indians from police brutality and demand more social services for urban Indians. AIM would later become a national movement that played a major role in many of the demonstrations of the era.

A few of the important leaders of the protest movements included Hank Adams, an Assiniboine-Sioux who led fish-ins in the Pacific Northwest to protest violations of Indians' fishing rights; Clyde Warrior, a Ponca and an aggressive leader of the NIYC who was considered by many as a major spokesman and essayist for the Red Power Movement; Ada Deer, a Menominee who fought for tribal restoration and later served as commissioner of Indian affairs; Vine Deloria Jr., a Standing Rock Sioux who wrote numerous books on Native American issues and supported many Indian causes; Ruth Muskrat Bronson, a Cherokee who devoted 60 years in various movements to aid Native Americans; Mary Brave Bird (aka Mary Crow Dog), a Sicangu Lakota who wrote two autobiographies that detailed her Indian activism; Russell Means, an Oglala Sioux; and Dennis Banks, an Ojibwa who led major AIM demonstrations throughout the United States in the 1960s and 1970s.

Indian activists hoped to attract national media coverage to expose federal Indian policy violations in several major demonstrations that included the occupation of Alcatraz Island in 1969; the Trail of Broken Treaties march in 1972 that resulted in the BIA takeover in Washington, D.C.; the occupation of Wounded Knee in 1973, known as Wounded Knee II; and the "Longest Walk" in 1978. These and other demonstrations indeed brought media attention to Indian needs and demands; however, because some activists engaged in violent acts, such physical confrontations often weakened the main reasons for the demonstrations and caused negative reactions from those who watched. In all of these examples, federal officials promised to study such issues as treaty violations and deplorable reservation conditions and to make recommendations.

During the last decades of the 20th century, Congress passed several pieces of federal legislation that addressed Indian sovereignty issues. The measures included the Indian Finance Act of 1974, which gave tribes federal grants and loans to promote economic development projects; the Indian Self-Determination and Educational Assistance Act of 1975, which allowed tribes, instead of the federal government, to administer such Indian programs as health care, education, and housing; the Indian Child Welfare Act of 1978, which gave Indians more control over non-Indians adopting Indian children; and the American Indian Religious Freedom Act of 1978, which recognized the religious freedom rights of Native Americans. In 1994, Congress amended the 1978 law by strengthening the right of peyote use in traditional ceremonies; passed the Indian Mineral Development Act of 1982, which encouraged tribes to engage in mining their mineral resources for economic development; approved the Indian Gaming Regulatory Act of 1988, which allowed tribes to develop casino gambling on reservations; and passed the Native American Graves Protection and Repatriation Act of 1990, which required museums and other facilities that contained Native American items to inform Indian tribes of their collections and return all human remains to the respective tribe. In addition to federal legislation, the U.S. Supreme Court also handed down decisions in favor of Indians recognizing their water, mineral, fishing, and hunting rights. Indians, too, took steps to achieve self-determination and established organizations like the National Tribal Chairmen's Association in 1971 to work with the BIA on major issues concerning Native Americans. The Native American Rights Fund was also founded in 1971 to provide legal assistance to tribes, and the Council of Energy Resource Tribes formed in 1975 to encourage development of mineral resources on reservations.

THE 21ST CENTURY

As the new century began, several major issues remained unresolved and/or extremely controversial regarding Indian and white relations. In 1996, Elouise Cobell, a Blackfeet, was lead plaintiff in a lawsuit representing hundreds of thousands of Indians against the Department of the Interior for mismanaging of Individual Indian Money trust accounts and not giving proper payments to those Indians whose lands were held in trust by the federal government. For more than 100 years, these trust lands were used by non-Indians for grazing and natural resource exploitation, and Indians claim they are entitled to billions of dollars in compensation. In mid-2008, the case remained unresolved.

Equally problematic are recent U.S. Supreme Court decisions that have challenged Indian sovereignty rights. A recent study revealed that since 1988, the Supreme Court has issued decisions against tribal interests in 33 of 44 cases. Examples include *Nevada v. Hicks* in 2001, which denied tribal civil jurisdiction of state personnel working on the reservation; *Atkinson Trading Co. v. Shirley* also in 2001, which declared that non-Indian businesses could not be taxed on fee land within the reservation by the Navajo Nation; and *City of Sherrill, New York v. Oneida Nation of New York* in 2007, which denied the Oneida the right to apply tax-exempt status to lands illegally taken from and later repurchased by them.

Among other issues are Indian gaming operations that tribes and states have to agree to in negotiated contracts that are then approved by the federal government. These tribal and state negotiations are often contentious and result in many tribes paying high percentage payments to the states on their casino profits. Moreover, more states are entering the casino business, which will directly reduce profits Indians generally used for improving conditions on reservations. Nevertheless, the successful Mashantucket Pequot Foxwoods Resort and Casino and the Mohegan Sun Hotel and Casino, both in Connecticut, have established major operations and use the profits for a number of economic development projects and even to assist other Indian nations.

Even though more Indians live off of reservations, those living on reservations continue to face major political, economic, and social challenges. At times, tribal councils and tribal leaders engage in bitter contests and accuse one another of not representing the interests of their tribal constituencies. The results can be devastating. In 1989, Peter MacDonald, Navajo chairman, and in 2006, Cecilia Fire Thunder, Oglala Sioux chairman, were removed from office by their tribal councils during such heated confrontations. Regarding other issues, many Indians remain in poverty and suffer from alarming rates of alcoholism, diabetes, tuberculosis, domestic violence, suicide, and even the appearance of Indian gang activities similar to the threatening teenage gangs found in large cities. Lack of economic development programs on reservations cause increased unemployment.

Finally, Indian identity issues have always been an area of contention. The use of Indian mascots, names, and gestures by sports teams still has not been settled. Indians claim they are being demeaned by such portrayals, while teams having Indian names and images believe they are honoring Native Americans.

Who is an Indian is not an easy question to answer. For the first time, the 2000 Census permitted people to list themselves in more than one racial category. As a result, approximately 2.5 million identified themselves as American Indian or Alaska Native, and about 1.6 million people listed themselves as part Indian, for a total of 4.1 million respondents claiming Indian heritage. The largest tribal identity claimed was Cherokee, followed by those reporting Navajo heritage. It has been estimated that by 2080, only approximately 8 percent of Native Americans will possess one-half or more Indian heritage.

The BIA, on the other hand, defines Indians as those belonging to federally recognized tribes or who have a blood quantum of one-half for some federal services or one-quarter ancestry for other programs. Of course, Indian nations have always determined their own membership. Indeed, in 2007, the Cherokee Nation voted to exclude Cherokee freedmen (descendents from African American slaves and Cherokee heritage) from its tribal rolls.

For many centuries, Native American movements demonstrated the need to improve relations between Indians and non-Indians. Too often, wars, disease, and assimilation policies devastated Indian America. It is truly amazing that Native Americans have survived these assaults. But they have, and in the final analysis, Indians should be able to retain their special status, which was established by the federal government, and, at the same time, demand more recognition of their sovereignty rights and their right to Indian self-determination.

Cecilia Fire Thunder. Photo by David Melmer, courtesy of Indian Country Today.

Charles A. Eastman. Courtesy of Gene Klotz and Raymond Wilson.

Elouise Cobell, third from the right. Photo by Jerry Reynolds, courtesy of Indian Country Today.

Winona LaDuke. Photo by Gale Courey Toensing, courtesy of Indian Country Today.

Peter MacDonald, in the black bolo tie, and Code Talkers. Photo by Brenda Norrell, courtesy of Indian Country Today.

Powwow. Photo by David Melmer, courtesy of Indian Country Today.

Vine Deloria Jr. Photo by Ardis McRae, courtesy of Indian Country Today.

Wilma Mankiller. Photo by David Melmer, courtesy of Indian Country Today.

Ætatis suæ 21. Aº .1616.

Matoaks als Rebecka daughter to the mighty Prince
Powhatan Emperour of Attanoughkomouck als Virginia
converted and baptized in the Christian faith, and
Wife to the worll Mr Tho: Rolff.

Pocahontas. Courtesy of the National Portrait Gallery of the Smithsonian Institution.

The Dictionary

- A -

ADAMS, HANK (1944–). Born on the Fort Peck Indian Reservation in Montana in 1944, Adams, an Assiniboine-Sioux, became a leading activist in support of Native American **fishing rights** in the state of Washington and other Native American protest movements and led the **Survival of American Indians Association**. He attended high school in Washington, where he was a gifted student scholar/athlete actively involved in such school activities as being the student body president, editing the school newspaper and yearbook, and playing football and basketball. Adams became aware of the mistreatment of Native Americans during his teenage years and joined the **National Indian Youth Council** in 1963. The following year he was among the Indians with actor Marlon Brando who demanded that Native American fishing rights be recognized along the Nisqually River in Washington, and he helped organize fish-in demonstrations when state officials and non-Indian fishermen threatened treaty fishing rights and wanted to place restrictions on Indian fishing. Adams helped in the arguments that resulted in the Boldt Decision of 1974, in which the treaty fishing rights of the Nisqually, Puyallup, and other Northwest tribes were recognized. He assisted in plans to help preserve salmon and steelhead in the region.

Another activist movement he played a significant role in was the **Trail of Broken Treaties** in 1972. Adams helped write the Twenty Points that dealt with treaty relations between Indians and the U.S. federal government, became involved in the subsequent Bureau of Indian Affairs takeover in Washington, D.C., and in the negotiations, and assisted in the return of **Bureau of Indian Affairs** documents taken from the building in an effort to make sure the materials were not lost, were not destroyed, and were available for future use. Other examples of his activism included helping in the negotiations during **Wounded Knee II**, working for indigenous rights for native peoples in Nicaragua, continuing his support of Indian fishing rights and water rights, lobbing for congressional funds for the Little Big Horn Battlefield National Monument Indian memorial, and counseling Northwest Indians on **gaming** issues. In 2006, *Indian Country Today*, a national Indian newspaper, presented Adams with its American Indian Visionary Award for the leadership roles he played in defending Native American rights.

ALASKA FEDERATION OF NATIVES (AFN). Founded in Anchorage, Alaska, in October 1966, the AFN was an organization that represented the aboriginal land claims, which included the **fishing rights** and **hunting rights** of about 80,000 Indians, Aleuts, and Eskimos in the state. Threats to their land claims came from oil discoveries in the region and Alaska achieving statehood in 1959. Because only a few **reservations** had been established in Alaska, the native population feared the loss of their traditional lands because the new state could select public domain lands that could also be claimed by Alaska natives.

The AFN engaged in serious negotiations with federal and state officials and convinced Secretary of the Interior Stewart Udall and his successor, Walter Hickel, who had been governor of the state, to cease land sales in Alaska until native land claims could be settled. The issue was resolved by the passage of the Alaska Native Claims Settlement Act (ANCSA) of 1971, in which Alaska natives relinquished their land claims and accepted $962 million and 44 million acres of land. In addition, the ANCSA created 174 village and 13 regional corporations and gave stock shares to Alaska natives. Finally, the ANCSA designated the AFN to administer land claim issues and help the corporations and native stockholders in economic development opportunities. Issues concerning native sovereignty rights, the special status that Indians have been granted by the U.S. federal government, the loss of land, and stockholding restrictions remain major areas of concern for Alaska natives. *See also* ALASKA NATIVE BROTHERHOOD (ANB).

ALASKA NATIVE BROTHERHOOD (ANB). Founded in 1912 in Sitka, Alaska, mostly by Tlingits, the ANB demanded the end of political, economic, and social discrimination against Alaska natives. A separated branch for native women, the **Alaska Native Sisterhood**, was later organized. Two primary objectives were the securing of U.S. citizenship for Alaska natives and better educational opportunities for native students.

Because of Presbyterian missionary influences, the ANB at first espoused assimilation and the abandonment of native ways, but the organization later adopted a more acculturation approach that recognized native traditions. The ANB published the newspapers *The Alaska Fisherman* and later *The Voice of Brotherhood* to promote its activities. Under the leadership of William L. Paul Sr., a mixed-blood Tlingit, in the 1920s and 1930s, the ANB protested the use of non-Indian fish traps for commercial fishing, segregated seating of Indians at movies, and voting restrictions in territorial elections. Paul also advocated protecting Alaska native land claims and stopping the creation of new **reservations**, which he perceived were threatened by the **Indian Reorganization Act** of 1934. However, the passage of the Alaska Reorganization Act of 1936 affected both issues and divided the ANB membership. Some believed that new reservation boundaries would provide more security and protection of property, while others contended that the new reserves threatened citizenship rights and encouraged segregation.

After World War II, the ANB continued its efforts to protect native land claims. It also demanded the end of segregated Indian schools, Indian administration reforms in which Alaska natives had more control, better medical care, and fair compensation for the sale of timber on native land. Discontent continued to weaken the organization because of clan and family issues, lack of representation of other Alaska native groups, and assimilation matters. Dissatisfied members formed a new organization, the **Alaska Federation of Natives**, which they felt would better meet their needs, particularly regarding the settlement of land claims. Nevertheless, the efforts of the ANB helped in the passage of the Alaska Native Claims Settlement Act (ANCSA) of 1971, which gave nearly a billion dollars to settle aboriginal land claims, provided 44 million acres of land, and created 13 regional and 174 village corporations in which Alaska natives held shares.

ALASKA NATIVE SISTERHOOD (ANS). *See* ALASKA NATIVE BROTHERHOOD (ANB).

ALCATRAZ, OCCUPATION OF. In 1964, six Lakota men occupied the closed federal prison on Alcatraz Island in San Francisco Bay off the coast of San Francisco, California. The men claimed that under the authority of the Fort Laramie Treaty of 1868, any abandoned federal facility would revert back to Indian ownership. Although treated as a publicity stunt, this occupation set the stage for a longer, more determined occupation that began in 1969. The second occupation became an international news sensation. The occupation of 1969 was organized in response to the **Bureau of Indian Affairs'** program of relocation as well as the abject poverty on the **reservations**. Leading the occupation was Adam Fortunate Eagle and **Richard Oakes**. The leaders drafted a petition stating that the **Indians of All Tribes** would purchase the facility for $24 in glass beads and red cloth, a reference to the Dutch purchase of Manhattan Island in the 17th century. The goal of the occupation was to establish an educational and cultural center inside of the prison facilities. Seventy-eight people arrived on the island on 20 November. Constant food and water shortages hindered the ability of the occupiers to remain on the island. On 11 June 1971, armed federal marshals removed the 11 remaining occupiers, thus ending the occupation of the island but not the spirit of activism that pushed Indian issues to the forefront of American politics.

ALCOHOL AND ALCOHOLISM. In Indian America north of Mesoamerica, few native peoples possessed fermented beverages before the arrival of Europeans. However, by 1800, so much alcohol could be found in Indian villages that communities began to decide whether to forbid its use. No other European trade good caused the demise of Indian communities more quickly than alcohol.

In the British colonies, alcohol became a commodity as early as 1650. Caribbean distillers began to produce vast quantities of rum. Eager to make quick cash, mainland colonists, especially those who lived in colonial cities and had few contacts with Indians, began to sell alcohol to Indians. By the early 18th century, a regular trade had developed when full-time traders began to transport liquor farther and further into the colonial backcountry. As white settlement expanded during the 19th century, Anglo-Americans came to dominate the trade in liquors even in the American southwest, where a few native peoples had a tradition of fermentation.

It is not possible to locate the exact point when Indians were first introduced to alcohol or why they continued to consume liquor once it was introduced. However, historians have argued that Indians turned to alcohol for many of the same reasons as their white counterparts: destruction of communities, the ravages of epidemic **disease** that decimated native peoples, the underhanded methods of land speculators who divested Indians of their homelands, and an increasing cycle of violence brought on by contact with ever-encroaching white settlement. Finally, Indians chose and choose, like their white contemporaries, to drink out of frustration. Social scientists have shown on numerous occasions that when a society undergoes rapid changes, the level of alcohol consumption rises.

However, there is evidence to suggest that some Indians enjoyed the heightened sense of power that often accompanied intoxication. Indians in the southwest believed that the disorienting effects of overconsumption of alcohol brought them closer to the divine. Indians in the Great Lakes region went so far as to incorporate alcohol use into some of their most sacred ceremonies, especially mourning rituals and those designed to put one in contact with the higher powers. Finally, as in white society, alcohol became part and parcel of the various hospitality ceremonies across Indian Country.

Indians knew the dangers of alcohol. Time and again in the historical records, Indians come forth to insist that the amount of alcohol flowing in Indian communities was destroying them. In fact, numerous colonial officials reported that stopping the alcohol trade was often a major point of contention at Indian councils. In nearly every colony, laws existed that forbade the trade of alcohol to Indians. The lack of strict enforcement, however, or the establishment of an effective colonial police force, often meant that liquor made its way into Indian hands whether or not a **law** had been passed. From the colonial period into the present, alcohol has been ever-present in Indian communities.

Attempts by the U.S. federal government well into the 20th century continued to fail to stop the flow of alcohol onto Indian lands. Thus, in 1953, at the height of the **termination** era, the government repealed its provisions against Indians alcohol use and turned full authority for the control of the trade over to tribal governments. Indian communities now had to decide whether alcohol would be allowed on **reservations**. As rates of alcohol consumption continue to rise, one of the growing problems on the nation's various reservations is Indian alcoholism.

Developing alongside the trade in alcohol during the colonial period was the stereotype of the "drunken Indian." Colonists argued that the "savage" nature of Indian cultures made itself clear when Indians became intoxicated. Since then, the idea that Indians are physically unable to handle their alcohol as well as whites do has remained popular. In fact, the idea that Indians are less able to control their drinking has found its way into many Indian communities. However, most social scientific studies suggest that Indian Country has an alarmingly high rate of alcoholism because of social destruction and the pressures of assimilation. Thus, medical practitioners and scholars alike argue that Indian alcoholism can be traced directly to the ravages of the situations surrounding their contact with Europeans and Americans.

The most recent reports suggest that Indians die of "alcoholism" at a rate five times the overall national average. A closer look at these deaths indicate that many are "alcohol-related" but are more accurately termed homicides, suicides, or accidents; the lumping together of these deaths with causes like cirrhosis increases the number of Indian deaths with alcohol as a cause. The various reports, however, fail to take into account the manner in which most Indian drinking occurs. Like the nation's college campuses, Indian reservations are often the sites for "binge drinking." After consuming large quantities of alcohol, drinkers generally pass out or find their supply gone; the aftereffects of such "binging" produce the symptoms of withdrawal. Thus, Indians are more prone to the symptoms of alcoholic withdrawal and suffer higher incidences of alcohol-related deaths than their white counterparts.

Alcohol use and abuse remains a very real problem across all of Indian Country. The problem facing the tribal governments that confront the issue today is that no single theory, racial, social, or otherwise, explains why Indians continue to drink despite the costs to their communities. The Indian Health Service, in recent years, has increased its budget for treating the chronic disorders associated with the pathologies of alcohol abuse.

ALL INDIAN PUEBLO COUNCIL (AIPC). Tenuously founded in 1600, the AIPC is comprised of 19 distinct pueblos in the Rio Grande Valley of New Mexico. For more than 400 years, the AIPC has worked to maintain cultural traditions and values as well as to defend Pueblo land rights and self-government. The first meetings seem to have taken place in the years before the revolt against Spanish occupiers in 1680. However, when the Spanish returned to the Rio Arriba in 1692, they recognized the rights that the council has fought to maintain ever since. The AIPC has aided the Pueblo people in their dealings with the Spanish crown, the Mexican government, and the U.S. federal government, but this promotion of culture and basic Pueblo rights has been an up and down struggle.

In the early 20th century, the AIPC faced its first major obstacle since Spanish entradas marched through their homeland—American squatters on Pueblo lands. In an effort to end the "problem" of more than 3,000 illegal squatters on Pueblo lands, Senator Holm Bursum of New Mexico introduced a bill that gave land title to the squatters. Working with such Anglos as **John Collier** and Mary Brady Luhan, the council was able to defeat the Bursum Bill. In the 1950s and 1960s, the AIPC assumed a more vigorous role in the lives of Pueblo people. On 16 October 1965, the 19 Pueblo governors met in Santo Domingo—the same meeting place as in 1680—and there leaders drafted a constitution, and AIPC was organized as a nonprofit organization under New Mexico law. The AIPC's stated purpose has remained unchanged since the 1600s: to promote justice and encourage the common welfare of all Pueblo Indians; to foster the social and economic advancement of all Pueblo people; and to preserve and protect the common interests and inherent rights of self-government and legal rights that are guaranteed to the Pueblo people. Since 1965, the AIPC has contracted with the **Bureau of Indian Affairs** to administer a variety of health, **education**, business development, and social welfare programs to the various pueblos of New Mexico.

AMERICAN ASSOCIATION ON INDIAN AFFAIRS. The American Association on Indian Affairs was officially founded in 1937 when the **American Indian Defense Association** and the National Association of Indian Affairs combined their efforts. The organization originally aimed to promote the integration of Indians into American culture by encouraging the settlement of Indian claims, economic self-sufficiency, **education**, and the retention of tribal traditions. In 1946, the name was changed to the **Association on American Indian Affairs**.

AMERICAN INDIAN ASSOCIATION (AIA). The AIA, which was the original name of the **Society of American Indians** established in 1911, was founded in 1922. The new AIA of the 1920s demanded that U.S. citizenship be granted to all Indians, more recognition of Indians' legal and civil rights, aid to elderly Indians and homeless Indians, and more Indian participation in issues affecting **reservation** life. Among its leadership was Sherman Coolidge, an Arapaho, and Joseph Strong Wolf, a Chippewa. The AIA allowed whites to join but excluded blacks from its membership and published a magazine that had various titles, like the *Indian Teepee*.

Additional AIA chapters and councils were established in Eastern and Midwestern cities, and these meeting places became among the first cultural centers for urban Indians to gather, especially in New York City. By the end of the 1920s, the AIA had become more of a fraternal organization that promoted social and educational issues.

AMERICAN INDIAN CHICAGO CONFERENCE. Many historians trace the beginning of Indian activist movements to the American Indian Chicago Conference held in June 1961 at the University of Chicago in Illinois. By the 1960s, worsening Indian conditions and federal policies like the **termination** of Indian treaties convinced many Native Americans to become more active in their protests. More than 400 Indians from approximately 65 tribes attended the Chicago conference, which was organized by the **National Congress of American Indians** and professor of anthropology Sol Tax, an advocate of Indian reform. A good number of the delegates were younger and more prone to activism than many of the older, more traditional delegates in attendance.

A "Declaration of Indian Purpose" proposal was presented to the incoming John F. Kennedy administration, calling for more recognition of tribal self-determination and improved health, **education**, economic, and social services. However, the more active delegates at the conference remained unhappy and demanded more aggressive action. They formed the **National Indian Youth Council** in 1961.

AMERICAN INDIAN CHRISTIAN TEPEE MISSION (AICTM). Founded in 1918 by Red Fox Francis St. James (Skiuhushu) on the Yakima Reservation, the AICTM was presumably organized like the Tepee Order of America. In 1915, St. James organized a secret society modeled after the Boy Scouts, but it was open only to young Native American men. The AICTM diverged from the Tepee Order of America when St. James became an ordained minister in the Disciples of Christ. The organization did not last for a significant length of time, and its influence is thought to have been limited.

AMERICAN INDIAN COMMUNITY HOUSE, INC. (AICH). The AICH was formed in 1969 and served as a social and cultural center for Indian people living in New York City. The organization provided a number of social services to Indian people, including but not limited to job training, legal aid, and adult education. A senior center and art gallery round out the AICH's offerings to the Indian community.

AMERICAN INDIAN DEFENSE ASSOCIATION (AIDA). Established in New York City in May 1923 and led by **John Collier**, who served as executive secretary from its founding until 1933, the AIDA became a national association for reformers who held similar concerns about protecting Pueblo Indian land titles in New Mexico threatened by proposed federal legislation. Much of what the AIDA demanded was later enacted in Indian New Deal legislation that emphasized a cultural pluralism approach rather than an assimilation approach to Indian affairs and stressed Indian self-determination. The association's objectives included ending land allotments on **reservations**, creating tribal governments, initiating economic development programs, recognizing Indians' civil and human rights, enforcing federal Indian treaties, and improving Indian health and medical and educational services. Membership in the AIDA was mostly non-Indian, and branch offices were established in several cities in the United States, including Los Angeles, California, Albuquerque, New Mexico, Milwaukee, Wisconsin, Minneapolis, Minnesota, and Washington, D.C. The AIDA issued a newsletter called *American Indian Life*, and by the early 1930s, membership stood at approximately 1,700 members.

The AIDA achieved many of its goals after Collier became commissioner of Indian affairs. In 1937, the association, which suffered some financial setbacks, merged with the National Association on Indian Affairs to form the **American Association on Indian Affairs**.

AMERICAN INDIAN DEVELOPMENT, INC. (AID). The AID was founded in 1952 by **D'Arcy McNickle** to educate Indian people on improving their communities through the utilization of homegrown talents. McNickle, the founder of the **National Congress of American Indians**, ensured that the board of directors included a wide variety of specialists, including lawyers, anthropologists, and other social scientists.

In 1953, the AID organized the Crownpoint Project, which gave technical assistance to Navajo tribal leaders in such areas as range management and irrigation. The organization later developed what became an annual conference on American Indian Affairs, which included a select group of Anglo and Indian authorities. The workshops were designed to help Indian students find meaning in college life and work and promote intellectual self-awareness.

AMERICAN INDIAN FEDERATION (AIF). Lasting from 1934 until the end of World War II, the AIF was a major voice of Native criticism of the Indian New Deal. The AIF had three major goals: that Commissioner of Indian Affairs **John Collier** be removed from office, that the **Indian Reorganization Act** of 1934 be overturned, and that the **Bureau of Indian Affairs (BIA)** be abolished.

Although most of the leadership was from Oklahoma, the AIF also included prominent Indian leaders from across the country. The Oklahoma group, led by AIF president Joseph Bruner, a Creek, reflected the apprehension of that state's allotted Indians with Collier's focus on tribal life and communal ideals. Bruner and other Oklahoma leaders argued that Indians needed to fully participate in mainstream

American politics rather than separate programs designed to keep them outside of American society.

The AIF held annual meetings that became increasingly militant and accused the BIA of perpetuating Bolshevik policies. In 1938, the Department of the Interior infiltrated the federation, spying on the national meetings, making use of confidential informants, and requesting Federal Bureau of Investigation surveillance of the leaders. Discredited by pro-Nazi, un-American sentiments, the AIF fell apart during the mid-1940s. The arguments proposed by the AIF contributed to the development of the post–World War II policy of **termination**.

AMERICAN INDIAN HIGHER EDUCATION CONSORTIUM (AIHEC). The AIHEC was formed in 1972 by six tribal college leaders who sought to protect the interests of their organizations. The goal of the consortium is to ensure the survival of tribal colleges and secure adequate funding for increasing their number. Promoting culturally sensitive training at tribal colleges, the AIHEC is dedicated to saving and teaching various Indian languages and promoting programs designed to increase native sovereignty.

The AIHEC sponsors annual conferences for faculty and students from the numerous tribal colleges and offers various workshops, seminars, and activities designed to ensure and expand the role of tribally operated colleges and universities. In recent years, the consortium has established the American Indian College Fund designed to promote personal, business, and foundation gift-giving to support tribal colleges. The consortium also publishes *Tribal College: Journal of the American Indian Higher Education Consortium*, which provides a forum for the discussion of all issues facing operations at tribal colleges. Through the actions of the AIHEC, the numerous tribal colleges and universities across the United States are connected to one another through a national association.

AMERICAN INDIAN INSTITUTE (ROE INSTITUTE). The basic outline for the American Indian Institute was first laid out by Reverend Walter Roe, who served as a missionary for many years among the tribes of the southwest. Roe believed that off-**reservation** boarding schools did not provide the Christian foundation necessary to create

Indian leaders who would lead their people to assimilate into American society. Roe, however, died in 1913 without realizing the dream of building his school. The plan for bringing his dream to life fell on Henry Roe Cloud, a Winnebago who was also an ordained Presbyterian minister.

Cloud was born in Nebraska in 1884 and educated at the Genoa Indian School; Santee Normal Training School; Dwight Moody's School at Mount Hermon, Massachusetts; and Yale University, where he earned both a bachelor of arts and a master of arts. During his school years, he became friends with Roe, whose name he later adopted for the school as a sign of gratitude. Since his earliest school days, Cloud argued in favor of Christian education and training for Indians. Cloud decided that his benefactor's institute would need a strategic location to succeed. He chose a site in Wichita, Kansas, because of its proximity to Oklahoma and the relative ease of travel from Indian centers in Nebraska and South Dakota. The site was a 21-acre farm outside town near Wichita University (now Wichita State University).

Cloud set the institute's goals at $250,000 in improvements and a $750,000 endowment to operate the school. From the outset, the institute was plagued with financial problems, and Cloud was only able to obtain funding for a few minor farm buildings. The main school building and superintendent's quarters would not be completed until the 1920s. Oversight of the Roe Institute, renamed the American Indian Institute in 1920, rested with a board of directors, which included local moneyed interests and those in the East.

Cloud argued that if Indian people were to survive in America, they needed Christian leaders to ease their assimilation into American culture. Thus, the objective of the institute was to select enrollees for their leadership potential and to instill in all students a sense of struggle and service. In short, Cloud wanted the American Indian Institute to serve the same purpose that Hampton and Tuskegee had for African Americans.

Despite lofty goals, the institute continued to suffer from financial shortcomings. Cloud launched a media blitz asking for funds through pamphlets, and in 1923, he lobbied for support in *The Indian Outlook*, a monthly newsletter. In a 1926 edition of the newsletter, Cloud argued that Indians were on the verge of extinction. He claimed that three forces had allied to ensure the destruction of Indian people: race mixture, dislodgement of Indians from the reservation, and a push in Congress to eliminate federal programs to Indians. The institute would continue to fulfill its mission because it would attract members of all tribes, and training leaders would continue to be important in a rapidly changing world. Despite the eloquent pleas, finances remained short.

In 1927, the Board of National Missions of the Presbyterian Church in the United States took control of the institute's funding. Cloud resigned his post as superintendent in 1931 and took a job in the Indian Service as a field agent. He was named superintendent of Haskell Institute in 1933. That same year, the students at the American Indian Institute entered the Wichita public school system in compliance with government policies. By 1935, only 40 students lived at the institute; all attended Wichita University and paid only for lodging.

The American Indian Institute came to an end in 1939. The Presbyterian Church sold the land to a local landowner, who remodeled the buildings and rented them to local college students. The institute failed to train the thousands of Christian Indian leaders Roe and Cloud envisioned, but its existence was an interesting experiment in Indian **education** and policy.

AMERICAN INDIAN LEAGUE (AIL). The AIL was organized in New York City in 1910 by a group of 100 like-minded Anglo reformers to assist Indian people on the road to assimilation. Like other Anglo reform movements of the early 20th century, the goals of the league were many. Organizers funded the distribution of Indian arts, especially baskets, and promoted economic development on **reservations**. The AIL's focus demonstrated a change in thinking in Indian affairs from the Christian ethos of the 19th century to one of cultural pluralism. By 1912, the AIL aided 24 tribes in 11 states and established distribution centers for Indian baskets in New York City, New Haven, Providence, and Boston. The end date for the AIL is difficult to determine.

AMERICAN INDIAN MOVEMENT (AIM). In July 1968, several Chippewas (Ojibwas) founded AIM in Minneapolis, Minnesota, in response to police harassment of Indians and to increase urban social services to Indians in the city. As one of several activist organizations formed in the turbulent 1960s to improve minority rights and protest other issues, like the Vietnam War, AIM adopted confrontational methods of demonstration from black civil rights movements and other protest groups. Successful AIM activities in Minneapolis resulted in additional chapters being created in other cities and on **reservations**. **Dennis Banks**, **Russell Means**, and **Clyde** and **Vernon Bellecourt** became leading figures in the movement.

AIM gained national attention by its participation in the occupation of **Alcatraz** Island in San Francisco Bay off the coast of San Francisco, California, in November 1969. Calling themselves **Indians of All Tribes**, the protesters occupied the abandoned federal prison and claimed it for Indian America based on a federal **law** concerning land reverting back to previous owners. Other major demonstrations involving AIM included their protests against the manner in which investigations of murdered Indians were being handled; the staging of "fish-ins" (*see* FISHING RIGHTS) in the Pacific Northwest; and the **Trail of Broken Treaties** caravan to Washington, D.C., resulting in the occupation and trashing of the **Bureau of Indian Affairs** in November 1972.

In February 1973, AIM played perhaps its most well-known role in the 71-day occupation of Wounded Knee, South Dakota, the historic site of the 1890 tragedy during the **Ghost Dance** disturbances at Pine Ridge Indian Reservation in December 1890. Known as **Wounded Knee II**, the occupation drew national attention to federal Indian policies and Oglala tribal politics on the reservation. As with other demonstrations, the U.S. federal government promised to investigate the issues and make recommendations. Indian factionalism continued at Pine Ridge; moreover, hundreds of federal charges were brought against AIM members, including Banks and Means. Nearly all of the indictments were dismissed, and both Banks and Means were acquitted of all charges due to federal improprieties at the trial.

In later years, AIM leadership began to factionalize, especially relations between Means and the Bellecourts. An urban organization, AIM was never able to recruit a membership representing the major tribal groups both on and off the reservations and achieve genuine **Pan-Indianism**. The Colorado Chapter of AIM claims to be the organization that truly represents AIM and has for the last several years protested **Columbus Day** activities in Denver.

AMERICAN INDIAN MOVEMENT FOR EQUAL RIGHTS (AMERIND).

The **National Indian Youth Council** established AMERIND, Inc., in 1969 to combat employment discrimination against and promote civil and economic rights for Native Americans. One hundred Indian employees of the **Bureau of Indian Affairs (BIA)** sued the agency for employment discrimination. In the suits, Indians complained that although the majority of BIA employees were Native Americans, only a small number held supervisory positions. Evidence of such discrimination was collected in BIA offices located in the southwest in cities like Albuquerque and Gallup, New Mexico.

A primary goal of AMERIND, Inc., is the establishment of a BIA composed of only Native Americans and free from federal supervision. The movement also demands the end of employment discrimination against Indians in other agencies that serve Indians.

AMERICAN INDIAN PROGRESSIVE ASSOCIATION (AIPA).

Established in January 1926 in Los Angeles, California, by a Pablo Narcha, presumably a California Indian, the AIPA is an example of several urban, often short-lived **Pan-Indian** groups, like the **National Society of Indian Women**, organized in various cities during the 1920s. These associations were more local or regional than national bodies, but they did offer places for urban Indians to gather and discuss Indian issues, especially those affecting the local members.

Only Indians who were approved by the AIPA members could join, and the association called on Indians to be proud of their heritage, work hard, and obtain an **education** to participate in mainstream America. The AIPA briefly published a periodical called *The OKeh*.

AMERICANS FOR INDIAN OPPORTUNITY (AIO).

AIO is a nonprofit organization founded in 1970 by **LaDonna Harris**, a Comanche. AIO is dedicated to the preservation and increased efficiency of tribal governments. Since its founding, Harris has served as president and executive director of the organization, focusing on improving the political and economic status of tribal governments and Indian people whether federally recognized or not.

AIO acts as an advisor to Congress and the president, promoting Indian and U.S. federal government cooperation to meet goals and bring together tribes, resources, and experts. The organization dedicates much of its time to economic development, environmental protection, and effective tribal governance.

Believing that non-Indians do not understand the rights and needs of Indian people, AIO has taken on a public relations role serving as educators to Congress, federal officials, and the non-Indian community. The organization's relationship with the federal government has resulted in the successful coordination of federal resources on behalf of tribes and both rural and urban Indian people. Additionally, AIO has negotiated with museums and private collectors for the return of sacred objects, aided in diversity training for the Federal Bureau of Investigation, and represented Indian interests at national and international conferences.

In recent years, AIO has organized its own conferences and projects on resource development, environmental protection, and tribal government operations. AIO combines environmental protection as an integral aspect of Indian economic development. The organization has worked closely with the Department of Agriculture and the Soil Conservation Service to ensure that tribes receive adequate flood protection assistance and irrigation technologies.

Since the 1980s, AIO has brought together tribal leaders, representatives of various federal agencies, and committed scholars to examine such important issues of governance as tribal representative government, separation of powers, the role of the federal executive in tribal affairs, issues of taxation, and ensuring Indian political rights. AIO continues its work at present.

ANNUITIES. As part of giving up their lands and way of life and agreeing to move to **reservations** during treaty negotiations, Native Americans were promised annuities, which were payments of money and/or such items as blankets and food rations for a certain period of time. Because the U.S. Senate ratified treaties and the House of Representatives appropriated the funds for annuity payments, both bodies often changed the amount of monies to be paid or the number of items to be given without informing Indians of the revisions.

Conflicts often resulted regarding reductions of annuity payments, substandard items given to Indians such as rancid bacon or flour, and annuities not arriving on time. Indian agents on reservations, who controlled the distribution of the annuity payments, frequently withheld annuities or selected Indians who supported federal Indian policies of assimilation to distribute the payments and items as ways to force Indians who resisted assimilation to rethink their position. In addition, unscrupulous white traders on reservations allowed Indians to purchase goods from them on credit with high interest rates. Many Indians fell into perpetual debt, and their meager monetary annuity payments were paid directly to these white traders. Native Americans organized movements to call attention to what they considered violations of annuity payments and voiced their concerns to federal officials and others. Sometimes violent confrontations erupted, as with the Dakota Conflict in Minnesota, led by **Little Crow** in 1862.

Finally, many Indian reformers questioned the use of annuity payments, particularly the distribution of money annuities because such payments allowed Indians to resist adoption of white farming methods. In place of monetary annuities, these reformers recommended the substitution of domestic animals and agricultural and mechanical implements. Still other reformers demanded that all annuities be abolished because Indians relied on them too much and remained "idle" and "lazy."

ANTHROPOLOGY AND INDIANS. American anthropology was founded on the study of American Indians, sometimes with the cooperation of the very Indian communities under examination. In the 19th century, the idea that Indians were a "vanishing race" was common among those interested in anthropological studies. That the belief has, by the 21st century, proven false does not negate the fact the anthropologists and Indians engaged in a practice that modern scholars call "salvage anthropology," wherein the scientist and in many cases their Indian aides preserve forever the cultural norms and ways of a given society.

The first major American anthropological study was Henry Lewis Morgan's *League of the Ho-de-no-sau-nee or Iroquois*, first published in 1851. However, Morgan's work could not have been completed without the assistance of **Ely Parker**, a Seneca from the Tonawanda Reservation, who became friends with Morgan and provided the "scientist" with intimate knowledge about the **Iroquois Confederacy** and its workings. With Morgan's work as a foundation, the Smithsonian Institution established the Bureau of American Ethnology in 1879. The single charge of the bureau was to document and study American Indian cultures. Over the next 50 years, numerous Indian peoples were involved in the study of their communities by a small cadre of professional anthropologists, led the **James Mooney**.

By the start of the 20th century, anthropology was quickly becoming a university-based social science, and Franz Boaz served as the leader of the professionalization movement. Museums began to fund field workers to gather information and cultural artifacts for their collections. Most impressive, however, is the number of professional Indian anthropologists who began to publish their works during the same period: Francis La Flesche, an Omaha; **Arthur C. Parker**, a Seneca and nephew to Ely; Ella Deloria, a Yankton Sioux; J. N. B. Hewitt, an Iroquois; Jesse Cornplanter, a Seneca; Essie Parrish, a Pomo; John J. Mathews, an Osage; William Jones, a Fox; James Murie, a Pawnee; and George Hunt, a Tlingit, all added scholarly materials to the growing volumes of information available about their respective cultures.

In the 1960s and 1970s, public pressures came to bear on the science of anthropology. The most damning argument against it was that the practitioners were in the business of exploiting Indian peoples. At the same time, many Indian peoples began to challenge the relationships they had with these bookish outsiders questioning whether non-Indians should hold interpretive power over Indian cultures. Perhaps the most eloquent critique of this nature and of this time can be found in **Vine Deloria Jr.**'s manifesto *Custer Died for Your Sins*. In many cases, tribes have responded to these pressures by requiring scholars to receive permission before beginning a research project, but in just as many cases, researchers continue to make their own arrangements with Indians willing to aid them.

Since the 1970s, the fields of cultural, physical, and linguistic anthropology have seen a decline in the number of American Indian scientists who specialize in North America. Only archaeology has seen growth—a result of laws passed by tribes and the U.S. federal government protecting archaeological sites and artifacts. Many tribes have established their own museums and cultural centers and have obtained copies of original documents first collected by those neophyte anthropologists and their Indian assistants. The practice of tribal control has borne considerable fruit, as many tribes have been able to rediscover parts of their lost cultural heritage because of the work of these early practitioners. Although the relationship between anthropologists and Indians remains strained, the benefits to Indian communities in terms of cultural revitalization must be taken into account when tribes seek to limit the number of researchers on their **reservations** or in their communities.

APESS, WILLIAM (1798–1839). Born in a tent in January 1798 somewhere near Colrain, Massachusetts, the difficulties of Apess's life were immediately apparent. Born to William, a mixed-race Pequot and European, and Candace, a mixed-race African slave, the world was set up against young William. At the age of five, he was sent to a neighboring family, the Furmans of Colchester, Connecticut, as a servant. Apess lived with the Furmans until the age of 11 and, during that time, he received his only "formal" education. He was then sold to a wealthy New York family, the Williams.

In April 1813, Apess ran away from his owners and ventured to New York City, where he joined a militia unit and served in the War of 1812. Mustered out in 1815, he spent the next 18 months living and working in Canada, attempting to overcome a drinking problem that he developed during his time in the militia. Determined to stop drinking, he returned to Connecticut and the Pequot people he never knew. During his time with the Pequots, Apess developed a strong sense of himself as an Indian, and more specifically, a Pequot.

With a solid Indian identity formed, Apess turned himself into a polemic writer becoming a critic of white Europeans' use of history and religion to spread racism against Indians. His autobiography entitled *A Son of the Forest* represents the first autobiography written by an American Indian. The work was written in an attempt to communicate with a world that understood Indians only as stereotypes and was designed to give readers a different view of Indian life.

In 1818, Apess began attending Methodist camp meetings because of the denomination's appeal to the dispossessed. In December of the same year, he converted and was baptized. He also met Mary Wood, who had also served elite families in New England. The two were married in December 1821 and remained together until Apess's death in 1839. Throughout the 1820s, Apess began to preach. Denied ordination by the Methodist Episcopal Church because of an injunction against Indians, he became an ordained minister under the auspices of the Protestant Methodist Church.

Apess's ordination began a public career that saw him minister to Indians, African Americans, and whites throughout New England. It was in this role that he first visited the Mashpees, who lived in the largest surviving Indian town in Massachusetts. The Mashpees were in the midst of a struggle to gain self-government and be free from the guardians appointed by Harvard College. The Mashpees immediately made Apess their spokesman. Apess put his writing skills to use and was so effective that Governor Levi Lincoln believed he faced a full-scale armed rebellion and began calling the incident the "Mashpee Revolt." In fact, Apess and the Mashpees were peaceably calling for the rights of self-government that belonged to any citizen of the United States. Apess's work, *Indian Nullification of the Unconstitutional Laws of Massachusetts*, remains the best account of the events. The Mashpees won most of their demands.

Apess last recorded public appearance came in 1836, when he delivered his controversial "Eulogy for King Philip." His death at the age of 41 seems to be the direct result of **alcoholism**, a problem he was never able to overcome. His works represent the greatest literary output by an Indian prior to the 20th century. In his works and his life, he argued that Indians were more than the stereotypes white people imagined.

AQUASH, ANNA MAE PICTOU (1945–1975). Born on the Micmac Reserve in Nova Scotia, Canada, in 1945, Aquash moved to Boston and became a teacher's aide in 1963. In Boston, she worked with urban Indians in the city and later helped plan the demonstration at *Mayflower II* on Thanksgiving Day in 1970. She became associated with such **American Indian Movement (AIM)** leaders as **Russell Means** and **Dennis Banks** and joined AIM and soon took on leadership roles.

She opposed the tribal government leadership at the Pine Ridge Indian Reservation in South Dakota and supported the removal of Richard Wilson, the tribal chairman. She was at **Wounded Knee II** in 1973 and even formally united in a traditional Sioux ceremony with Nogeeshik Aquash, a Chippewa Canadian she had been with since her time in Boston during the occupation in April 1973. Later, she apparently had an affair with Banks. Aquash continued her AIM activities at Pine Ridge and elsewhere. However, because of the Federal Bureau of Investigation (FBI) infiltrations of AIM in attempts to destroy the movement, she was suspected of possibly being an FBI informant, and some AIM members questioned her loyalty.

Aquash was murdered in mid-December 1975 on the Pine Ridge Indian Reservation, but her body was not discovered until February 1976. Who killed her remains shrouded in controversy and mystery. In March 2003, two men were indicted for the slaying of Aquash. Arlo Looking Cloud, an Oglala Sioux, was convicted of the murder and sentenced to life in prison in April 2004, while John Graham (aka John Boy Patton), a Yukon native, was also charged in the killing of Aquash; but since he lived in Canada, Graham appealed his extradition to the United States but lost his appeal in June 2007. Each man declares that he did not kill Aquash. Many Indians remain skeptical of the murder and speculate that Aquash could have been set up as an informant and murdered by an FBI agent instead of by Indians. *See also* WOMEN.

ARROW, INC. Arrow, Inc., was originally founded as an independent agency under the auspices of the **National Congress of American Indians (NCAI)**. The original intent of Arrow, Inc., was to assist Southwest Indians who were suffering the effects of a terrible winter in 1948 and 1949. However, by 1952, the organization had developed a larger initiative and grew increasingly independent of the NCAI.

Arrow, Inc., sponsors projects to promote the general well-being of Indian people and provides information on the conditions of Indians to the general public. The organization initiates projects at the **reservation** level using direct aid and federal grants. In recent years, Arrow, Inc., has focused on recruiting qualified nurses and doctors to work on reservations to meet deep staffing shortages. A direct result of the work of Arrow, Inc., has been the creation of the **National American Indian Court Judges Association**.

ASSOCIATION ON AMERICAN INDIAN AFFAIRS (AAIA). Founded in 1922 in New York, the AAIA has undergone several name changes in its long history of helping Native Americans. The

AAIA was originally called the **Eastern Association on Indian Affairs**, then the National Association on Indian Affairs in 1933 for a more national title, then the **American Association on Indian Affairs** after it merged with the **American Indian Defense Association** in 1937 because of similar objectives and for financial reasons, and finally the Association on American Indian Affairs to better emphasize its identity in 1946.

In 1930, anthropologist and author Oliver La Farge began his long association with the AAIA that lasted for more than three decades. The AAIA supported Indian New Deal programs and conducted investigations of conditions on **reservations**. Among the publications of the association were *The American Indian* (1943–1959), a quarterly journal; studies on Indian health, Indian families, racism in American history textbooks, Indian and Eskimo authors, and Indian **education**; and a newsletter called *Indian Affairs*. The AAIA also opposed **termination**, a federal policy to "liberate" Indians from their special status.

Still in existence, the AAIA continues promoting the welfare of Native Americans and Alaska native peoples. Recent activities included supporting the Indian Child Welfare Act of 1978 and the Native American Graves Protection and Repatriation Act of 1990, advocating the protection of Native American sacred sites, establishing health programs, awarding educational scholarships, and even creating a Dakota-language Scrabble game and tournament in 2006.

– B –

BANKS, DENNIS (1937–). Born on 12 April 1937, on the Leech Lake Indian Reservation in Minnesota, Banks, an Ojibwa, is one of the founders of the **American Indian Movement (AIM)** and is among the leading figures in the Indian activist movement that began in the late 1960s. Initially raised by his grandparents in traditional ways, at a young age, Banks was forced to attend an off-**reservation** federal boarding school and then other schools in both North Dakota and South Dakota before returning to Leach Lake. He joined the U.S. air force in 1953 and was stationed in Japan and Korea. After his tour of duty, Banks returned home to the poverty of his reservation and then to the slums of Minneapolis, drinking and getting thrown into jail for participating in illegal activities.

Determined to make a better life for himself, Banks became involved in community activities in Minneapolis to help Indians and learned more about Indian affairs. He briefly worked as a recruiter to hire Indians to work for the Honeywell Corporation in 1968. Influenced by African American movements and activism for civil rights, Banks and other Indians in Minneapolis decided that Native Americans must also become more active and vocal in their demands. In 1968, he helped found AIM and later planned and led many of the demonstration movements of the organization. He was among the demonstrators who seized the *Mayflower II* on Thanksgiving Day 1970 to remind the nation of the atrocities committed against the Indians by the English settlers; he played major roles in the **Trail of Broken Treaties** in 1972, **Wounded Knee II** in 1973, and the **Longest Walk** in 1978; and he fought for Indian civil rights and better investigations and proper punishment of whites accused of murdering Indians.

Found guilty of assault during an AIM demonstration in Custer, South Dakota, that protested the sentence given to a white man who had murdered an Indian in 1973, Banks jumped bail and fled to California, where Governor Jerry Brown refused to extradite him to South Dakota. Banks contended that if he were incarcerated in South Dakota, he would be killed there. In 1983, Banks left California because the new governor was going to accept the extradition and moved to New York, where he lived on the Onondaga Reservation. Banks surrendered himself to South Dakota authorities later in 1983 and served one year in prison.

During the last decades of the 20th century and into the 21st century, Banks continued his involvement with Native Americans, serving as an **alcohol** and drug counselor on the Pine Ridge Indian Reservation in South Dakota; supporting the return of Indian remains and artifacts to tribes; organizing "Sacred Runs" for Indian youths; and giving lectures on Indian history, **religion**, and philosophy. He has also appeared in several films, including *The Last of the Mohicans* (1992). A member of the Colorado AIM, Banks owns a tribal business that manufactures natural foods in Minnesota. His autobiography, *Ojibwa Warrior: Dennis Banks and the Rise of the American Indian*

Movement, was published in 2004. To commemorate the 30th anniversary of the 1978 **Longest Walk**, Banks helped coordinate the Longest Walk II, another march on Washington, D.C., which focused on environmental protection issues and Indian rights.

BELLECOURT, CLYDE (1939–). Born on 8 May 1936, on the White Earth Reservation in Minnesota, Clyde Bellecourt, an Anishinabe/Ojibwe, was one of the founders of the **American Indian Movement (AIM)** in 1968. Bellecourt came from a large family, having 11 siblings, including his brother **Vernon Bellecourt**, another well-known Indian activist. He had a troubled youth, spending time in and out of reform schools and prison. While in prison, Bellecourt obtained a license as a steam plant engineer, developed his speaking abilities, and learned about Indian religions and cultures.

For several decades, Bellecourt has been involved in movements to help Native Americans. He worked to improve housing conditions and **education**; helped organize the **Trail of Broken Treaties** march on Washington, D.C., in 1972 and the 71-day occupation known as **Wounded Knee II** in 1973; helped plan the **Longest Walk** in 1978; worked to prevent gang-related activities among troubled Indian youth; and promoted Native American religious, environmental, and cultural issues. He and some other AIM leaders, most notably **Russell Means**, have parted ways, and Bellecourt is among those members of the Colorado AIM.

BELLECOURT, VERNON (1931–2007). Born on 17 October 1931 on the White Earth Reservation in Minnesota, Vernon Bellecourt, an Anishinabe/Ojibwe and older brother of **Clyde Bellecourt**, came from a large family and like his brother had several confrontations with the law that resulted in his incarceration. While in prison, he acquired skills as a barber, and he later became a hairstylist in Minneapolis.

Bellecourt played a leading role in the **American Indian Movement (AIM)** demonstrations in the 1960s and 1970s, including the 1972 Bureau of Indian Affairs takeover in Washington, D.C. He has also protested the use of Indians as **mascots**, especially by the Washington Redskins; helped found and served as executive director of the Colorado AIM; expressed contempt toward other AIM leaders, like

Russell Means; and held membership in the White Earth Tribal Government. He died on 13 October 2007 in Minneapolis, Minnesota.

BLACK DRINK. Southeastern Indians of the United States, like the Creeks, Choctaws, and Cherokees, consumed the Black Drink on a daily basis. This caffeinated beverage was made by boiling the stems and leaves of the yaupon holly (*Ilex vomitoria Ait*), which was native to the region, and was believed to provide purification and wisdom. The Black Drink was consumed in massive quantities at council meetings and rituals, and the drink served as an emetic, causing a vomiting effect. In other rituals, beverages derived from other plants were also called "black drinks," and Southeastern Indians and those removed to present-day Oklahoma still use black drink beverages in their ceremonies.

BLACK HAWK (c. 1767–1838). A Sauk war leader and spokesman, Black Hawk came of age during a time of great turmoil for the Indian people of the Upper Mississippi Valley. British victory in the Seven Years' War expelled the French from America, but a few French traders still moved at will among the tribes of the Mississippi Valley. French activities brought the British and Spanish into the area seeking lucrative Indian trade and military alliances. In his early years, Black Hawk watched the Sauk economy fall apart, their hunting territories shrink, and their remaining lands threatened by the ever-expanding Americans. As a war leader, Black Hawk helped foster resistance to the inevitable and disastrous changes to tribal life.

Black Hawk rose to prominence in the Sauk Nation during the late 18th century by allying with the Mesquakies (Fox) and leading successful raids against neighboring tribes. In war and diplomacy, Black Hawk served as a leader of his people. Until 1804, when the Americans took over St. Louis from the Spanish, Black Hawk viewed the Europeans as his friends and allies. The Americans, however, were different. From the first meeting with the Americans, the Sauks distrusted the motives of these newcomers. Distrust led to violence and, in that same year, settlers faced a series of attacks. The American settlers demanded punishment of the Indians of the Mississippi Valley. A small Sauk delegation traveled to St. Louis, and federal officials forced them to sign a treaty ceding all of their lands east of the Mississippi River.

It seems to have taken a number of years for the majority of the Sauk nation to learn of the 1804 treaty, but when they did, a large portion of the tribe rejected it. At the start of the War of 1812, large numbers of Sauk warriors—Black Hawk among them—joined the British in an effort to fight off American expansion. During the war, Black Hawk led warriors first to Detroit and then into other portions of the Old Northwest, campaigning in Michigan, Indiana, and as far east as Ohio. When the warriors returned to Illinois in late 1813, a young warrior named **Keokuk** was chosen as village leader. Chosen for his oratorical and political skills, Keokuk relegated Black Hawk to the fringes of Sauk life. Black Hawk turned to the one thing that had brought him renown throughout his life: war. In 1814, he and a number of warriors defeated a force led by Zachary Taylor, who was ordered to the Mississippi Valley to punish the Sauks for their siding with the British. Hostilities ended in 1816.

By 1831, Black Hawk was the spokesmen for a ragtag group of Sauks, Mesquakies, and other Indians who refused to recognize treaties with the United States and move to lands west of the Mississippi. In 1832, Black Hawk led his group across the Mississippi River into Illinois in an attempt to establish a new village and begin farming. Pioneer and politician protests forced President Andrew Jackson to call in federal troops. By April of that year, American troops chased Indians up and down the Mississippi Valley as far north as southern Wisconsin, eventually pushing them to the western side of the river. Troops overtook the exhausted band at the mouth of the Bad Axe River and massacred many of them. Black Hawk was captured and sent to prison in Virginia. He returned to his tribe in disgrace and died in 1838.

Black Hawk remains a symbol of cultural pride for the Sauks and Mesquakies because his actions, despite their outcomes, were based on Sauk beliefs and traditions; however, by 1832, the American onslaught was too great to withstand.

BLACK MESA LEGAL DEFENSE FUND. In 1969, traditional Navajos and Hopis organized the Black Mesa Legal Defense Fund in an effort to stop strip mining on **reservation** lands. The work of the fund helped bring about increased knowledge of environmental issues in the United States, especially in the desert southwest. Representatives testified before the United Nations Conference on the Human Environment in 1972. Their testimony created an outpouring of support, and dangerous strip-mining operations on Navajo and Hopi lands came to an end.

BLACKFOOT CONFEDERACY. The Blackfoot Confederacy consists of four tribes: the Pikuni/Peigan, North Peigan Pikuni, Blood/Kainai, and Blackfoot/Siksika. Members of the confederation live in Montana and across the border in Alberta, Canada. When the Canadian government/British Crown sought to enter into a treaty with the Niitsitapi (the Real People), they made initial contact with the Siksika, who lived on the north and northeastern frontiers of Blackfoot territory. They made the incorrect assumption that all Niitsitapi were Blackfoot and as such, the confederacy was born.

BOARD OF INDIAN COMMISSIONERS. Created by an act of Congress in 1869, the Board of Indian Commissioners served as an advisory body to the Department of the Interior regarding Indian affairs, especially the allocation of funds for Indian programs. The board was composed of 10 members appointed by the president of the United States who served without pay. The board was part of the larger federal Indian policy reform movement that focused on assimilation programs after the cessation of the American Civil War. Board members were usually white reformers who demanded that Indians abandon their traditional ways and assimilate into mainstream America.

The board engaged in such activities as visiting Indian **reservations**, investigating complaints against Indian agents, examining the use of the treaty-making system, inspecting annuity payments to Indians, exposing graft and corruption in the **Bureau of Indian Affairs**, and studying the increasing conflict between civil versus military control over Indian issues. Board members often became increasingly upset with the Department of the Interior for not implementing their recommendations, and disgruntled members resigned in protest.

Although the Board of Indian Commissioners could only recommend changes to federal Indian policies, issues that needed addressing were nevertheless exposed, and some, like health and **education** reforms, were acted upon. The board continued to support assimilation programs during the 1920s and 1930s. In 1933, it was abolished because it was out of step with the Indian New Deal policies.

BONNIN, GERTRUDE SIMMONS (AKA ZITKALA-SA) (1876–1938). Born on the Yankton Sioux Reservation in South Dakota on 22 February 1876, Bonnin's Indian name was Zitkala-Sa, meaning Red Bird; her mother was Yankton Nakota, and her father was white. At the age of eight, she was convinced to attend a Quaker school in Indiana, and in 1895, she enrolled at Earlham College, also in Indiana, where she excelled in oratory and music. In 1898, Bonnin accepted a position as a teacher at Carlisle Indian School in Pennsylvania, and in 1899 she attended the Boston Conservatory of Music, studying the violin. In 1900, she toured Europe with the Carlisle Indian Band, receiving high praise for her violin performances.

These years of education caused her to reconsider her life and relationship with her mother and people, which had become estranged. Bonnin began to write articles that were published in such magazines as the *Atlantic Monthly* and *Harper's*, which questioned federal assimilation policies and the general mistreatment of Indians, and these articles and others were later published in two books, *Old Indian Legends* (1901) and *American Indian Stories* (1921).

Bonnin became engaged to Dr. **Carlos Montezuma**, a Yavapai, but later broke off the engagement and married Raymond Bonnin, a Yankton Nakota and **Bureau of Indian Affairs** employee, in 1902. The Bonnins worked at the Uintah Ouray Ute Agency in Utah from 1902 to 1916. Bonnin also became active in the **Society of American Indians (SAI)**, founded in 1911, and she later served as the SAI secretary and editor of its quarterly journal in 1916. She demanded U.S. citizenship for Indians, banning **peyote** use among Indians, ending white corruption and graft perpetrated against the Five Tribes in Oklahoma, and improving **reservation** conditions and opportunities. After the demise of the SAI, Bonnin founded the **National Council of American Indians** in 1926 and worked with other groups to improve political, economic, and social issues affecting Native Americans. Bonnin died on 25 January 1938, and is buried in Arlington Cemetery. She represented an educated female Indian who identified injustices that Native Americans endured and became involved in movements to reform federal Indian policy to eradicate these problems. *See also* WOMEN.

BRANT, JOSEPH (c. 1742–1807). A Mohawk warrior and diplomat, Brant is best remembered as a Loyalist military hero during the American Revolution, the founder of a pan-tribal alliance designed to protect Indian lands after the American Revolution, and the founder of an Indian community on the Grand River in Canada. Brant was truly a man of both worlds. He learned English and attended Eleazar Wheelock's school in Connecticut from 1761 to 1763. When he returned to his people, he taught them to farm in European fashion, assisted the Christian missionaries active in the area, and served as interpreter for British superintendent of Indian affairs Guy Johnson.

Brant became alarmed by threats to Indian lands in the years before the American Revolution. Traveling to London, England, in 1775, he attempted to break the neutral position of the **Iroquois Confederacy** at his reception with King George III. Brant was convinced that the British would provide him with support and future protection if he took up arms for their side. On 6 August 1777, Brant, leading a force of Indians and white volunteers, attacked an American militia in Oriskany, New York. For the next five years, he led forces against the Americans in New York and Ohio. Working with other Loyalists and Indians, Brant's force struck across a wide swath of land helping harass superior militias, destroy supply lines, level settlements, and divert Continental forces from battles in the East. Despite his battlefield successes, Brant's cause was lost. The war divided the Iroquois and destroyed Indian villages. Much worse, the British abandoned their Indian allies in the Treaty of Paris of 1783, ceding all territory south of the Great Lakes to the Americans without mention of the Indian occupants.

In 1784, Brant moved to Canada on a plot of land awarded to him and his followers. Almost 2,000 Indian Loyalists, mostly Mohawks, moved to the grant near the site of present-day Brantford. Two years later, Brant again traveled to London to secure payment for Indian losses during the American Revolution.

He continued to urge the Indians south of the Great Lakes to resist the idea that the United States had secured title to their territory by right of conquest. Under Brant's leadership, the Indians of the Ohio Valley formed the Western Confederacy. The confederacy argued that the boundary between the new nation and Indian land was still that as defined in the 1768 Treaty of Fort Stanwix. Fear of losing Indian trade kept the British installed at interior forts despite stipulating otherwise in the Treaty of Paris, and these outposts supplied the confederacy with ammunition. Brant gave up his leadership when the United States moved away from Conquest Theory and began to acquire Indian lands by purchase and treaty.

At home on the Grand River, Brant exhibited all the problems of a man operating in two cultures. He encouraged Indians to improve their economy, convert to Christianity, and send their children to British schools. He translated the Gospel of St. Mark and the Book of Common Prayer into Mohawk in 1787. Yet, he remained proud of his Mohawk heritage, encouraging many traditional ceremonies and speaking out against total assimilation. Brant died at his home in Burlington on 24 November 1807.

BRAVE BIRD, MARY (AKA MARY CROW DOG) (1953–). Born on the Rosebud Reservation in South Dakota in 1953, Mary Brave Bird, a Sicangu Lakota, recalled her experiences as an Indian woman growing up in poverty on and off the **reservation** and as an Indian activist in two autobiographies, *Lakota Woman* (1990) and *Ohitika Woman* (1993). As a child, she lived in a small cabin that lacked electricity and indoor plumbing, and her father had abandoned the family. Brave Bird later attended a Catholic boarding school, where she encountered both physical and cultural abuse. Her troubled teenage years were filled with **alcohol** and other abusive activities. Brave Bird saw hope for her and other Indians in the **American Indian Movement (AIM)** and joined the organization. She was among those who took part in the **Trail of Broken Treaties** and the Bureau of Indian Affairs takeover in 1972, and in 1973, she participated in the occupation known as **Wounded Knee II** in South Dakota, where she delivered a baby during the siege and later married, "Indian style," Leonard Crow Dog, a leading medicine man of AIM. She learned about her heritage and traditions from him, topics that Brave Bird's mother refused to discuss with her because she feared it would hamper her daughter's assimilation into white society. Mary and Leonard Crow Dog later parted ways, and she reassumed her last name of Brave Bird.

Brave Bird provides a female perspective of an activist involved in significant experiences and movements that were dominated by Indian males. Three films portray her involvement in movements, including *Incident at Oglala, The Leonard Peltier Story* (1991); *Thunderheart* (1992), which has a female character patterned after her; and *Lakota Woman, Siege at Wounded Knee* (1994), a TNT film. *See also* WOMEN.

BRONSON, RUTH MUSKRAT (1897–1982). Born in **Indian Territory** in 1897, Bronson, a Cherokee, lived a long life devoted to helping Native Americans. Her father was Cherokee and her mother was white, and the family engaged in farming. She saw how assimilation policies and land allotments had caused many problems for her people. In 1912, Bronson attended preparatory school in Tonkawa, Oklahoma, and later took courses at the University of Oklahoma and the University of Kansas, and received a bachelor of arts degree from Mount Holyoke College in 1925. Before her graduation, she worked at a summer recreation program for Mescalero Apache girls on their **reservation** in New Mexico in 1921, and she later traveled to Asia with a student Christian group, becoming acquainted with different cultures.

Bronson believed in Indian self-determination and campaigned for better educational programs and opportunities for Native Americans. She was a member of the Committee of One Hundred, a group of non-Indians and Indians organized by the secretary of the interior in 1923 to review federal Indian policy. Their findings were published in 1924 as *The Indian Problem*. Bronson, dressed in Indian garb, was among those meeting with President Calvin Coolidge, and a photograph was taken of them in which she presented the president with a book on Indian history. Included among the recommendations of the committee were more attention to Native American education, improvements in reservation health services, support of the Pueblo Indian land claims in New Mexico, a thorough study of **peyote** use, and protection of Indian land holdings.

In 1925, Bronson began her career with the **Bureau of Indian Affairs (BIA)**, working as a teacher at Haskell Institute in Lawrence, Kansas. In 1928, she married John Bronson, who supported her work. She left Haskell in 1930 and took a BIA position that helped find jobs for Native American graduates and later helped them secure U.S. federal government loans for additional schooling. She retired in 1943, having helped approximately 2,500 students in these loan programs.

In 1944, Bronson wrote *Indians Are People Too*, which attempted to dispel Indian stereotypes. In 1945, she joined the **National Congress of American Indians (NCAI)** and soon became an active member in its campaigns to combat new assimilation programs. In 1946, she became executive secretary of the NCAI.

Bronson then accepted a position with the Indian Health Service in 1957, moving to San Carlos Apache Indian Reservation in Arizona. She provided health service education and worked with Indian **women** to develop leadership skills. Bronson again retired in 1962 and moved to Tucson, where she worked as a representative of the Save the Children Foundation among Yaqui and Tohono O'odham Indians. On 14 May 1982, she died. Her career that spanned six decades of working with and helping Native Americans is truly remarkable.

BROTHERHOOD OF NORTH AMERICAN INDIANS. Founded in 1912 mainly as a fraternal and cultural organization, the Brotherhood of North American Indians may have been an alternative choice to the more effective and well-known **Society of American Indians**. The body stressed the preservation of Native American traditions and **Pan-Indianism**. Membership was two-fold: Native Americans could hold full membership, while others, like important personalities in arts, sciences, and literature, could be honorary members. Those holding office in the body had special titles, for example, calling the director the "Great Sachem."

BUREAU OF INDIAN AFFAIRS (BIA). Created by the secretary of war, John C. Calhoun, in 1824 and sometimes referred to as the Office of Indian Affairs, the Indian Bureau, and the Indian Service, the BIA is a Department of the Interior agency that administers to and manages federal relationships with more than 560 Native American nations and Alaska natives. It holds 55.7 million acres of land in trust and provides educational services to approximately 48,000 Indian students.

During the Colonial Period, European powers attempted to convince Native Americans to become their exclusive allies in war and in trade. Acquiring Indian lands was always a major objective as well. To achieve these objectives, the Spanish, French, and English designated certain officials and agencies to negotiate with Indian peoples. Similarly, after the United States won its independence, Indian affairs were placed under the jurisdiction of the Department of War. New laws were enacted to restrict the liquor trade and require licenses to trade with Indians, and treaty negotiations to acquire more Indian lands continued.

New federal assimilation programs were also implemented in the early 1800s to hasten the Indians' abandonment of their traditional ways, and Thomas McKenney directed these efforts and handled other aspects of Indian and white relations, including correspondence, expenditures, and treaty issues. In 1832, Congress created the position of commissioner of Indian affairs to head the BIA.

As the nation expanded, so did the duties and responsibilities of the BIA. The creation of **Indian Territory** in the 1820s, the passage of the **Indian Removal Act** of 1830, the organization of territories west of the Mississippi before and after the Civil War, and the establishment of many new Indian **reservations** contributed to the expansion of the bureau. Conflicts and competition between military and nonmilitary jurisdiction concerning Indians also increased, resulting in the transfer of the BIA from the Department of War to newly created Department of the Interior in 1849. It was believed that nonmilitary control of Indian affairs was a better way to achieve assimilation programs on reservations.

After the Civil War, assimilation efforts intensified. The appointment of **Ely Parker** as the first Indian to become commissioner of Indian affairs, the creation of the **Board of Indian Commissioners** to serve as a "watchdog" of BIA activities, the increased funding for Indian schools, and the attempts to select more qualified Indian agents to head reservations are some examples of these efforts to force Indians to assimilate.

The passage of the **Dawes Severalty Act** in 1887 was viewed as the panacea to convince Indians to abandon their traditional ways, accept individual land allotments, and engage in farming activities. The BIA managed the mammoth process, assigning and later selling reservation land. The land allotment policy was a miserable failure but operated until 1934.

The BIA expanded its operations as the 19th century ended and the 20th century began. Besides divisions of the bureau dealing with land, civilization, and finances and records, new divisions were established that concerned depredations and medical and educational matters. Indian agents enforced legislation that denied Indians the right to practice traditional ceremonies. By 1911, the BIA had approximately 6,000 employees, compared with its original workforce of about three members. At the end of the 20th century, approximately 13,000 employees, most of whom were Native Americans, worked for the bureau, which had a budget of more than $800 million.

Calls to reform or even abolish the BIA became more vocal in the early 1900s. Many Native American members of the **Society of American Indians**, founded in 1911, demanded its abolishment, while others criticized the bureau for providing inadequate services and engaging in wasteful practices. During the 1920s, **John Collier** declared that the BIA needed to abolish land allotments, refocus on Indian needs, and improve reservation conditions. Government and nongovernment groups conducted studies that revealed the problems Indians endured under BIA-directed programs.

When Collier became commissioner of Indian affairs in 1933, he initiated an Indian New Deal, which slowed down the pace of assimilation and recognized Indians' rights to be Indians. Many reformers and government officials did not support Collier's cultural pluralism approach to Indian and white relations. When World War II ended, Collier resigned in disgust, and the pendulum swung back to more aggressive assimilation policies, like the **termination** of the special relationship Indians had with the U.S. federal government and relocation of Indians from reservations to urban areas for better economic and other opportunities. These policies again proved disastrous, and Indians, like other discontented Americans, staged protest movements throughout the nation in the 1960s and 1970s, demanding recognition of their rights. In 1972, for example, Indians joined the **Trail of Broken Treaties** march on Washington, D.C., and occupied the BIA headquarters. Native American protest movements convinced the federal government to abandon its assimilation policies and pass legislation that granted Indians more control over services and programs provided by the bureau.

Since 1966, only Native Americans have held the position of commissioner of Indian affairs, presently called assistant secretary for Indian affairs, and by the last decades of the 20th century, a growing number of Indian tribes were exercising their sovereignty and self-determination rights, while maintaining their special status with the federal government. Many problems still exist, however. A primary concern is the **Cobell case**, a major lawsuit against the Department of the Interior for mismanaging hundreds of thousands of individual Indian trust land accounts and not properly compensating the landowners. Nevertheless, the BIA no longer patronizes Indians and no longer demands that Indians abandon their native traditions.

BUREAU OF INDIAN AFFAIRS (BIA) TAKEOVER. *See* TRAIL OF BROKEN TREATIES.

– C –

CACIQUE. Cacique is a word of Arawakan (Caribbean Indian) origin that Spanish explorers and colonists applied to Indian religious leaders. When applied to the Pueblos of the American southwest, the term denoted the supreme priest in the town or village. Among the Pueblos, the cacique is considered the deciding authority in all town matters, both religious and secular.

CALUMET. A calumet, or peace pipe, was the name the French gave to this sacred pipe used by many Native Americans in their ceremonies. Although types of calumets differed among Indian tribes, the pipe stems were usually adorned with feathers, furs, or other ornaments, and the detachable pipe bowls were made of clay, stone, or the highly prized red pipestone and were decorated as well. The adornments and decorations dictated how the pipes were to be used. Indians believed that the calumet possessed spiritual powers and smoked it at peace conferences, before going to war or on a hunt, at healing ceremonies, and during other important ceremonies. Specially trained individuals cared for the pipes, and certain protocols at events were observed in its usage, for example, how it was presented and the order in which it was smoked by participants.

CAPTIVES. Taking captives was a widely used war tactic in Indian America, even before the arrival of Europeans. Although often used by Europeans to justify their wars against Native Americans, tribes used captives as slaves both for religious ceremonies and other important functions.

In the British colonies, death, torture, adoption, or ransom were the fates of captives secured by Indians from time immemorial until the American Revolution. During the 17th and 18th centuries, Indian **women** were the determining factors in the fate of captives. Female elders decided whether their men would go to war, and a family who lost a member in battle could choose from the returning captives and adopt the prisoner into their family to replace the lost member.

In most cases, the age and sex of the captive determined the fate. Men generally endured a number of physical trials, including torture with the result likely being death. Adoption was possible if a man bore his trials in a manner satisfying to his captors, but adoption would also mean that the man would have to become one with his enemies. Women and small children had a very different fate. Although psychologically terrorized by their ordeal and frequently witnessing the murder of their parents and loved ones, they were often adopted into the enemy tribe and took on roles that sought to stabilize family and village life.

Europeans also kidnapped their share of Indians. Early explorers captured Indians and brought them back to Europe as specimens. From the 1600s through the 19th century, when **disease**, warfare, and overwork destroyed Indian populations, millions of Africans were captured in an effort to supply a ready labor force in the colonies. The taking of captives is not an Indian phenomenon, but more likely a universal one.

However, it was the stories of whites captured by Indians that caught the imagination of the colonists and their ancestors. The writings of Puritan ministers and of some captives began as statements of religious experience. For them, God punished his children for their misdeeds by having them captured by the Indians. Later, these writings evolved into works of ethnography, with the captive giving whites the only glimpse into Indian cultures they may have ever had. Later still, in the 19th century, captivity stories became grist for the propaganda mills and an easy sale at the book counters. Captivity themes became a staple of art and popular culture. Although the Puritans confined their narratives toward Biblical speculation, captivity stories of later years are full of gore, folklore, and wild, speculative fictions.

Despite the gross exaggerations of most captivity narratives, these stories provide a window into Anglo-American, Indian, and French interactions along the North American frontier. Vacillating between adventure story and spiritual struggle, the depiction of capture and encounters between Indians and whites in the wilderness has left a lasting mark on the American mind. The narratives reached all aspects of politics and history and discussions of race and gender and even influenced the arts and popular conceptions.

CATAWBA. Both a tribe and a movement, the group of people known collectively as Catawbas have a unique history. Among the most prominent Indian people met by the first Spanish explorers in the southeast, Catawba life has changed drastically. Between the years 1698 and 1759, epidemic **disease** tore through Catawba territory, reducing their numbers to less than 500. In an effort to ward off extinction, the Catawbas began incorporating their neighbors—Waterees, Cheraws, Pedees, Saponis, and others—into their nation. So successful was this incorporation that those calling themselves Catawba spoke more than 20 different languages. The Treaty of Nation Ford removed the Catawbas from South Carolina in 1840. They were to receive a **reservation** elsewhere in the Carolinas and a cash payment, though neither was ever received. In the 1850s, a number of Catawbas began returning to their South Carolina homeland. On 29 November 1993, they reached a formal settlement with the governments of South Carolina and the United States, receiving federal recognition and $50 million for land purchases, economic development, and **education**.

CHURCHILL, WARD (1947–). Born 2 October 1947 in Elmwood, Illinois, Churchill, who claims Cherokee and Creek ancestry and membership in the United Keetoowah Band of Cherokee in Oklahoma, was a professor and former chair of Ethnic studies at the University of Colorado and is a leader and an active member of the **American Indian Movement (AIM)** in Colorado. He received a bachelor of arts and a master of arts in communications from Sangamon State University, now the University of Illinois at Springfield, and an honorary doctorate of humane letters from Alfred University.

Churchill has presented a number of lectures annually throughout the United States and has many publications on Native American history and culture, nearly all of which are highly controversial. His September 2001 essay, "Some People Push Back: On the Justice of Roosting Chickens," which first appeared on the Internet and later in one of his books, *On the Justice of Roosting Chickens: Reflections on the Consequences of U.S. Imperial Arrogance and Criminality* (2003), created a national uproar. In the piece, Churchill argued that the 11 September 2001 attacks on the World Trade Center were provoked by genocidal U.S. foreign policies and that those killed in the attacks were not all innocent victims but "little Eichmanns," referring to the Nazi Adolf Eichmann and his role in the Holocaust. Churchill borrowed the "chickens coming home to roost" reference from Malcolm X's comment on the assassination of President John F. Kennedy, suggesting that he perhaps had it coming.

As a result, many offended Americans called for his dismissal as a university professor. In January 2005, Churchill resigned as department chair but maintained his academic rank. Governor Bill Owens of Colorado called for his removal. Factionalism in AIM was apparent when **Russell Means** supported Churchill, while **Dennis Banks** condemned his actions and claims of being an Indian. The University of Colorado conducted investigations concerning such issues as the remarks Churchill made in his essay, research improprieties, and his receiving tenure early. In 2006, a faculty investigating committee concluded that Churchill's remarks in the essay were protected speech—First Amendment rights and academic freedom—but supported charges of academic research misconduct that included manufacturing facts and plagiarizing other publications. Churchill appealed the findings. Both the University of Colorado acting chancellor Phil DiStefano and later president Hank Brown called for his dismissal.

In July 2007, the University of Colorado Board of Regents voted 8–1 in favor of his dismissal. Churchill filed a lawsuit to retain his teaching position. He remains a controversial figure in Native American movements.

CLIFF DWELLERS. Cliff Dwellers is the common name given to Indians of the Anasazi culture of the desert southwest who built their large living structures into the sides of cliffs. These structures are found on mesas and in canyons throughout the southwest, principally along the tributaries of the Rio Grande River and Colorado River in Utah, Arizona, New Mexico, and Colorado. Archaeologists once thought that these ruins were the work of an extinct people, but science has established that the ancestors of the present-day Pueblos built the structures between the 11th and 14th centuries. The dwellings were large communal structures built on ledges in the canyon walls and on the flat tops of the mesas. This setting provided an easily defensible position against raids by migrating groups. The Cliff Dwellers were sedentary agriculturists who planted crops and used complex irrigation systems. The presence of numerous **kivas** at these structures demonstrates that their religious ceremonies were also like those of the Pueblos. Many of the dwellings are now preserved in national parks. Some of the better-known ones include Mesa Verde, in Colorado, where there are more than 300 dwellings; Hovenweep National Monument, in Utah; Bandelier National Monument, in New Mexico; and Canyon de Chelly, in Arizona.

COBELL CASE (AKA *COBELL V. BABBITT*; *COBELL V. NORTON*; and *COBELL V. KEMPTHORNE*). Named after the lead plaintiff, Elouise Cobell, a Blackfeet, and filed against the U.S. Department of the Interior and the **Bureau of Indian Affairs** in U.S. District Court in June 1996, the case was initially called *Cobell v. Babbitt* (the title of the case changed each time a new secretary of the interior was appointed). It was a class-action Indian trust suit demanding an accounting of between 300,000 and 500,000 Individual Indian Money (IIM) trust accounts that the plaintiffs charged were mismanaged, lost, and frequently underpaid, estimating payment as high as $10 billion without interest (the amount could reach $40 billion or more counting interest). Because of the special status held by Native Americans, many individual Indians' property was held in trust by the U.S. federal government, which, in turn, leased these trust lands to private companies for grazing and natural resource use, usually without Indian participation in the negotiations. Distribution of payments and royalties to Indians for more than 100 years was often fraught with corruption and graft and was not being properly distributed to Indians. Therefore, the Cobell case lawsuit was filed.

For more than a decade, Cobell, who had expertise in accounting and banking, steadfastly continued to pursue the case. Significant highlights of the case are as follows: In February 1999, federal judge Royce Lamberth found interior secretary Bruce Babbitt, treasury secretary Robert Rubin, and assistant interior secretary Kevin Gover in contempt for failure to produce and protect records. In June and July 1999, "Trial One" began, which focused on ways to reform the trust accounting system. A federal mediator was appointed in October 1999; however, by December 1999 mediation had failed, and Judge Lamberth stated that the Department of the Interior had breached its Indian trust responsibilities and ordered quarterly reports on its efforts to reform the trust system. In November 2000, the Department of the Treasury revealed that it had destroyed trust documents. In February 2001, the U.S. Court of Appeals found in favor of the plaintiffs. In September 2001, a report found IIM trust fund data incomplete and mismanaged. In September 2002, interior secretary Gale Norton and assistant secretary Neil McCaleb were found in contempt for withholding evidence (charges were later dropped in July 2003). In May 2003, "Trial Two" began to determine what was owed the IIM trustees. In April 2004, two mediators were appointed, but mediation was declared a failure in October 2004. In December 2004, the U.S. Court of Appeals overruled the September 2007 deadline that Lamberth had ordered for "full and accurate accounting" by the Department of the Interior and allowed the department to devise its own sampling system and reform plans. In March 2005, Senator John McCain, chairman of the Senate Committee on Indian Affairs, pledged to study the trust issue and offer a solution. In August 2005, the Department of Justice recommended the removal of Lamberth from the case, which was done in July 2006. McCain proposed an $8 billion settlement to the IIM trustees in July 2006, and in October 2006, the IIM plaintiffs rejected McCain's proposal. In December 2006, Judge James Robertson was appointed to replace Lamberth. In early 2007, the George W. Bush administration proposed to the Senate Committee on Indian Affairs that $7 billion be paid over a 10-year period to settle all IIM accounts.

The Cobell case remains unsettled. In an effort to resolve the case, Robertson has ordered the Department of the Interior to present its accounting of the IIM trust accounts in October 2007. Following this meeting, in January 2008. Robertson ruled that the Interior Department had "unreasonably delayed" presenting their findings for billions of dollars owed to individual Indian landowners. Meanwhile, plaintiff attorneys estimated their clients' losses at $58 billion. Robertson has scheduled a trial to resolve the trust breach for June 2008 and hopes to have the entire matter resolved by the end of summer 2008. *See also* LAW.

CODY, IRON EYES (1904–1999). Born Espera DeCorti on 3 April 1904, in Kaplan, Louisiana, to Sicilian parents, he claimed Cherokee and Cree descent. While his birth certificate proves he was not Native American, he lived most of his adult life as an Indian, marrying an Indian woman, changing his name to Iron Eyes Cody, and becoming an actor in the 1920s and pledging his life to Native American causes.

Cody appeared in more than 100 films, including *A Man Called Horse* (1970), but he is most well known for his role as the "Crying Indian" in a television commercial and poster as part of the *Keep America Beautiful* campaign, "People Start Pollution; People Can Stop Pollution." Cody brought public awareness to the ecology movement as an Indian who represented a special relationship with the environment, agonizing over its destruction.

Most Native Americans overlooked the fact that Cody was not an Indian. Indeed, in 1999, Native Americans and California government officials gathered at a memorial service for Cody at the Southwest Museum in Los Angeles, California, and posthumously honored him for his commitment to Native American movements. He died on 4 January 1999, and was buried in Hollywood, California.

COLLIER, JOHN (1884–1968). Collier was born in Atlanta, Georgia, on 4 May 1884. He learned from his father, a banker and politician, that the social ills of society could only be changed by communal, cooperative efforts. Collier never graduated from college, but he attended Columbia University and the College de France. In 1907, he became secretary of the People's Institute in New York City and engaged in social work with immigrants. This work convinced him that to become Americanized, one did not have to abandon one's heritage.

In 1919, Collier became director of adult education in California, a post that he held for only one year because of his "Bolshevik" approach. Mabel Dodge, an old friend from New York, invited Collier to her residence in Taos, New Mexico, where he became enthralled with the Pueblo Indians and their survival strategies based on communal lifestyles. They had created, he opined, a "red Atlantis," which he believed sustained his approach to helping minorities. He dedicated the rest of his life to helping Native Americans.

Collier became a research agent for the Indian Welfare Committee of the General Federation of Women's Clubs in 1922 and gained national attention in a successful fight against the passage of the Bursum Bill, which threatened Spanish land grant titles to the Pueblo Indians. In 1923, he founded and became executive secretary of the **American Indian Defense Association**, an organization that called for Indian reforms citing the devastating effects of the **Dawes Severalty Act** of 1887, which allotted Indian **reservation** lands and forced Indians to become white farmers, as well as the deplorable political, economic, and social conditions of Native Americans in the United States. To Collier, Indians could retain certain aspects of their heritage and still become part of mainstream America.

In 1933, Collier became commissioner of Indian affairs and served in that position for 12 years, holding the post longer than any other commissioner. Borrowing from President Franklin D. Roosevelt's New Deal slogan, he proclaimed an Indian New Deal, which was a major reversal of past Indian policies, although it can be argued that it was a different way to assimilate Indians into white society. In addition to providing aid to Indians from the New Deal programs, Collier's Indian New Deal had three major pieces of legislation specifically for Indians enacted: the **Indian Reorganization Act (IRA)** of 1934, which was the centerpiece of the Indian New Deal and among other reforms ended land allotments and created tribal governments and businesses; the **Johnson-O'Malley Act** of 1934, which dealt with federal and state contracts for Indian **education**, agricultural assistance, medical aid, and welfare services; and the **Indian Arts and Crafts Board**, created in 1935 to promote, preserve, and protect Indian-made products.

The coming of World War II and increasing criticism of Collier's views on allowing Indians to be Indians and at the same time having them acculturate seriously weakened the Indian New Deal. Collier resigned in 1945 and later taught at the City College of New York and at Knox College. In analyzing Collier's approach to Indian policy reform, historians generally believe he improved Indian conditions, but at the same time they point out that he failed to recognize the diversity of Indian tribes and still demanded too much federal approval of changes, even though Indians had more participation in matters affecting them than ever before. Collier died in Talpa, New Mexico, on 8 May 1968.

COLUMBUS DAY. Non-Indians celebrate Columbus Day on October 12 in recognition of the "discovery" of America by Christopher Columbus in 1492. Indian people, however, look upon Columbus as the "destroyer," not the "discoverer," of America. During the last decades of the 20th century and into the 21st century, Native Americans have protested Columbus Day activities. In Denver, Colorado, especially, the Colorado branch of the **American Indian Movement (AIM)** has staged major demonstrations in which **Russell Means** and other AIM leaders have participated. It is interesting to note that Colorado became the first state to establish a Columbus Day holiday in 1907. Italian Americans tend to argue that they are honoring their Italian heritage in such events, while Native Americans do not see it that way. Columbus Day ceremonies continue to be contested and controversial.

COUNCIL OF ENERGY RESOURCE TRIBES (CERT). Established in September 1975 by Indian representatives from more than 20 tribes, CERT, headquartered in Denver, Colorado, promotes tribal management of mineral resources on Indian lands. Navajo leader **Peter MacDonald** served as its first chairman.

Before the creation of CERT, the **Bureau of Indian Affairs (BIA)** negotiated energy extraction leases on **reservations** with corporations with very little Indian input in contract provisions that generally provided monetary compensation that was below market levels. With the movement for Indian self-determination and rising energy costs in the 1970s, Indian tribes demanded more control regarding their participation in the negotiations, especially because of the large supplies of such energy resources as coal, uranium, and petroleum on

Indian lands and the potential for tribal economic development programs to improve reservation conditions.

Included among CERT's achievements are restructuring the BIA leasing programs, developing Indian partnerships with corporations, providing assistance programs to educate tribes in energy-related issues and management skills, and supporting such legislation as the Indian Mineral Development Act of 1982 and amending other environmental pieces of legislation that provided more tribal control of environmental regulations and issues on reservations. CERT continues to provide valuable reservation mineral development services, and in 1999, more than 60 tribal leaders met and developed the National Tribal Energy Vision, which has as its goal supplying reasonably priced electricity to sovereign Indian tribes by 2010.

CRAZY HORSE (c. 1842–1877). Born in the 1840s in the Black Hills of South Dakota, Crazy Horse (Tasunke Witko) was an Oglala Lakota military leader. His grandfather and father also had the same honored name, which he received in his late teen years. Early in life, he had a **vision quest** that foretold of his prowess as a warrior and protector of his people. Crazy Horse also developed a strong resentment toward whites, whom he condemned for their wanton killing of Indians and believed could not be trusted. Continuing to excel in battle, Crazy Horse became a shirtwearer, a high honor among his people. In that capacity, he served as a role model for others to emulate, even though he later had to relinquish the honor due to a love triangle he became involved in. Regardless, he continued to have the respect of his people. Crazy Horse was not a flamboyant figure and did not flaunt his successes.

Crazy Horse fought with **Sitting Bull** against the U.S. army and led forces in two successful battles, one at Rosebud Creek against General George Crook and the other at the Little Bighorn against Lieutenant Colonel George Armstrong Custer in June 1876. However, within a year, the Indians were defeated, and Crazy Horse surrendered in 1877. Crazy Horse was killed by a soldier's bayonet at Fort Robinson in Nebraska on 5 September 1877, when he refused to be incarcerated. Sioux people continue to admire his dignity, prestige, and stature, and a memorial sculpture of the great leader is still being constructed in the Black Hills. Interestingly, there is no authenticated photograph of Crazy Horse.

CRAZY HORSE MEMORIAL FOUNDATION. Famous sculptor Korczak Ziolkowski (1908–1982) began working on a massive sculpture of **Crazy Horse**, the well-known and respected Oglala leader, at Thunderbird Mountain in the Black Hills of South Dakota in 1947. The impressive structure is roughly 20 miles from the carved presidential heads at Mount Rushmore. At the time of Ziolkowski's death, more than seven million tons of granite had been blasted off the mountain; the project still continues to be directed by family members 60 years after the project began.

The finished sculpture will be an impressive 563 feet high and 641 feet long, and its primary purpose is to remind Sioux people to be proud of the greatness of Crazy Horse and his commitment to his people and to give them strength to meet future challenges. The Crazy Horse Memorial Foundation also provides additional services, including an Indian museum and learning center and education and nursing scholarships to aid Native American students. Publications about the project are available for purchase. Ziolkowski's body is buried at the site, and both Indian and non-Indian contributors continue to support completion of the world's largest sculpture honoring the great Sioux leader.

CROW DOG, MARY. *See* BRAVE BIRD, MARY (AKA MARY CROW DOG).

– D –

DAUGHTERS OF POCAHONTAS. Established in Philadelphia, Pennsylvania, in 1887 and named after the famous Indian woman, the Daughters of Pocahontas had as its goals the teaching of loyalty, love, charity, and kindness to America. An Indian woman, flanked by two American flags, and wearing a shield with the words "Degree of Pocahontas" on her chest, is the organization's insignia. The Daughters of Pocahontas was the ladies auxiliary of the **Improved Order of Red Men,** a secret group that claimed to be the oldest in America, with roots traced back to the Sons of Liberty in 1763.

To become a member, **women** had to be more than 18 years old and possess high moral character. In 1907, there were approximately

26,000 members, and in 1977, in figures last reported, there were roughly 22,800 members. Until 1974, only white women could be members.

The Daughters of Pocahontas included among their charity work providing food, clothing, and other necessities to Indians; purchasing Braille books; and aiding retarded children. They also honored unknown soldiers at Arlington Cemetery, advocated safe driving programs, and provided financial assistance to fight communism.

Structured on local, state, and national levels, the Daughters of Pocahontas uses a number of Indian names in its operation. Two examples are calling a meeting place a "teepee" and a male counselor the "Powhatan." *See also* POCAHONTAS.

DAUGHTERS OF SACAJAWEA. Organized during the 1920s, the Daughters of Sacajawea was most likely a New York City chapter of the **Teepee Order of America**, one of several fraternal organizations established by Red Fox St. James, who claimed Indian heritage, in 1915. Although not much is know about the organization, by 1926, Princess Chinquilla, a Cheyenne, was a "Great Sacajawea," and with St. James, she unsuccessfully planned a cultural center for Indians in New York City. Causes for the failure included financial difficulties, religious considerations, and most likely racial issues. St. James was intolerant of Catholics and blacks, causing Indians of that faith and those with black ancestry to oppose organizations affiliated with him. After the demise of the Daughters of Sacajawea, Princess Chinquilla joined other women in New York City, who called themselves the Ojistah Council, a group that sent needed items to **reservation** Indians. *See also* SACAJAWEA.

DAWES SEVERALTY ACT (DAWES GENERAL ALLOTMENT ACT), 1887. After the American Civil War and especially during the 1880s, a growing number of Indian reformers and organizations like the **Indian Rights Association** and the **Lake Mohonk Conference of Friends of the Indian** supported the concept of allotment of **reservation** lands to ultimately achieve assimilation of Native Americans into mainstream culture. Reformers believed that breaking up reservation lands held in common into land allotments held by individual Indians would rapidly hasten assimilation efforts to Christianize and civilize Indians and convince them to adopt white farming practices.

Senator Henry Dawes of Massachusetts ultimately sponsored the bill that Congress passed in 1887. Officially called the Dawes General Allotment Act, but more commonly referred to as the Dawes Severalty Act or the Dawes Act, the legislation authorized the president of the United States to select reservations—based on recommendations from the secretary of the interior, Indian agents, and other officials—that were considered "ready" to be allotted. Because of treaty provisions or other circumstances, several tribes, like the **Five Civilized Tribes**, other tribes in **Indian Territory**, and the Seneca in New York, were initially exempted from the Dawes Act. Land allotments were as follows: Each Indian family head received 160 acres; single people more than 18 years of age received 80 acres, as did orphans less than 18 years old; and single people under 18 years of age received 40 acres of land.

Indians could choose their own land allotments, but those who resisted had land chosen for them. To prevent Indians from selling their individual land holdings, title to the property was placed in trust for 25 years. In addition, the surplus reservation land was generally sold to whites with the proceeds held in the U.S. Treasury, ideally for Indian use. Finally, Indians became U.S. citizens after receiving their land allotments.

The Dawes Act was not the panacea that Indian reformers had envisioned. In fact, its results were devastating. As the years passed, new legislation allowed Indians to receive title to their lands before the 25-year trust period ended, which often resulted in Indians selling their land allotments and becoming landless and destitute. Indians also leased their lands to whites for grazing purposes instead of working the land themselves.

After nearly 75 years in operation and despite evidence of its tremendous negative effects on Native Americans, reservation land allotments did not end until the passage of the **Indian Reorganization Act** of 1934. During those years, Indians lost more than 90 million acres of land. *See also* LAW.

DEER, ADA (1935–). Born on 7 August 1935, on the Menominee Reservation in Wisconsin, Deer's mother was white, and her father was Menominee. She moved with her family to Milwaukee for more economic opportunity in 1940. Deer faced discrimination while in elementary school there. In 1945, the family moved back to their cabin that had no electricity or running water on the **reservation** and raised goats. Deer attended public schools in Shawano, Wisconsin, and did quite well in nearly all of her courses; she won an oratory award, edited the yearbook for the senior class, and became a member of the Youth Advisory Board to the state's Commission on Human Rights. In her senior year, she also traveled to Hollywood and spoke one line in a western movie, *The Battle of Rogue River*, because her mother had submitted a picture of her to an Indian beauty contest that she won. In 1953, she entered the premed program at the University of Wisconsin and received financial aid of $1,000 a year from her tribe.

Deer became more interested in Native American issues during her college years and later changed her major to social work, graduating with a bachelor of science in 1957. She then entered Columbia University, where she received her master of science in social work in 1961. Deer then accepted a position to work with urban Indians in Minneapolis, Minnesota.

Deer also kept abreast of her tribe's efforts to fight federal **termination** of services and programs on the Menominee Reservation because the Menominee had been considered "qualified" to be terminated and had to agree to termination before they could receive a monetary settlement case they had won. In 1963, she met with the commissioner of Indian affairs in Washington, D.C., to discuss termination issues. The commissioner was impressed with her and offered her a **Bureau of Indian Affairs (BIA)** position as a community services coordinator in Minneapolis, which she accepted in 1964. In her new BIA job, she traveled to other urban Indian communities across the United States and learned firsthand the issues they faced. In 1966, Deer resigned her BIA position because her job was eliminated, and she did not like her new assignment as an employment counselor. Other jobs she held as the 1960s ended included working for the Minneapolis Board of Education as a school social worker and as an Upward Bound director at the University of Wisconsin, Stevens Point campus. Because she had gained a national reputation, she was called to serve on several boards, including the Girl Scouts of America; the Urban Task Force of the United States Department of Health,

Education, and Welfare; and **Americans for Indian Opportunity**. The issue of termination, however, still remained paramount in her life.

Deer helped found **Menominee Drums** to reverse termination and regain her tribe's special status with the U.S. federal government. Her lobbying efforts proved valuable to the movement, and the Menominee were restored to their former status in 1973. Deer also helped unite different Menominee factions after the restoration. She was selected to serve on the American Indian Policy Review Commission in 1975, and its final report two years later recommended more than 200 reforms that included a major reorganization of the BIA and more emphasis on Indian self-determination. Deer remained active as the 1970s ended, being appointed a Harvard Institute of Politics fellow; holding a senior lecturer position in the School of Social Work and Native American Studies at the University of Wisconsin in Madison; and working with the **Native American Rights Fund**, an organization concerned with helping tribes with legal issues, which she had called upon during the Menominee restoration.

An active member of the Democratic Party, Deer unsuccessfully ran for state offices in Wisconsin but continued to influence national and state Indian policy reform, and she lost to a republican opponent for a seat in the U.S. House of Representatives in 1992. President Bill Clinton appointed her as the new assistant secretary of the interior for Indian affairs—the new and elevated name for the former commissioner of Indian affairs post—in 1993. Under her leadership, more than 200 Alaska native villages and 12 tribes received federal recognition that qualified them for special status and federal programs and services, and there was an increase in tribes contracting for their own services. Deer also supported **gaming** contracts for economic development on reservations, improvements in Native American religious rights and educational opportunities, and increased recognition of Indian self-determination initiatives. Her advocacy of more Indian sovereignty made her superiors unhappy, which resulted in her resignation in 1997.

A recipient of many awards, including the Woman of the Year from the Girl Scouts of America, the **Indian Council Fire** Achievement Award, and the National Distinguished Achievement Award, Deer has devoted her life to helping Native Americans and serves as an excellent role model. *See also* WOMEN.

DEGANAWIDA. An Iroquois spiritual figure who, according to Iroquois tradition, allied with **Hiawatha** to form the political and social structure of the five Iroquois tribes. Traditional accounts of his origin vary from being of virgin birth to a Huron woman who attempted to drown him for being born Onondaga and later adopted by the Mohawks. He is credited with exceptional diplomatic skills and establishing the **Iroquois Confederacy** by laying out its laws, regulations, and customs.

DELORIA, VINE, JR. (1933–2005). Recognized as one of the premier scholars on Indian issues, Vine Deloria Jr., a Standing Rock Sioux, was born on 26 March 1933, in Martin, South Dakota, near the Pine Ridge Indian Reservation. Deloria's grandfather and father were well-known Episcopal ministers, and his aunt, Ella Deloria, was a prominent anthropologist. After serving in the U.S. marine corps, Deloria received a bachelor of arts in general science from Iowa State University in 1958, a master of arts in theology from the Lutheran School of Theology in Illinois in 1963, and a law degree from the University of Colorado School of Law in 1970. He initially wanted to follow in the footsteps of his grandfather and father, working as a minister, but instead he became executive director of the **National Congress of American Indians (NCAI)**, a position he held from 1964 to 1967. As head of the NCAI, Deloria rejuvenated the organization to once again become a leading movement in addressing Indian affairs.

For the reminder of the 20th century and into the early 21st century, Deloria's achievements have been remarkable. They included opposing **termination** of federal services to and programs for Native Americans, helping found the National Museum of the American Indian, advocating protection of Indian sacred sites and repatriating Indian remains, supporting Indian sovereignty, and providing profound arguments on Indian **gaming** issues. Perhaps his greatest contribution was the more than 20 books he wrote, beginning in 1969 with *Custer Died for Your Sins: An Indian Manifesto*, and ending with his posthumous *The World We Used to Live In: Remembering the Powers of the Medicine Men* in 2006.

Deloria placed his works into three categories: political essays, legal works, and theological writings. Besides providing valuable and thought-provoking information on Native Americans through his many publications, he also taught at the college level, first at the University of Arizona from 1978 to 1990, and then at the University of Colorado from 1990 to 2000. Among his many awards were the Wordcraft Circle Writer of the Year Award in 1999, the Wallace Stegner Award in 2002, the American Indian Festival of Words Author Award in 2003, and the American Indian Visionary Award in 2005.

Deloria was an intellectual but was also a down-to-earth human being, with a keen sense of humor. He died on 13 November 2005.

DETERMINED RESIDENTS UNITED FOR MOHAWK SOVEREIGNTY (DRUMS). DRUMS was founded in 1974 on the Akwesasne Mohawk Reservation. Also called the St. Regis Reserve, the **reservation** straddles the international boundary between the United States and Canada. DRUMS was originally established to stop smuggling operations. The organization's focus was the various illegal drinking establishments that were increasing the number of traffic accidents on the reservation. By June 1989, DRUMS members were planning a blockade of the reservation's main road to keep away patrons of illegal casinos. The plan for the blockade was abandoned when 200 Federal Bureau of Investigation agents and New York state troopers raided seven illegal gambling operations on the reservation. DRUMS continued to oppose smuggling and illegal **gaming** until 1990, when two members were killed in a shoot-out and authorities from New York, Ontario, and Quebec occupied the reservation and permanently ended the illegal operations.

DISEASE. Diseases that originated in the Old World and were transplanted to the New World have had a major impact on the biological history of Indian Country. If one accepts the Beringia Migration Theory, then one must also assume that Indians either brought with them or encountered pathogens that affected open wounds and dental decay. These oldest forms of New World disease, along with arthritis, are found in the remains of ancient hunters and gatherers discovered by archaeologists.

When Europeans arrived in the Americas, Indians were less genetically diverse than their Old World counterparts. This biological homogeneity had disastrous consequences when the Columbian

Exchange—the transfer of people, pathogens, animals, and plants—
began when Christopher Columbus first set foot on the island of Hispaniola in 1492. European newcomers and their African slaves trans-
mitted the most contagious diseases that evolved in the Old World to
Indians. Most scholars now agree that whatever the real number, the
Indian population in Mesoamerica fell by 5 to 10 percent between
1519 and 1619. The numbers for North America prove more controversial. The documentary records of disease and Indian populations
cover a much shorter time period than do the records of the quickly
colonized south.

However, it is clear that the disease epidemics that ravaged Indian
peoples began with the second voyage of Columbus. Livestock transported by Columbus's colonizing fleet carried an influenza virus that
spread among the Indians with catastrophic consequence. Native ca-
noes likely transported the virus to Cuba and Florida; however, there
is no way to verify whether this is true. Smallpox first broke out on
Hispaniola in 1518. Archaeological evidence suggests that the virus
spread northward among all intervening populations all the way to
the Canadian border. Measles ravaged Mexico in 1531 and spread
northward, the last Spanish observer noting an outbreak in Sonora,
just south of present-day Arizona. As viruses do not stop at colonial
borders, it is likely that the disease spread even farther north.

The diseases that Europeans brought with them from the Old
World caused what epidemiologists call "Virgin Soil" outbreaks; the
Indians who contracted the diseases were very susceptible because
they had not developed an effective immunity to these new
pathogens. Unfortunately, for the affected Indians, native cures often
caused as much death as the disease. One general Indian cure was the
sweat lodge ceremony, in which an individual sweats in a heated
lodge and later plunges into cold water. This treatment, although an
effective ritual previously, now weakened patients to the point that
the disease was able to take over their body. Despite the best attempts
of Indians and newcomers, diseases continued to destroy entire Indian villages.

In 1613, the bubonic plague halved Florida's Indian population.
By 1619, the epidemic had reached New England. So many Indians
died in the epidemic that when the Puritans arrived one year later,
they were convinced that God had rid the land of its native inhabi-

tants before their arrival. This belief, in the divine favor of God, governed the relationship between Puritan colonists and Indians for the rest of their history. But disease continued as the shock troop of European arrivals.

Smallpox recurred in 1649, 1662, 1669, and 1687. Measles ravaged Indian Country in 1658 and 1692, influenza took its toll in 1647 and 1675, and diphtheria raged in 1659. Malaria reached the southern shores of North America as early as the 1690s. Old World diseases continued to reach epidemic proportions through the 18th century. In all, 16 major epidemics destroyed large portions of Indian America by the turn of the 19th century. The new century brought new diseases. In the 19th century, as a result of steamship travel, cholera reached Indian communities by 1832.

Some Indian groups began to recover their lost populations in the latter years of the 19th century, though again suffering epidemic tuberculosis. Others began recovery in the first years of the 20th century, just in time to be decimated by the influenza outbreak of 1918. After World War II, just as modern medical practices developed to affect earlier epidemics, diabetes developed as a major killer of Indian peoples. As Indians become increasingly integrated into American society, they suffer from the same diseases as other North Americans.

DREAMER RELIGION. *See* SMOHALLA.

– E –

EASTERN ASSOCIATION ON INDIAN AFFAIRS (EAIA). Founded in the fall of 1922, the EAIA was established to protest the Bursum Bill of 1922, which, if enacted, would have favored non-Indian land claims of Pueblo Indian lands. EAIA membership was led by white reformers mainly from Boston and New York City. They admired Pueblo Indian culture and wanted to protect them from losing their lands, as did other organizations, like the **American Indian Defense Association (AIDA)**, although EAIA leaders were not as critical of federal policymakers as the AIDA.

Successful in defeating the Bursum Bill, the EAIA also studied problems of poverty, malnutrition, and trachoma on Indian **reservations** and secured funds to help combat these conditions. The EAIA also wanted to protect and preserve native arts and crafts, which later helped influence the establishment of the **Indian Arts and Crafts Board** in 1935. Much of the EAIA's success can be attributed to the leadership of Oliver La Farge, a white Indian reformer. He changed the name of the organization to the National Association on Indian Affairs in 1933, which increased membership, and he got along well with commissioner of Indian affairs **John Collier**. In 1937, the National Association on Indian Affairs and the AIDA joined together to form the **American Association on Indian Affairs**, and in 1946, it became known as the **Association on American Indian Affairs**.

EASTMAN, CHARLES ALEXANDER (1858–1939). Born on 19 February 1858, near Redwood Falls, Minnesota, Eastman was first named Hakadah, meaning "Pitiful Last," because his mother, who was the mixed-blood daughter of noted artist Captain Seth Eastman, died shortly after giving birth. At the age of four, he received the name of Ohiyesa, meaning "Winner," because of an Indian **lacrosse** game that his village won and because he was the child chosen by the winning team to gain the honor. A Wahpeton and Mdewakanton Santee Sioux, Ohiyesa fled to Canada after the unsuccessful Santee Sioux uprising in Minnesota in 1862. Believing his father had died during the conflict, Ohiyesa was raised by his paternal grandmother and uncle in the traditional ways of a Sioux boy. He developed his hunting skills and prepared to become a successful warrior. However, in 1872, his believed deceased father, who had been imprisoned for his role in the uprising and who became a Christian while in confinement, found his son in Canada and convinced him to return with him to his Flandreau, South Dakota, homestead. Ohiyesa became Charles Alexander Eastman and, for the next 17 years, sought his formal education in white schools.

Before going to Dartmouth College in 1883, Eastman attended several schools, including Santee Normal Training School in Nebraska, Beloit College in Wisconsin, Knox College in Illinois, and Kimball Union Academy in New Hampshire. He graduated from Dartmouth in 1887 and entered Boston University School of Medicine, receiving his medical degree in 1890.

Wanting to work among his people, Eastman became a government physician at Pine Ridge Indian Reservation in South Dakota and witnessed the **Ghost Dance** movement and the Wounded Knee tragedy in 1890. He became disillusioned working as a **Bureau of Indian Affairs (BIA)** employee and resigned in 1893. Unable to establish a successful private practice, he later held other BIA positions, including an outing agent at Carlisle Indian School in Pennsylvania in 1899; a government physician at the Crow Creek Reservation in South Dakota from 1900 to 1903; renaming the Sioux project from 1903 to 1909; and Indian inspector from 1923 to 1925.

Eastman was hailed by white Indian reformers and such organizations as the **Lake Mohonk Conference of Friends of the Indian** and the **Indian Rights Association** as the "poster child" of what an Indian could achieve through assimilation. What these reformers failed to recognize was that Eastman was an acculturated Indian—he picked and chose which aspects of the dominant society he wanted and did not abandon his Indian ways.

Eastman's greatest contributions were his writings. In 11 books and numerous articles, all of which were edited by his non-Indian wife, Elaine Goodale Eastman, he explained Indian beliefs and customs to non-Indians. Two of his books, *Indian Boyhood* (1902) and *From the Deep Woods to Civilization* (1916), were autobiographies. Several others, like *Red Hunters and the Animal People* (1904) and *Old Indian Days* (1907), concerned Indian customs and traditions and were written especially for young readers. And two books, *The Soul of the Indian* (1911) and *The Indian Today* (1915), contained valuable information on Indian **religion** and many issues affecting Indians. Eastman also became a popular speaker on the lecture circuit.

Considered by many as the foremost educated Indian living in the United States at the beginning of the 20th century, Eastman engaged in other activities and movements related to Native Americans, including helping establish the **Society of American Indians** in 1911; providing information on Indians for the Boy Scouts of America; supporting U.S. citizenship for all Indians; and serving on the Committee of One Hundred, a national body formed in 1923 to study Indian conditions and make recommendations. Eastman also traveled to England on two occasions, presenting lectures at universities and elsewhere.

During his last years, Eastman lived in Canada and, during the winter months, with his son in Detroit. Eastman and his wife parted ways, keeping their separation a secret because of the possible stigma attached to their mixed marriage not working and because of financial and personal concerns. He continued to give lectures and write but was unable to have his works published. In 1933, the **Indian Council Fire**, a **Pan-Indian** organization, presented Eastman with its first Indian Achievement Award, recognizing his many efforts to help Native Americans. He died on 8 January 1939, in Detroit, Michigan.

EDUCATION. Since the time of the first European arrivals in the New World, Indian education has been directed toward assimilating Indians to Euro-American values. Until the 19th century, Indian education was the province of missionaries and churches that established their own schools. When the American nation was born, the U.S. federal government continued the practice of religious education and even began to fund some missions/schools. In fact, much early American Indian policy was directed by religious groups who lobbied for the creation of **reservations** with corresponding reservation schools. The groups believed that if they could teach Indians in isolation and remove the influence of whites, then their assimilationist agendas would be far more effective.

In the years after the Civil War, the federal government took responsibility for Indian education. The **Bureau of Indian Affairs (BIA)** argued that the only way to end the violence underway in the West was to speed the process of assimilation. Because Indian reservations were ultimately under the guardianship of the federal government, the responsibility for Indian education would become that of the federal government as well.

How the new education policies were to be carried out was a source of much debate. Colonel Richard Henry Pratt, a retired army officer and founder of the Carlisle Indian Industrial School, believed that removing Indian children from their reservations and educating them in eastern boarding schools was the best practice. Boarding schools, Pratt contended, would cut the cultural ties between the children and their families, thus allowing them to learn English and receive a traditional mechanical education. Few students would receive the more classical education that prepared them for college. Other reformers argued that Pratt's model was too expensive for the federal government, and instead, they called for the creation of schools on the various reservations, either as day schools or boarding schools. Pratt's views won the day. The federal government created a number of off-reservation boarding schools across the nation, including institutions in Santa Fe, Carson, Phoenix, and Flandreau. By the 20th century, 25 nonreservation schools were in operation serving more than 10,000 students.

At these off-reservation schools, the curriculum was always the same: Designed to speed the pace of assimilation, the schools were often very severe. Discipline was strict, and the environment was English-only. Students were forbidden to speak their native languages and frequently beaten if they did so. New students were often forced to convert to Christianity, and they celebrated American holidays and learned job skills. Doubts quickly arose about the effectiveness of the nonreservation schools. The programs were expensive, and Indian graduates frequently returned to their reservations and resumed their Indian lives. Because of these failures, the federal government began supporting the development of vocational curriculums for reservation day schools. By 1910, the federal government was actively aiding in the placement of Indians in public schools.

As part of the Indian New Deal in the 1930s, major changes affected Indian education. Commissioner of Indian affairs **John Collier** ended religious instruction in the schools and pushed for the passage of the **Johnson-O'Malley Act** of 1934. The act allowed the BIA to contract the states to provide education for Indian students. Indian students would face new problems by the middle of the 20th century, including racism, discrimination, and lack of interest on the part of the state for their educational needs.

The problem of discrimination led to calls among Indians for educational self-determination. In an effort to protect Indian students from racism, preserve their traditional cultures, and prevent the undue influence of government officials, Indian peoples began calling for Indian control of educational resources and curricula. In 1972, the federal government passed the Indian Education Act, which called for tribal participation in all federal aid programs to public schools, encouraged the establishment of community schools, provided funds for the creation of bilingual curriculum, funded adult education initiatives, and established the Office of Indian Education. In 1975, Congress moved further by passing the Indian Self-Determination and Education Assistance Act. The act mandated that all schools receiving funds through the Johnson-O'Malley Act had to ensure that the money was being used on Indian students. The act further stated that when Indians were not in control of school boards serving Indian students, an Indian Parents Committee must be established and consulted on all decisions affecting Native American students. Although not perfect, Indian education is no longer another tool in the assimilationist arsenal, and Indian students find many of the same opportunities as their non-Indian counterparts.

– F –

FIRE THUNDER, CECILIA (1946–). Born on 24 October 1946, on the Pine Ridge Indian Reservation in South Dakota, Fire Thunder, an Oglala Lakota, defeated **Russell Means** in the November 2004 election by a narrow margin of 622 votes to become the first female tribal president of the Oglala Lakota. When she was 16 years old, her family moved to Los Angeles, California, where she graduated from high school. Fire Thunder became a practical nurse and worked as a community organizer among the poor, teaching them nutritional habits and helping start a free clinic in Los Angeles for Indians. She spent more than two decades working in Los Angeles and San Diego before returning to Pine Ridge and obtaining a nursing position at Bennett County Hospital.

In 1988, Fire Thunder began a women's society that studied **reservation** problems, which included helping battered women and also establishing Cangleska Shelter for them. She also worked on such important issues as fetal alcohol syndrome and the revival of the Lakota language. In 1994, she failed in an attempt to become tribal president. Ten years later, she won the presidency.

As tribal president, Fire Thunder challenged the Oglala Sioux Tribal Council to address such important reservation issues as providing more economic development opportunities and improving **education**, health, and medical services. She wanted all Oglalas to be proud of their heritage and work together to make the Oglala Nation stronger. Her relations with the tribal council, however, deteriorated, and Fire Thunder faced impeachment charges on three separate occasions, the third resulting in her removal from office six months short of completing her two-year term.

The two earlier, unsuccessful attempts at impeachment involved charges of perjury, trespassing, fraud, disloyalty, and assault and battery. The main complaint, however, concerned a $38 million loan she negotiated to pay tribal debts and expand tribal **gaming** operations. Those demanding her removal claimed that she failed to properly consult tribal members during the loan negotiations. Having fended off the charges, Fire Thunder was impeached and subsequently removed from office because she started a health clinic that her opponents declared was an abortion clinic and, therefore, was in violation of a recent state law that virtually banned all abortions in South Dakota.

Fire Thunder declared that the tribal council violated tribal constitutional requirements and federal laws in their actions against her and that members wanted to remove her because she demanded more accountability from them. In 2006, Fire Thunder failed in her attempt to be reelected tribal president, but she continues to be involved in health, women's issues, and other issues affecting her people. *See also* WOMEN.

FISHING RIGHTS. Native American tribes engaged in fishing and hunting as a way of life and for subsistence thousands of years before European contact. Indians developed a special relationship to the land and with the fish, animals, and other items provided to them for their survival. Indeed, provisions in numerous treaties that Europeans and later the United States negotiated with Indians recognized their fishing and **hunting rights**. However, as the non-Indian population continued to increase and occupied Indian lands, Indian fishing rights were challenged. The demands to eliminate or reduce Indian fishing rights came from those advocating commercial, recreational, and environmental and conservation interests.

States began passing fishing laws that violated federal treaties, and Indians organized movements to protest these infringements and prohibitions on their fishing rights. To complicate matters even further, state laws affected fishing rights both on and off Indian **reservations**.

Indians were usually more successful in retaining their treaty fishing right on reservation land than off the reservation. In the Pacific Northwest, for example, **Hank Adams** and the **Survival of American Indians Association** fought for Indians' fishing rights and staged fish-ins in the 1960s to protest state laws curtailing their rights to fish in "usual and accustomed places."

Such important federal judicial decisions as the Boldt Decision and the three Puyallup Tribe cases against the Washington State Department of Game found in favor of Indian fishing rights and allowed Indians to annually harvest a certain number of fish for private and commercial purposes. Tribes and states now often cooperate in non-Indian fishing regulations on Indian and non-Indian owned lands on reservations and in fishing conservation programs.

FIVE CIVILIZED TRIBES. The Five Civilized Tribes is the name commonly given to the five major tribes of the southeastern United States: the Cherokees, Chickasaws, Choctaws, Creeks, and Seminoles. These tribes came into contact with Europeans in the 16th century and quickly adjusted to their new condition. Intermarriage with whites produced a number of mixed-race tribal leaders, as well as successful southern planters and important businessmen within tribal communities. Each tribe developed its own constitution, **law** code, judicial system, and other aspects of "civilization." By the early 19th century, they were known collectively as the "Civilized Tribes." *See also* FIVE CIVILIZED TRIBES FOUNDATION, INC.

FIVE CIVILIZED TRIBES FOUNDATION, INC. Incorporated in Muskogee, Oklahoma, on 25 October 1965, the Five Civilized Tribes Foundation, Inc., focused on increasing economic development opportunities for the **Five Civilized Tribes**: the Cherokees, Chickasaws, Choctaws, Creeks, and Seminoles. A board of trustees composed of principal leaders from the tribes directed the foundation. Not much was accomplished during the 1960s; however, during the 1970s, Robert Anderson, a Choctaw, served as executive director and broadened the board membership and developed action plans that secured federal funds to promote such economic and industrial activities as acquiring better Indian management and planning skills. In 1975, the foundation began publishing a journal called the *Five*

Tribes Journal. As the 1970s ended, the foundation again became inactive and by 1980 was defunct; nevertheless, it was a movement that attempted to provide needed economic development projects through federal funding for the Five Civilized Tribes.

FORT BERTHOLD INDIAN DEFENSE ASSOCIATION (FBIDA). The FBIDA was created in 1946 by representatives of the Mandan, Arikara, and Gros Ventres, in opposition to plans by the U. S. federal government to build a dam on the Upper Missouri River near the Fort Berthold Reservation. The dam would have dislocated more than 1,500 tribal members and flooded more than 275,000 acres. Although the tribes were to receive compensatory lands in exchange for the flooded acreage, the FBIDA organized a massive resistance campaign.

In an effort to block the dam, which was to provide hydroelectric power, the FBIDA hired an engineer to complete a feasibility study examining land 70 miles north of the federally proposed site. The study concluded that the dam was more practical at the northern site, and the association immediately lobbied the federal government to build the dam at the second site. In its sole mission, the FBIDA was unsuccessful. The dam was built, the land was flooded, the tribal members were displaced, and the tribal members received compensation. Despite the reparation, many people chose to leave the **reservation** rather than try to build a life on new lands. After their failure to block to the dam, the FBIDA shut down.

FUR TRADE. The trade of furs was important to the development of European colonial enterprises and had a major impact on Native American cultures. The demand for furs, sparked by new fashion trends in Europe, prompted European rivalries and the desire on the part of numerous entrepreneurs to establish trading posts for the benefit of their mother country. The Indians, who procured the furs for the European traders, were pulled into these rivalries, which often resulted in competing companies and tribes going to war against one another. Fur traders also introduced Indians to such European manufactured items as metal tools and guns. Indian desires to obtain these trade items accelerated their involvement in the trade. As Indian hunting increased, fur-bearing animals became extremely hard to come by. Thus, Indians became tied to European traders and were forced to travel ever further to procure pelts.

The rapid depletion of fur-bearing animals, especially beaver, led tribes into new territories and caused conflict between Indian peoples. European fur companies made efforts to encourage Indians to attack their neighbors in efforts to control trade in a particular region. The result was that intertribal warfare quickly developed into struggles between competing commercial entities. Before European involvement, most Indian wars were **mourning wars**, but the new commercial wars would have a deleterious effect on Indian life. These "Beaver Wars" were particularly disastrous to the tribes who called the **Iroquois Confederacy** their neighbors. In most cases, especially among the Huron, the Iroquois engaged in successful wars of extermination, a type of warfare unheard of in Indian America before the European arrival.

In addition to its cost in human life, Indian overhunting had a severe impact on Indian peoples. Fur trading activities took up more time among tribal males, leading to neglect of other basic needs, including the procurement of food. Hunters were forced to travel farther and farther from home in an effort to capture more pelts. The workload of tribal **women** increased as they were forced to plant larger fields, harvest more crops, clean more furs, and perform tasks traditionally performed by men. Inability to produce the needed materials led Indians into an ever-tightening noose of dependency on European traders, who supplemented Indian shortcomings with trade items. In short, the fur trade came to symbolize the hold Europeans had on Indian peoples in America.

– G –

GAMBLING. *See* GAMING.

GAMING. During the final decades of the 20th century, as a result of mismanagement and misappropriation of funds by the **Bureau of Indian Affairs**, Indian **reservations** were in the midst of financial disaster. Along with drastic cuts in federal services—the result of President Ronald Reagan's policies—reservations became some of the poorest areas in the United States. Less than 20 percent of reservations contained the natural resources necessary to generate enough revenue to sustain tribes. In a search for increased tribal revenues and a new path to sovereignty, Indian peoples across the nation turned to casino operations.

The desire on the part of tribes to open their own gaming operations caused controversy around the nation. Indians claimed that state jurisdiction stopped at reservation borders; therefore, state gaming laws had no force in Indian Country. By the early 1980s, 183 tribes owned bingo houses, and 20 operated full-scale casino gaming businesses. In 1987, the U.S. Supreme Court upheld Indian tribes' rights to operate gaming facilities in the landmark case *California v. Cabazon Band of Mission Indians*. The decision had a ripple effect across Indian America, and by 1995, 102 bingo houses and 61 casinos dotted the nation's various Indian reservations.

State officials complained that Indian reservations, with their Las Vegas–style gaming operations, would draw a disproportionate amount of state tourist dollars. Congress responded in 1988 with the Indian Gaming Regulatory Act (IGRA), which legalized Indian casinos so long as there was a specific tribal ordinance on record and a compact had been agreed upon between the tribe and the state. They further stated that the U.S. federal government, through the Department of the Interior, was the official regulatory body for all Indian gaming operations. Finally, the act created the **National Indian Gaming Commission** to enforce any and all regulations. Many state governments, in their refusal to negotiate with a tribe for the required compact, cited the IGRA and argued that the act violated the Eleventh Amendment to the U.S. Constitution.

The Supreme Court again took up the matter of Indian gaming in *Seminole Tribe of Florida v. Florida* (1996). The Supreme Court, upholding the decision of the 11th Circuit Court, stated that the tribe could not force the state to negotiate for a compact. According to then chief justice William Rehnquist, the section of the IGRA that ordered the creation of a compact was a violation of the Eleventh Amendment because it brought "undue incursion on state sovereignty." The *Seminole Tribe v. Florida* decision created political turmoil in Indian Country, especially where white business leaders sought to close down Indian-owned casinos. However, Indian-operated casinos continue to thrive. Although tribes still need to negotiate with states, and every casino venture faces stiff opposition, gaming operations, especially the Foxwoods Resort and Casino and the Mohegan Sun Hotel and Casino, both in Connecticut, have provided tribes with heretofore unknown revenues and increased amounts of sovereignty over the basic services offered to their people.

GERONIMO (c. 1829–1909). Born in the late 1820s near Clifton, Arizona, Geronimo, whose Apache name was Goyahkla, meaning "One Who Yawns," was an Apache religious and military leader. As a member of the Chiricahua Apache band, Geronimo (Spanish for Jerome; the name was given to him by Mexicans who apparently called upon St. Jerome for assistance in fighting Geronimo) gained a reputation as a spiritual leader and fierce warrior in his battles against Mexican forces, who had killed his mother, wife, and children in 1850. When the United States acquired the southwest after the Mexican War, Geronimo now faced another enemy who threatened his peoples' existence.

Geronimo fought with Cochise and other Apache leaders in the Apache Wars between 1860 and 1886. The guerrilla tactics that the Apaches employed forced the United States to negotiate treaties in which Apache leaders agreed to accept **reservations**. In the 1876, Geronimo was forced to move to the San Carlos Reservation, where conditions were deplorable. On more than one occasion, Geronimo bolted the reservation and resumed his raiding activities in Mexico and the United States. General George Crook and later General Nelson Miles, two famous Indian fighters, pursued the Apache leader, who finally surrendered to Miles in September 1886.

Now prisoners of war, Geronimo and other Chiricahuas, even those who scouted for Crook and Miles, were exiled first to Fort Pickens in Florida and later to Mount Vernon Barracks in Alabama. In 1892, after several years of suffering and deaths of loved ones, the Apache prisoners were sent to Fort Sill in Oklahoma, where Geronimo adopted Christianity but kept his traditional beliefs and engaged in farming activities. His people still regarded him as their leader. Geronimo's fame grew, and he appeared at such national events as the 1898 Trans-Mississippi and International Exposition in Omaha, the 1901 Pan-American Exposition in Buffalo, and the 1904

Louisiana Purchase Exposition in St. Louis. In 1905, he rode in President Theodore Roosevelt's inaugural parade. Geronimo received payments for his appearances at such events and sold autographed pictures. His autobiography was published in 1907.

Geronimo failed to convince federal officials to allow his people to return to their Arizona homeland. On 17 February 1909, he died of pneumonia at Fort Sill and is buried there.

GHOST DANCE. The Ghost Dance is the common name given to a series of **revitalization movements** begun in the late 19th century on the Walker River Indian Reservation in Nevada. During the 1870s and again in the 1890s, western Indian tribes adopted new rituals that focused on a circular dance and the belief that long dead relatives and diminished resources would be restored and thus revive struggling Indian communities.

In the 1870s, a Paiute named Wodziwob fell into a trance. Upon waking, he preached that Indians could recreate the old life by practicing a series of common rituals. Wodziwob's vision spread westward, where various tribes adapted the ceremonies to meet their own specific circumstances. Despite this adaptation, the core of the ritual was a dance in which each person joined hands and sidestepped counterclockwise. Wodziwob's movement gradually lost support and ended sometime in the late 1870s or early 1880s.

In 1889, a new Ghost Dance movement appeared. A Paiute named **Wovoka** fell into a trance and returned espousing a doctrine that offered a paradise on earth. By performing a circular dance and paying strict attention to a series of specific peaceful virtues, Indian people could restore their lost lands and resources, bring back dead ancestors, and rid the world of white people. Wovoka's teachings spread far and wide among the tribes of the Western United States. He won followers among the Arapaho, Caddo, Cheyenne, Kiowa, Paiute, and most famously, the Lakota. Like the 1870s ceremony, the new ceremony called for a circular dance. However, the ceremony lasted several days, and participants sought visions at the culmination of the day's events.

Among the Lakota, the ceremony became a central focus of young people dissatisfied with **reservation** conditions. The spread of the Ghost Dance among the Lakota culminated in the events that led to the massacre at Wounded Knee in December 1890. Despite the tragic events of the winter of 1890, Wovoka's Ghost Dance continued to be practiced among various tribes, and some still practice aspects of the ritual; Wovoka remained a recognized prophet until his death in 1932.

GREAT LAKES INTER-TRIBAL COUNCIL (GLITC). Established in 1961, the GLITC was created by 10 Wisconsin tribes to combat federal **termination** policies that threatened them since the Menominees, the largest Indian tribe in the state, had been terminated (see MENOMINEE DRUMS). The 10 tribes included the Wisconsin-Winnebago, the Stockbridge-Munsee (Mohican), the Oneida, the Forest County Potawatomi, and the Bad River, Lac Courte Oreilles, Lac du Flambeau, Mole Lake, Red Cliff, and St. Croix bands of the Ojibwa (Chippewa).

The GLITC promoted Indian self-determination; better economic, educational, and health conditions on **reservations**; and programs to educate non-Indians about Indian cultures. The council was quite successful in receiving federal funding from such programs as President Lyndon Johnson's War on Poverty and the Office of Economic Opportunity and using the funds to create more than 40 community action programs for the 10 tribes. Lac du Flambeau Reservation is the headquarters of the GLITC.

GREEN CORN CEREMONY. The Green Corn Ceremony is also known as the Busk ceremony from the Creek word "pushkita," meaning "to fast." The Creeks originally practiced the ceremony as a new year celebration. Believed to be one of the oldest ceremonies practiced in the New World because of its links to the precontact Mississippian cultures, the ceremony is the major religious rite of the Creeks, Seminoles, Yuchi, and other southeastern tribes through the present day.

The ceremony starts when the green corn ripens. Besides its clear association with agriculture, the ceremony is also a time for renewal and thanksgiving. Participants ritually prepare to eat the green corn through a series of purification rituals. A new sacred fire is kindled and amnesty is granted for last year's transgressions. The ceremony is and was conducted for four to eight days in the town square or center of a tribal community. *See also* RELIGION.

– H –

HANDSOME LAKE (c. 1735–1815). Handsome Lake, a Seneca, was born in 1735 in present-day New York. Little is known of his early years, but in July 1777, he and his brother, Cornplanter, attended a large council between the **Iroquois Confederacy** and the British in Oswego, New York. Both brothers initially maintained a position of neutrality but later fought alongside the British against the American revolutionaries. At the time, Handsome Lake was said to be a man ravaged by **alcohol**. From the end of the American Revolution until 1799, he lived with Cornplanter as an invalid.

On 15 June 1799, Handsome Lake was assumed dead, and his family dressed him for burial. He awoke and recounted three visions that came to him while he was sick. In the first, he had been visited by three strangers all dressed alike and carrying blueberry saplings. These men prescribed medicine to cure Handsome Lake's illness. Handsome Lake vowed to these men that if they allowed him to return to his family, he would repent and change his ways. The men told him that the Creator had chosen him for a special mission. In the second vision, a fourth stranger arrived, displaying holes in his hands and feet and showing Handsome Lake the paths to heaven and hell. Finally, in the third vision, Handsome Lake received his instructions from the Creator. The recounting of the instructions became known as the Code of Handsome Lake: *ohnega* (alcohol) was the worst of all evils and had to be renounced; *otgo* (witchcraft) was to be used to heal and be given freely rather than for evil; *onohwet* (love medicine) was used to attract a mate, and those who refused to stop using it found themselves on the path to hell; marriage, family, and children were to be cherished because they were the future of the people.

Handsome Lake preached more than these four tenets: He argued that the Seneca must learn white ways by attending school, railed against vanity, touted the virtues of white housing and farming, cautioned that traditional clothing be worn only for ceremonial purposes, and held out the virtue of a confession of sins. The Code of Handsome Lake also contained four sacred rituals: the Great Father Dance, to honor children; the Drum Dance, to honor the spirits who watch over the Iroquois; the Men's Chant, to honor the Creator; and the Peach Pit Bowl Game. All ceremonies were performed at a specific time in mid-winter. Finally, Handsome Lake argued that he could see into the future. He foretold of a time when the Iroquois chiefs would abandon the Great Council, the people would abandon their ceremonies, an old woman would give birth, and a child would give birth to a bear. These signs marked the end of the world.

In 1802, Handsome Lake traveled to Washington, D.C., where he met with President Thomas Jefferson. Jefferson congratulated Handsome Lake and called on other Iroquois to follow his teachings. Returning home, Handsome Lake moved to the village of Tonawanda and began to receive dignitaries from the other members of the Iroquois Confederacy. The Onondaga Nation sent word that they wanted Handsome Lake to preach to them personally. Handsome Lake had another vision in which the three men from his initial vision returned to him and told him that he must travel to the Onondaga (modern Syracuse, New York), where he would meet four men who would take him to the Sky Trail. Handsome Lake and his followers set out for Onondaga. By the time the contingent arrived, Handsome Lake was very sick. The Onondaga quickly put together a **lacrosse** game hoping to revive the ailing prophet. However, on 10 August 1815, Handsome Lake embarked on his final journey on the Sky Trail. Though Handsome Lake was dead, his code lived on. Members of the Iroquois Nation have met in Tonawanda every fall since his death to agree on arrangements for the mid-winter ceremonies. The Code of Handsome Lake remains a centerpiece in the faith of the Iroquois people and a testament to the perseverance of tradition. *See also* RELIGION.

HARRIS, LADONNA (1931–). Born LaDonna Crawford on 15 February 1931, in Temple, Oklahoma, her mother was Comanche and her father was white. She was raised by her grandparents and spoke only Comanche until she started public school. Times were hard for her family during the Great Depression, but she did graduate from high school, where she dated her future husband, Fred Harris, whom she married in 1949. Fred attended the University of Oklahoma, while LaDonna worked at the university library. In 1954, Fred passed the bar exam, and the Harris family moved back to Lawton, where he opened a law practice.

In 1956, Fred entered politics and won a seat in the Oklahoma state senate. LaDonna took care of their two children and became involved in community activities. When Fred decided to run for the U.S. Senate, LaDonna, as usual, was his help mate. She traveled with him on the campaign trail, and many voters were aware of her Indian heritage. He defeated Bud Wilkinson, the famous Oklahoma football coach, in 1964, and the Harris family headed east to the nation's capital. They lived in McLean, Virginia, close to the Robert F. Kennedy family, and both families soon became good friends. Political and social connections with the Kennedys helped LaDonna meet influential politicians and their wives, including other members of the Kennedy clan, the Udalls, the Humphreys, and the Mondales. She later toured Indian **reservations** in Minnesota with Mrs. Joan Mondale.

These associations with other Democrats convinced LaDonna to become more active in civil rights movements by supporting programs to promote educational and employment opportunities for poverty-stricken minorities. In 1965, she returned to Oklahoma to focus on the needs of American Indians and founded Oklahomans for Indian Opportunity (OIO), an organization aimed at improving the socioeconomic conditions of Oklahoma Indians. Funded by an Office of Economic Opportunity grant, the OIO relied on local community action committees to help Indians help themselves by offering programs concerning leadership skills, **education** assistance, employment, health conditions, and housing issues. These empowerment programs provided Indians with skills that would increase their self-confidence and motivation and allow them to become more actively involved in the larger community. In 1970, she established **Americans for Indian Opportunity (AIO)**, a national body based on the OIO. Her tireless work for both organizations in securing funding and helping Indians further enhanced her reputation as an advocate who supported political, economic, and social movements to improve conditions among Native Americans. Both the OIO and the AIO continue to operate in the 21st century.

In 1976, she supported her husband's unsuccessful campaign to secure the Democratic presidential nomination, and in the 1980 presidential election, she ran as the Citizens' Party vice presidential candidate of Barry Commoner, an environmentalist advocate. Also in

1980, LaDonna and Fred divorced due in part to their active careers that kept them separated and strained their marriage. They parted amicably.

LaDonna continued her work in Indian movements during the last two decades of the 20th century and into the 21st century. She became active in world peace movements and participated in a number of international conferences. She has served on numerous national boards, including the National Organization for Women, National Museum of the American Indian, and National Institute for Women of Color, and has received many honors for her work, which include an honorary doctorate from Dartmouth College. *See also* WOMEN.

HAUDENOSAUNEE. Pronounced "Ho-day-no-show-nee," it is the Iroquois word describing "the people of the Long House," also known as the **Iroquois Confederacy**.

HERDING AND RANCHING. For many Indian communities, the care of livestock has been central to both their economy and their culture. Livestock in the form of **horses**, cattle, and sheep came with Europeans, but the herding of animals preceded their arrival. When Europeans brought these animals with them, they encountered problems keeping them for themselves. On occasion, Europeans gave stock to Indians as part of their Indian policy in an effort to win over the community. Missionaries in the American southwest encouraged their Indian charges to herd sheep and cattle as part of acculturation programs.

Despite the common misconception that Indians had no concept of ownership, Indian peoples took great pains to exercise control over livestock. Ownership may not have rested with an individual but rather with a family or clan, but it was ownership nonetheless. After Indians were pushed onto **reservations**, livestock offered a way for people to retain their identities and forge new ones. In many cases, raising livestock had long been a central aspect of the economy and culture of a particular group—the Navajo for example. In the case of other groups, federal initiatives were passed to bring animal rearing to the reservation.

The Navajo again serve as an example. After being settled on their reservation in 1868, the Navajo took major steps to increase their land holdings and flocks of sheep. This increase, which the U.S. federal government hailed as a sign of progress, later caused problems with soil erosion on the reservation. The land base quickly reached its carrying capacity and could not be expanded to accommodate the ever-rising number of sheep. Despite later issues of stock reduction, the sheep allowed the Navajo to rebuild their broken culture and destroyed economy.

On the Great Plains, herding also had a long history. For centuries, hunters herded buffalo and then stampeded them, forcing the animals to run off of cliffs; hunters then only had to gather the meat. The destruction of the buffalo, however, did not end the Plains Indians' love affair with herding. Horses had quickly taken the place of buffalo run-offs in Plains Indian culture. Some well-intentioned and pragmatic Indian agents sought to introduce cattle ranching to the Indian peoples who so admired the horse. For the Comanches, **Quanah Parker** led the way to the development of a major ranching operation. Among the Apaches, Indian agents worked with important leaders to develop full-fledged Apache livestock associations.

On the Northern Plains, Indian ranchers were in direct competition with whites for land. Whites argued that the area was a destination, and Indians argued that the land was theirs. Both sides wanted to increase the land under cultivation or set aside for pasture. Whites emerged victorious, and their demands for acreage were a great force behind the federal government's passage of the **Dawes Severalty Act**. Undaunted, the Sioux reservations actually developed their own cattle ranching operations, as did the Blackfeet, Crow, Northern Cheyenne, and Gros Ventres. This progress was achieved despite the government's best efforts to push farming onto the Indians. In other cases, Indian cowboys went to work for white ranchers in the area.

The involvement of Indians in the cattle ranching business also spurred an interest among Indians in rodeo. Since the 1920s, Indians ranchers have developed an alliance with their white counterparts, who face many of the same complications and difficulties. Indian herding and ranching continue to provide for some tribes. The animals form the basis of a cultural identity that is both old and new, and the continuity of the ranching experience demonstrates that Indian communities are here to stay.

HIAWATHA (c. 1525–c. 1575). The most complete account of the life of this legendary Mohawk credited with founding the **Haudenosaunee** comes from **Joseph Brant**, who wrote a biography of Hiawatha in the 19th century. Hiawatha's name is most familiar from its use in the Henry Wadsworth Longfellow poem, "The Song of Hiawatha." Longfellow's poem, however, is set on the Great Lakes and has almost nothing to do with Hiawatha, the historical figure.

Iroquois tradition and Brant's work tells that Hiawatha lived alone in the woods and survived by being a cannibal. One day, after having waylaid a traveler and preparing him for the pot, Hiawatha looked into his cooking pot and saw a face. The face was that of **Deganawida**, who promptly convinced Hiawatha to give up cannibalism and eat venison instead. Hiawatha vowed to atone for his past behavior by spreading Deganawida's message among the Iroquois.

Hiawatha first went to his people, the Mohawks, preaching Deganawida's message of peace. He lived happily among the Mohawks, marrying and even having a family. However, Tadadaho, the leader of the Onondaga, opposed Hiawatha's work and led an attack on Hiawatha, which ended in the slaughter of his family. Stricken with grief, Hiawatha returned to the woods, where he created a string of shells known as **wampum**. The wampum symbolized his plan for Iroquois unification.

Hiawatha again traveled among the Iroquois preaching Deganawida's message. This time, Tadadaho was convinced and pledged to end all violence among the Iroquois, thus forming a large league based on the principles of internal peace, respect for ancestors, warriors, clan mothers, and the stability of community. Tadadaho's homeland at Onondaga was chosen as the site for all future meetings between the members of the **Iroquois Confederacy**.

Hiawatha also developed two ceremonies designed to ensure the stability of the confederacy. The first was a condolence ceremony designed to ease grief in times of loss. The ceremony was to take the place of retaliatory violence or blood feuds among confederacy members. If a tribe outside of the confederacy killed an Iroquois, then a requickening ceremony was performed. In this ceremony, the deceased position in the family was filled by adoption. An integral part of the ceremony was the **mourning war**, a style of warfare designed to secure **captives**.

Hiawatha's later years and death passed without notice, but his ceremonies and teachings lived on. His work helped the Iroquois become one of the most powerful Indian groups in America. The Iroquois Confederacy acted as an allied front against European aggression and conducted diplomatic relations with competing imperial interests for the betterment of the league as a whole. *See also* RELIGION.

HILLIS HADJO (c. 1770–1818). A noted Seminole leader of the **Green Corn Ceremony.** Hillis Hadjo was known among whites as Francis the Prophet. Active in the Seminole Wars, he was accused of being one of the chief instigators of the second Seminole uprising. Told by British merchants that the 1814 Treaty of Ghent guaranteed the return of the Seminole homeland, and in hope of gaining support for his people against the Americans, Hillis Hadjo traveled to England, where he enjoyed an audience with the king and much court attention. His diplomatic mission netted no results. In 1817, an American trader by the name of McKrimmon was captured by a Seminole war party and turned over to the Seminole leader. Hillis Hadjo ordered the American burned to death. Only the intervention of the chief's eldest daughter, Milly, spared the trader. Shortly after the McKrimmon incident, the chief was captured by an American patrol and hanged. His wife and daughters later surrendered to the Americans in St. Mark's, Florida.

HORSES AND INDIANS. Horses were brought to North America by Spanish explorers, and it is likely that the Indian acquisition of the animal was a gradual process. The transfer of horses from Spaniards to Indians began when the conquistadores taught Indians to ride in return for acting as guides and caretakers during their expeditions. Later, trained Indian horsemen brought horses to other Indians through trading and raiding. Thus, the first tribes to take horses into their possession were those with direct access to the Spanish.

Indians carried out an active horse trade, and many were skilled in training and raising horses even before they met their first Euro-Americans. The image of the Plains Indian and the centrality of the horse have come to define the American ideal of Indians. However, it is likely that the diffusion of the horse among the tribes of the

Northern Plains did not begin until sometime after 1640 and before 1885. As tribes learned the value of horses, the animals became war prizes. Horse raiding became an acceptable method of obtaining horses as soon as Indians learned the art of stealth horsemanship. Among the Plains Indians, horse raiding quickly became an integral part of their culture.

Scholars often argue that horses dramatically changed the way of life of Indian people. However, it is more appropriate to state that horses altered and made easier the preexisting cultural way of life. Nomadic tribes were able to carry more items with them because they could use the horse as a pack animal. The horse, however, did not make them nomadic. These tribes could transport themselves farther and with less effort, thus making life easier. Finally, elements of horsemanship were transferred with the animal. Methods of breaking horses and the use of quirts instead of spurs became generalized Indian practices. The most interesting aspect of Indian horsemanship was that the horses received no brand. Owners simply identified their horses by sight and were able to do so with remarkable accuracy. The affinity between Indians and horses continues though the present-day. *See also* HERDING AND RANCHING.

HUNTING RIGHTS. An essential element in Native American cultures is hunting. Indians believed animals were placed on the earth primarily as a food source (some animals, like the buffalo, provided many other needed items, like hides for clothing and shelter), and Indians performed special rituals honoring the killed animal. Like **fishing rights**, hunting rights were frequently guaranteed in treaty provisions that Europeans and the United States negotiated with Indian tribes.

As the 19th century ended states—mainly influenced by non-Indian sport hunters—began enacting legislation that attempted to regulate or curtail Indian hunting rights both on and off **reservation** lands. Indians were blamed for causing the extinction of certain animals and not initiating animal preservation programs. It would not be until the last half of the 20th century that Indians organized movements and demanded recognition of their treaty hunting rights. Several federal court cases, like *New Mexico v. Mescalero Apache Tribe* (1983), upheld Indian treaty hunting rights. Tribes also developed commercial hunting programs and animal management programs, the latter often in cooperation with state agencies.

– I –

IMPROVED ORDER OF RED MEN. The Improved Order of Red Men was established in 1833 in Baltimore, Maryland, tracing its beginnings back to 1813 with the founding of the Society of Red Men. The non-Indian membership stressed the preservation of Indian traditions and supported the founding of the **Society of American Indians (SAI)** in 1911, and many even became SAI members. The order also assisted the SAI in organizing their first two national conferences. Social activities played an important role as well, with the holding of several ceremonial rituals and granting of certain levels of degrees, including the "Warrior's Degree" and the "Chief's Degree." By the mid-1920s, the order claimed to have more than half a million members and had a women's auxiliary called the **Daughters of Pocahontas**. The Improved Order of Red Men also published the *Quarterly Journal*.

INDIAN ACTORS ASSOCIATION (IAA). Founded in 1936 as a replacement for the **War Paint Club**, the IAA wanted Indian actors to stop competing with other Indian actors for parts in films for lower pay, which became apparent with the casting of *The Last of the Mohicans* in 1936, and to only have Indians play Indians in films. The IAA chairman, Bill Hazlett, a Blackfeet, reported that after a few years in existence the IAA had become affiliated with the Screen Actors Guild (SAG) and secured better salaries for Indian actors. The IAA also helped Indian actors out of work by providing them monetary aid that the group derived from membership dues, performances at various events, and powwows. Later in the 1960s, **Jay Silverheels**, a Mohawk, who played Tonto in the 1950s television show *The Lone Ranger* and acted in a number of movies, founded the Indian Actors Workshop to help improve Indians' acting skills and have a better and more accurate representation of Indians in theater and film.

In 1983, Will Sampson, a Creek, and other Indian entertainers, founded the American Indian Registry for the Performing Arts, which continued the efforts of the War Paint Club, the IAA, and the Indian Actors Workshop. The registry ceased functioning in 1992 due to financial problems. In 1985, Sonny Skyhawk, a Sicangu Lakota, established American Indians in Film and Television to help Indians in these media and provide more accurate depictions of Indian culture and history. The SAG later created a subcommittee of Native American members to address issues regarding Native Americans in the entertainment industry.

INDIAN ARTS AND CRAFTS BOARD (IACB). Established by Congress in 1935 as part of the Indian New Deal program of the commissioner of Indian affairs **John Collier**, the IACB promoted Native American economic development by protecting and marketing Indian-made products. To improve the market for authentic Indian arts and crafts and undermine the production of mass-produced copies, the board issued government trademarks for Indian-made products to ensure their authenticity. Those involved in misrepresenting Indian-made products faced possible imprisonment of up to six months in prison, a fine of $2,000, or both. The IACB wanted Indians to be proud of preserving their heritage and wanted non-Indians to gain a deeper understanding and respect for Indian cultural expressions.

The IACB offered classes to help Indians improve their art and craft skills in such areas as weaving, silverwork, beadwork, and drawing. At the 1939 San Francisco World's Fair, Indian products on display received rave reviews. In 1990, Congress passed additional legislation that provided stiffer penalties for fraudulent or misrepresented products. First time individual offenders could be fined up to $250,000, receive a five year prison term, or both. A business could be fined up to $1,000,000.

The IACB is headquartered in Washington, D.C., and operates three regional museums in Anadarko, Oklahoma; Browning, Montana; and Rapid City, South Dakota.

INDIAN ASSOCIATION OF AMERICA (IAA). The IAA was founded in the 1930s by Red Fox Francis St. James, who had organized the **Teepee Order of America** years earlier. The organization called for the establishment of an all-Indians' claims commission, advocated the representation of Indians in Congress, proposed that appointed commissioners of Indian affairs and superintendents be approved by tribes, and proposed a plan to have all forest rangers and guides selected from tribal members.

There is no evidence to suggest that the IAA was very active other than a few local chapters in New York City. Why the organization failed remains a mystery. The association ceased all operations in 1961.

INDIAN CENTERS, INC (ICI). Founded in Los Angeles, California, in 1935 by Mira Frye Bartlett, a Kickapoo, and originally called the "Lowansa Tipi" and then the Los Angeles Indian Center, it became the Indian Centers, Inc., in 1971 and served as a place for urban Indians to meet and share their experiences. The ICI soon broadened its scope after World War II to provide community assistance to the increasing number of Indians moving to Los Angeles. By 1985, the ICI had acquired several federal, state, county, and city grants to offer programs on job training skills, aid to senior citizens, and provide housing assistance. Additional programs deal with domestic violence, discrimination, child welfare, and educational opportunities. The ICI publishes a periodical called the *Talking Leaf*.

INDIAN CONFEDERATION OF AMERICA (ICA). Organized in New York City in 1933, the ICA was founded to provide a cultural and social setting for New York's urban Indians and whites who wished to learn more about Indian traditions. By offering to aid recent Indian arrivals to the city, the ICA served as a model for current urban Indian centers.

INDIAN COUNCIL FIRE. Founded in 1923 in Chicago, Illinois, as the Grand Council Fire of the American Indians and renamed the Indian Council Fire in 1932, the organization was a **Pan-Indian** body that promoted Native American achievements, had a profound interest in improving Indian **education** programs, and originally had both Indians and non-Indians in its membership. Other activities included holding events in Chicago for Native Americans, sending needed items to Indian **reservations**, and giving aid to sick and needy Indians.

Scott Peters, a Chippewa, effectively led the organization in the 1920s and early 1930s. Titles of its officers included "chief of chiefs," "chief medicine man," and "chief wampum keeper." Marion Gridley, an adopted Omaha, later became a primary force in the organization for many decades. She served as editor of *Indians of Today*, a book on prominent Native Americans that went through several updated editions. One of the Indian Council Fire's most well-known events was the presentation of the Indian Achievement Award to Native Americans who became prominent in mainstream America but also retained their Indian identities and helped their people. In 1933, Dr. **Charles A. Eastman**, a Santee Sioux, received the first award in recognition of his achievements. The Indian Council Fire endured well into the 20th century as a movement promoting Native American achievements and needs.

INDIAN DEFENSE LEAGUE OF AMERICA (IDLA). Organized in 1926 by members of the **Iroquois Confederacy**, the IDLA argued that the restrictive immigration policies of both the Untied States and Canada violated the statement of Iroquois sovereignty in the 1794 Jay's Treaty. Although both Congress and the courts have upheld the Indians' position, immigration officials still harass Iroquois people crossing the international bridges connecting New York and Canada.

In recent years, in addition to continuing its fight, the IDLA has organized an annual celebration of Jay's Treaty every July with a parade route that crosses the International Bridge between Niagara Falls, Ontario, and Niagara Falls, New York. The IDLA members have also sought to correct the impression of Indian people in mainstream America by seeking to place American Indians—especially the Iroquois—in their proper place in American history. The IDLA also appealed to the United Nations for recognition in its struggles against the New York State Power Authority and the U.S. Army Corp of Engineers over the Kinzua Dam project in 1949.

INDIAN HOPE ASSOCIATION. The Indian Hope Association was established in the 1870s, perhaps in 1877, by Eastern white Indian reformers who were appalled by the mistreatment of the Piegans, Nez Perces, Poncas, and Cheyennes by the United States in the 1870s. The association strongly supported assimilation policies, and Mary C. Morgan was an effective spokesperson of assimilating Indians into American society. As the 1880s began, newer and stronger organizations formed, including the **Indian Rights Association** and the **Lake Mohonk Conference of Friends of the Indian**—two powerful organizations that continued to advocate Indian assimilation and allotment of **reservation** lands. The influence of these organizations resulted in the passage of the **Dawes Severalty Act** in 1887, which attempted to break-up Indian reservations and apply forced assimilation. Indian Hope Association members most likely joined the new organizations, since the association stopped functioning in the 1880s.

INDIAN LAW RESOURCE CENTER. The Indian Law Resource Center aids tribes fighting to retain their rights by supporting educational and research work in the fields of Indian **law**, policy, and history. Founded in 1978, by Tim Coulter, a Potawatomi, the center is charitably funded, receiving the majority of its operating budget from churches, individual donors, and tribes.

The Indian Law Resource Center has aided numerous tribes in the United States and Canada in their efforts to retain their rights to self-government, land, water, and natural resources, as well as treaty rights and basic human rights. Since the late 1970s, the center has assisted the Western Shoshone Sacred Lands Association in its effort to block a U.S. Court of Claims award that extinguished, without Shoshone consent, title to ancestral lands for the construction of an MX missile site. The center has also filed three detailed complaints with the United Nations Human Rights Commission on the part of the **Iroquois Confederacy** and the Hopi and Shoshone nations.

Coulter also played a leading role in organizing the center's annual international conference under the auspices of the United Nations Nongovernmental Organizations in Geneva, Switzerland. The center distributes its material on an international basis, and it also played a major role in the development of the United Nations Working Group on Indigenous Populations.

In recent years, the Indian Law Resource Center has sought alternatives to litigation to protect Indian rights and explored avenues of legal research and **education** programs directed at the general public—an effort to sway public opinion. The three areas in which the center has been the most active are Indian property rights, the plenary power of Congress, and legal discriminations against Indian people.

INDIAN REMOVAL ACT, 1830. After the American Revolution came to an end, Great Britain ceded all territory between the Appalachian Mountains and the Mississippi River south of Canada to the new United States. American settlers poured into the territory the British had once claimed to be off limits to whites. The influx of settlers into the region sparked numerous violent confrontations between Americans and the various Indian nations who called the area home.

American officials—none more prominent than Thomas Jefferson—began to push for the relocation of all Indians west of the Mississippi River. In fact, the removal of Indians to this territory was one of the reasons why Jefferson, after he became president, purchased the Louisiana Territory from Napoleon in 1803. Jefferson's thinking was twofold. First, he believed that few whites would want to live in the Louisiana Territory. Second, he and many like-minded reformers were convinced that removal was the best way to end violence against Indians and ensure their assimilation into the dominant society. In short, removing Indians across the Mississippi River would provide a venue for Americans to instruct Indians on white ways in safety and peace. Wealthy merchants and farmers also supported the idea because removal would open vast tracts of Indian land.

In 1830, Congress passed the Indian Removal Act, which President Andrew Jackson quickly signed. The act provided for the relocation of all Indians living east of the Mississippi River to **reservations** west of the river. The legislation also created a parcel of land known as **Indian Territory**, which was to serve as the Indians' new home.

The majority of Indian people did not want to relocate; resistance was frequent, sometimes violent, and at times through legal measures went all the way to the U.S. Supreme Court. The Cherokees attempted to sue in court to block their removal. Despite the court finding in their favor, President Jackson used federal troops to evict the Cherokees from their homeland. Other tribes, like the Seminoles in Florida and the Sac and Fox under **Black Hawk** in the Old Northwest, chose violent means to resist removal. In the end, under increasing pressure from white settlers and the U.S. federal government, large numbers of Indians across the United States, often constituting the majority of their nation, were removed to lands west of the Mississippi River.

INDIAN REORGANIZATION ACT (IRA), 1934. In 1933, **John Collier** became commissioner of Indian affairs and proclaimed an Indian New Deal, which took a more cultural pluralism approach to Indian affairs than an assimilation one. Rather than trying to "get the Indian out of the Indian," the Indian New Deal policies recognized Indian traditions and believed Indians could acculturate into mainstream America and still retain their heritage, similar to the experiences of immigrants who came to America and became part of the dominant society. The IRA of 1934 was the cornerstone of the new direction in federal Indian policy.

The IRA was a comprehensive piece of legislation. Proposed as the Wheeler-Howard Bill, the final version weakened or eliminated areas that Collier sought to implement, including increasing the powers of tribal governments and establishing a special Indian court. Nevertheless, the enacted IRA brought about significant changes. The act prohibited further allotments of Indian **reservation** land, restored surplus reservation lands that were created by the **Dawes Severalty Act** of 1887 to Indian tribes, provided an annual $2 million congressional appropriation for the acquisition of additional lands for Indians, and proposed the creation of tribal governments and, in turn, the creation of tribal corporations that were to be funded by annual congressional appropriations of $250,000 for creating tribal governments and a $10 million revolving credit fund for providing loans to tribal corporations. A $250,000 appropriation also established a fund for Indian students who wanted to attend colleges and vocational schools, and civil service requirements were modified to allow more Indians to be qualified to work for the **Bureau of Indian Affairs (BIA)**. Indians in Oklahoma and Alaska were excluded from certain provisions of the IRA for various reasons, but the passage of laws in 1936 allowed Alaska natives to establish tribal corporations and the Oklahoma Indians to create tribal governments and corporations.

Tribes were permitted to vote on whether to accept or reject the IRA. If a tribe accepted, then it could hold additional elections to create a tribal government and then tribal corporations. Although figures vary, approximately 181 tribes, with a population of 129,750, accepted the IRA, while 77 tribes numbering 86,365 rejected it. Those who rejected the IRA tended to be tribes who had had terrible experiences with the U.S. federal government, including the Navajo, the largest Indian tribe at the time, who voted against the IRA. Ninety-three tribes wrote tribal constitutions, and 73 established tribal corporation charters. In Alaska, 49 villages with a total population of approximately 10,899 Indians voted to create tribal constitutions and incorporation charters, while in Oklahoma, 18 tribes numbering 13,241 in population wrote tribal constitutions, and 13 tribes with a population of 5,741 drew up charters of incorporation.

The IRA did not accomplish the Indian millennium that Collier had envisioned. Although it ended the devastating policy of land allotments, helped Indians acquire additional lands, granted tribes more political and economic control, promoted Indian culture, provided funds for **education** opportunities, and allowed more Indians to be employed by the BIA, many Indians and non-Indians criticized the act. A number of congressional and other federal officials never embraced Collier's cultural pluralism approach and still believed assimilation was the better policy. In the past, Indians often came to decisions by consensus rather than majority rule. A number of Indians refused to vote, however, federal officials counted votes of eligible participants who did not vote as votes for the IRA. In addition, congressional appropriations were often not fully funded. Collier is also criticized for his inability to recognize the complexities of Indian tribes. Finally, although Indians had more participation in the process, final approval still rested in non-Indian hands.

INDIAN RIGHTS ASSOCIATION (IRA). Founded in December 1882 in Philadelphia, Pennsylvania, by Herbert Welsh, a philanthropist, and Henry Pancoast, a lawyer, the IRA, like the **Lake Mohonk Conference of Friends of the Indian**, formed as a result of deplorable conditions on Indian **reservations**. Unlike the Lake Mohonk conferences, which held forums to discuss Indian issues, the IRA was more of a lobbying organization that met with members of Congress to influence changes in federal Indian policies. Both reform groups had similar goals and strongly supported assimilation policies, especially the enactment of the **Dawes Severalty Act** of 1887, which divided reservations into individual land allotments in an effort to make Indians live like white, Christian farmers.

The IRA also advocated such changes as civil service reform in the Bureau of Indian Affairs; improved education, economic, health, and medical services for Indians; and Indian citizenship. The IRA personnel visited Indian reservations, reported on conditions, and recommended changes concerning issues that needed addressing, including those of fraud and corruption or rivalries between Indian agents and Indians on reservations. These reports were then often published as pamphlets and distributed to members of Congress and other Indian reformers.

In the 1930s, the IRA vehemently opposed **John Collier** and his Indian New Deal programs, especially the **Indian Reorganization Act** of 1934. In the 1950s, the IRA opposed federal **termination** of Indian treaties, and in the 1960s and 1970s, the association supported Indian self-determination. By the early 1990s, the IRA no longer functioned.

INDIAN SHAKER CHURCH. Founded in 1881 by Squsachtun (John Slocum), a Squaxin Indian, around Puget Sound, the Indian Shaker Church did not, like some other Indian religious movements, totally reject white ways. There was a syncretism, or blending, of Christian and traditional ways in an effort to encourage better relations with whites. A central feature of the Shaker Church was the holding of services to heal the sick.

Before establishing the church, Squsachtun lived a life of drinking and gambling. Such hard living resulted in his apparent death and then resurrection. He told of visiting heaven, speaking with God, and receiving instructions to improve conditions between Indians and whites. Squsachtun later returned to his previous way of living and again fell ill. While getting him water, his wife started shaking, and the body movements helped Squsachtun recover. He again pledged himself to religious teaching, and body trembling or shaking was interpreted as spiritual intervention to help cure sickness.

White missionaries and government officials attempted to destroy the movement, viewing such blending of religious beliefs as a sacrilege. Squsachtun continued to argue that Indians needed separate churches for their Christian and traditional practices. The matter was settled when a lawyer successfully argued that Shaker Church members had freedom of religion rights as Indians living on allotted lands created by the **Dawes Severalty Act** of 1887, which established land allotments on **reservations**. Today, members of the Indian Shaker

Church still believe in the healing powers of its ceremonies. *See also* RELIGION.

INDIAN TERRITORY. Officially created in the 1820s, Indian Territory was unorganized territory west of the states of Missouri and Arkansas specifically established for Native Americans to move to in the 19th century, resulting from federal Indian removals from their native homelands. The term should not be confused with Indian Country, which usually means areas occupied by Native Americans.

Although some tribes, particularly members of the **Five Civilized Tribes**, began relocating themselves before the passage of the **Indian Removal Act** of 1830, the process accelerated after its enactment and included many tribes both east and later west of the Mississippi River. The Five Civilized Tribes, for example, occupied most of what would eventually become the state of Oklahoma and reestablished their tribal governments and businesses. Unaccustomed to the region's climate and at times involved in conflicts with other removed tribes, life was often extremely difficult for all of the displaced tribes.

After the creation of Kansas Territory in 1854, Indian Territory became primarily present-day Oklahoma. Because factions of the Five Civilized Tribes supported the South during the Civil War, they were forced to cede lands to the U.S. federal government that were used for removals of other tribes, such as the Cheyenne and Arapaho, Comanche, Kickapoo, Sauk and Fox, Osage, and Modoc, to the region.

During the 1880s and 1890s, the tribes in Indian Territory faced further challenges. The passage of the **Dawes Severalty Act** of 1887 called for the severing of **reservation** lands and ending of tribal governments, which initially did not apply to the Five Civilized Tribes due to provisions in their former treaties. More and more non-Indians also began coveting lands in Indian Territory, resulting in the division of Indian Territory into Oklahoma Territory, occupying the western half of the region, in 1890. Tens of thousands of non-Indians rushed into the newly created territory.

It was only a matter of time before the Five Civilized Tribes would be forced to accept land allotments, which began in 1898. In an effort to retain their tribal identities, the Five Civilized Tribes proposed to Congress the creation of the state of Sequoyah as part of the United States in 1905. The proposal was rejected, and, instead, Congress approved the creation of the state of Oklahoma in 1907, extinguishing what remained of Indian Territory.

INDIANS OF ALL TRIBES. On 20 November 1969, more than 80 young, urban, educated Indians calling themselves the "Indians of All Tribes" occupied **Alcatraz** Island off the coast of San Francisco, California. Originally called the "United Native Americans," the group recognized that the name was not representative of their mission. While searching for a proper name, a Lakota woman, Belvia Cottier, suggested the name that eventually stuck—Indians of All Tribes. The group found this name more appropriate because various tribes from all over the United States worked to make the occupation possible. The name was quickly adopted and remained until legal actions forced them to incorporate and become Indians of All Tribes, Inc., in 1970.

The group's purpose was to promote the welfare of Indian people on Alcatraz Island and across the United States. The group promised to administer Alcatraz Island; promote the general welfare of the inhabitants of the island; negotiate with the U.S. federal government for the title to Alcatraz Island; establish Indian cultural and education centers on the island; sign contracts and enter into agreements; and receive and distribute money. All six promises met the criteria for incorporation under the California Nonprofit Corporation Law.

Membership on the board of directors changed often throughout the 19 month occupation. Provisions were made for regular elections so that leadership position continued to reflect the will of the people on the island. Throughout the occupation, the corporation provided the framework for the daily chores of security, housing, financing, public relations, sanitation, cooking, cleaning, day care, medical care, and negotiating with federal officials. Indians of All Tribes ceased to exist on 11 June 1971, when the occupation ended.

INSTITUTE FOR THE DEVELOPMENT OF INDIAN LAW. Founded by **Vine Deloria Jr.**, Franklin D. Ducheeaux, and Kirke Kickingbird in 1971, the Institute for the Development of Indian Law provides research, publication, and legal assistance to Indian tribes and is dedicated to increasing tribal sovereignty and fostering self-determination. Headquartered in Oklahoma City, Oklahoma, the institute has led the way in litigating Indian civil rights cases and has dedicated itself to aiding tribes in forming like-minded organizations.

INSTITUTE OF AMERICAN INDIAN ARTS (IAIA). In 1961, the **Bureau of Indian Affairs** authorized the opening of a school for Indian artists in the old Santa Fe Indian School in Santa Fe, New Mexico. The curriculum was designed to incorporate Indian arts into the mainstream of American culture and assimilate Indian artists. The IAIA opened in 1962 to students of at least one-quarter Indian blood who were between the ages of 15 and 22. The IAIA served grades ten through twelve and offered two years of college training. The institute offered programs in creative writing, metal work, textiles, ceramics, sculpture, painting, music, and theater arts. By the 1970s, the offerings were expanded to include filmmaking, merchandising, and museum curating.

A series of funding issues plagued the IAIA in the 1970s and 1980s that appeared to spell the end for the institute. However, administrators chose to focus on its postsecondary offerings. In 1986, the U.S. federal government declared the IAIA a charter institution and allowed it to actively raise funds as a nonprofit organization, hire faculty without civil service restrictions, and appoint its own governing body. Overcoming financial worries, the institute opened a museum and gift shop in downtown Santa Fe in 1992.

The IAIA is credited with revitalizing interest in Indian arts, especially painting. More than 3,000 students have graduated from the institute since its inception. The IAIA has been home to some of the leading and most famous Indian artists.

IROQUOIS CONFEDERACY. The Iroquois Confederacy is a political union in which all members act as one in making decisions concerning war and peace, trade alliances, and treaty making. The most powerful and populous group of tribes east of the Mississippi, the Iroquois Confederacy was originally made up of the Senecas, Cayugas, Onondagas, Oneidas, and Mohawks. Through the skilled diplomacy of **Deganawida** and **Hiawatha**, the members of the confederacy vowed to end hostilities and bloodshed against one another and join together in peace. The symbols of the league are the wampum belt with the representation of Onondaga at its center and the Longhouse, structures that held the extended families of the various nations. Each longhouse represents the respective clan mothers of the specific tribe and provides for their protection. Thus, each matrilineal clan is united and peace and friendship link together all of the nations of the Confederacy in a bond of kinship.

The English colonists knew them as the Five Nations. In 1722, the Tuscaroras migrated from the South and joined the confederacy, changing the name to the Six Nations Confederacy. Continuous contact with colonial powers began in 1609, when Samuel de Champlain led a force against the Mohawks in the New York valley that now bears the explorer's name. Champlain's attack led to sporadic warfare between France and the Iroquois until 1624, when the two agreed to peace terms—the first treaty signed between the confederacy and a colonial power. From that time onward, contact with Europeans was an everyday occurrence. One of the first English actions, after expelling the Dutch from New York, was to forge a treaty with the confederacy. Through a complex set of treaties and arrangements, the confederacy controlled trade routes and access to hunting territories as far west as Illinois and as far south as Kentucky. In the wars for empire between Britain and France, the confederacy maintained a position of neutrality. However, the member nations had closer cultural and economic ties with the English.

When the American Revolution began, the confederacy again attempted to maintain neutrality. It would be unable to do so this time for a number of reasons, namely competing religious loyalties that led some individuals to side with the British and others with the Americans and a devastating epidemic that killed many leaders who favored neutrality. The result of this uneven response was disaster. In 1779, General George Washington ordered General John Sullivan to travel to Iroquoia and burn crops, level villages, and scatter the population.

The confederacy was able to withstand Sullivan's assault, and throughout the 19th century it continued to function as both a political alliance and a cultural entity. However, in the wake of the American Revolution and Sullivan's campaign, the confederacy split into two grand councils, one at the traditional home at Onondaga and the other on the Grand River in Canada, where **Joseph Brant** and his followers settled.

Although the two councils meet and act as one body when a situation affects both groups, the Grand River Council primarily negotiates with Canada, while the Grand Council at Onondaga is the primary negotiator with the U.S. federal government. The political culture of the confederacy, now celebrating its 500th birthday, continues to function in the present-day.

– J –

JOHNSON-O'MALLEY ACT (JOM), 1934. The Johnson-O'Malley Act of 1934 was another piece of important Indian New Deal legislation supported by the commissioner of Indian affairs, **John Collier**. The JOM Act authorized the secretary of the interior to enter into contracts with states to provide monetary payments for services to rural, low-income Indians who generally lived off **reservations**. Most funds were primarily directed for Indian **education** but could be used for medical, agricultural, and social welfare services.

A major problem soon developed when public school districts that received the JOM funding, which was specifically designated to create special programs for their Indian students, often put the money into their general operating budget instead of hiring bilingual teachers, providing supplies, and revising the curriculum. Prejudice from non-Indian students and even teachers continued. Over the years, these problems have been largely rectified in most cases, and tribes have taken more control of the process. The JOM funds continue to provide Indian students in public schools better opportunities to succeed. In 2007, the George W. Bush administration proposed eliminating the JOM funding for 2008.

– K –

KACHINA. (Also spelled cachina, kacina, katcina, katchina, and katzina.) A Hopi term that has become the general term for spirits of this type found among the Pueblo Indians. Kachinas are powerful spirits of departed ancestors who have taken the form of plants, animals, and other humans who function to bring rain, secure crops, and ensure the continuity of Pueblo life. The spirits once inhabited the San Francisco Peaks and visited the people annually to dance and sing. The spirits eventually stopped coming, and now powerful members of the community invest themselves with the spirit and carry out the sacred duties. Masked male dancers, after a period of ritual initiation, become kachinas, losing their personal identity and acquiring all the powers of the spirit they portray.

Although the kachinas are not worshiped, they require that certain rituals be performed in their honor. Proper ritual and state of mind permit the kachinas to respond and bring benefits to the Pueblos; failure to conduct the rituals properly or improper behavior may cause the kachinas to withhold rains. Kachinas visit the numerous Pueblo villages at various times throughout the year, and the number of visitors varies from pueblo to pueblo. Among the Hopis, kachinas are viewed as friends with the exception of the ogre kachina, who punishes those who violate ceremonial laws. In addition to the masked dancers, kachinas are often depicted as dolls. *See also* RELIGION.

KEETOWAH. A Cherokee word derived from the name of one of the seven Cherokee "mother towns," Kituhwa. The town was originally situated on the Tuckasegee River in present-day North Carolina. The settlement served as the northernmost outpost of the Cherokee people and therefore was responsible for the protection of the northern frontier.

After Cherokee removal in 1838, a secret society formed within the tribe, calling themselves Keetowah. Keetowahs were traditionalists who sought to preserve their culture despite living in **Indian Territory**. At the turn of the 20th century, they fought against allotment and protested Oklahoma statehood. Today, the organization serves as the keeper of many of the most sacred Cherokee rituals and traditions.

Separate from the secret society is the United Keetowah Band of Cherokees, a federally recognized group that believes they are the representatives of the Cherokee people and not the Cherokee government.

KEOKUK (c. 1783–1848). Keokuk was a Sauk leader born near Rock River, Illinois, around 1780. Although not a chief by birth, he rose to command his people through the force of his personality and unquestionable skills as an orator. He assumed a leadership position when he was named tribal guestkeeper. In this position, Keokuk lived at tribal expense with all the abilities to greet guests with great hospitality. He played the role of genial host with such success that his lodge became the virtual center of all village activity. Keokuk quickly capitalized on his ever-expanding popularity and used his position to further his ambitions. Contrary to other men who held this position, he was not above violating customs if he would profit; he worked his will against Sauk custom not in an open and aggressive manner, but from behind the scenes using his diplomatic acumen. In time, he became the leading spokesman for the Sauk Nation and enjoyed great popularity among his people.

Keokuk's rise to power took a dramatic turn when the U.S. federal government signed a treaty with a small band of Sauk camped out near a St. Louis trading post. The agreement stated that the Sauk were to give up control of the Rock River country. As soon as the larger tribal body learned of the treaty, the Black Hawk War erupted. Throughout the fighting, Keokuk took a passive stance. Those who favored military action united under **Black Hawk**. Keokuk and those who feared military action sought protection from the Fox chief, Paweshik.

Although he was not part of the fighting force, Keokuk returned to the Sauk Nation to negotiate the peace that ended Black Hawk's War. He so deftly dealt with government officials that he was made chief of the Sauk Nation. Tribal legend states that the naming of Keokuk as tribal chief was done in open council, and when Black Hawk heard the translation, he became angry, ripped off his clout, and slapped Keokuk across the face with it.

Despite his difficulties in coming to power, Keokuk proved to be no pushover to the federal government. In Washington, D.C., Keokuk used his diplomatic skills to secure a claim for the Sauk and Fox nations to a territory that comprised the entire modern state of Iowa. Unable to hold the territory against U.S. advances, Keokuk and the Sauks were removed to **Indian Territory** in 1845. Keokuk died three years later, and his position as chief was handed to his eldest son. In 1883, Keokuk's remains were removed from Kansas and interred in a city park in Keokuk, Iowa, where a large bronze marker stands over his grave.

KING PHILIP'S WAR. Under the leadership of **Metacom** (King Philip), the Indians of colonial New England united against the colonists in a last ditch attempt to end a series of land disputes. In an effort to retain power in a corrupt political environment, sachems in New England sold tracts of land to competing colonies. Conflicts over the borders of these tracts soon developed and were rarely decided in favor of the Indians. Tribes were also angered by the colonists' attempts to meddle in the internal politics of the tribe and raged against the damage done by sales of liquor to Indian people. Making matters worse, English livestock often wandered into Indian fields and destroyed crops. In retaliation, Indians killed the livestock and sold the meat back to the colonists. Land conflicts became a matter of daily routine by 1667, when Plymouth violated an agreement with Metacom and authorized the purchase of land within his territory from *any* Indian.

In 1671, Plymouth demanded a meeting with Metacom, and when he arrived, he was forced at gunpoint to turn over his firearms and sign a treaty binding him and his dead father retroactively to the authority of the Plymouth colony. By making the treaty retroactive, Plymouth negated the land sales made by Metacom to other colonies. Returning home, Metacom began planning for war. Rather than strike against the colony on his own, he sought to build an alliance of all the Indians of New England. He won the support of the Wampanoags and Nipmucks, but he was forced into long negotiations with the Narragansetts, who were traditional enemies of the Wampanoags. Word of Metacom's plan reached colonial officials from Indian informants. When one of these informants turned up dead, Plymouth arrested three Wampanoags and tried them for murder. All three were found guilty and hanged.

In July 1675, Metacom and a group of warriors appeared outside of Swansea and attacked the town's cattle herd. A townsman shot one warrior. The uprising began more from lack of patience than any plan. When the colonial army attempted to arrest Metacom, he fled to his home on Mount Hope in present-day Bristol, Rhode Island. From his home, he gathered his warriors and family and fled to join the Nipmucks. With his Nipmuck allies, Metacom sacked villages west and south of Boston causing great alarm. The uprising spread when settlers in the Connecticut River Valley overreacted to the news and began attacking Indian settlements. During the winter, attacks continued, and Boston became a virtual refugee camp. Although Metacom did not actually command an Indian army, his presence seems to have been everywhere.

While attempting to find new allies, Metacom and his warriors were attacked by Mohawks allied with New York. All but 40 of his men died, and Metacom lost prestige. The Mohawks continued their assaults from the west while a revived colonial militia attacked from the east, putting Metacom in an untenable situation. By the spring of 1676, Metacom's alliance began to fall apart. He returned to Mount Hope when his allies threatened to send his head to the British as a peace offering. On 12 August 1675, an Indian force working for the British surrounded Metacom. He was shot, and his head was cut off. His body was quartered, and the pieces were sent to the various colonial capitals.

The defeat destroyed the Indian population of New England, but the colonists, who also suffered high casualties, did not return to their abandoned town for several years. Metacom's death marked the end of Indian independence in the region.

KIVA. Kivas are windowless, sacred structures where religious ceremonies occur. The structures are predominant among the Pueblo people of the southwest and have been part of their religious traditions since time immemorial. The kiva serves as the spiritual center of the Pueblo communities and is a meeting place for the spiritual and the sacred.

According to Pueblo traditions, the spirit beings of the "world below" instructed the people of the "world above" to build kivas in the shape of a *sipapu*, the opening through which humans emerged from their previous existence. People entered the kiva via a ladder from the top as the structure was built into the ground to bring the two worlds closer together.

Men dominated the rituals and ceremonies practiced inside the kiva. Kivas held sacred items, the walls were often elaborately decorated, and altars held representations of the appropriate deities. When the Spanish arrived in the area in the 16th century, they violated many of the kivas, destroying their contents in an effort to force the Pueblo people to convert to Catholicism. *See also* RELIGION.

– L –

LACROSSE. Lacrosse was just one of many stickball games played by Indians prior to the arrival of Europeans. Exclusively a male game, it is separated from the other stickball games by its use of a netted racket designed to pick the ball up off the ground and throw, catch, and shoot it into or past a goal to score a point. The game played a serious role in Indian cultures. Rooted in myths and legends, the game had curative and restorative powers and was surrounded by ceremony. A medicine man must bless game equipment and participants, and victory is determined to be the will of supernatural forces. Lacrosse also served as an outlet for frustration and, in some languages, the term used for the game translates into "little war." Lacrosse was often used to peacefully settle territorial and tribal disputes.

Lacrosse was given its name by early French settlers who used simple generic terms to describe a game played with a curved stick (*crosse*) and a ball. Early descriptions of the game come from French Jesuit missionaries among the Hurons and a few English explorers who navigated the Great Lakes. The oldest surviving equipment comes from the 19th century, and early data is so lacking that a real history of the game is impossible.

The spread of nonnative lacrosse, first seen in the Montreal area, has made the game one of the fastest growing sports in the world. The game is now controlled by written rules and governing bodies and played with manufactured rather than handmade equipment. Ironically, the women's game of today with its wooden sticks, lack of protective equipment, unmarked sidelines, and tendency toward frenetic attack most closely resembles the Indian game.

LADUKE, WINONA (1959–). Active in American Indian issues since her teens, LaDuke gained national attention in 1996 as the vice presidential running mate of Ralph Nader on the Green Party ticket. She and Nader would put the ticket back together in 2000. The daughter of an Anishinabe (Ojibwa) father and Jewish mother, LaDuke earned a degree in economics from Harvard University. She then moved to the White Earth Reservation, the traditional home of the Anishinabe people. On the **reservation**, she became involved in a land recovery lawsuit and founded the White Earth Land Recovery Project, which seeks to buy back tribal lands. The author of numerous articles, LaDuke wrote her first novel, *Last Standing Woman*, in 1997. The final chapter of her novel was written entirely in the Ojibwa language. *See also* WOMEN.

LAKE MOHONK CONFERENCE OF FRIENDS OF THE INDIAN (LMC). Founded in 1883 by Indian reformer Albert K. Smiley, the LMC was an annual event held at the Lake Mohonk resort, owned by Smiley and his twin brother, Alfred, in the Catskill Mountains in New York. The meetings at Lake Mohonk lasted for several days, and leading Indian reformers, both non-Indians and Indians, gathered to discuss Indian issues in an attempt to solve the "Indian problem." Indian reformers organized the LMC and also the **Indian Rights Association** because of what they conceived as major federal Indian policy failures and blatant mistreatment of Indian tribes during previous decades, especially in the 1870s.

Major reforms proposed by the LMC included supporting civil service reform in the **Bureau of Indian Affairs**, increasing appropriations for Indian **education**, and improving Indian schools. Since most of the conference attendees were staunch assimilationists who saw little value in Indian lifestyles, they supported the passage of the **Dawes Severalty Act** of 1887, which broke up **reservations** by assigning land allotments to the Indian inhabitants in an effort to have them become like white, Christian farmers. Additional issues addressed were protecting Indians' civil and legal rights, exposing graft and corruption on reservations, supporting Indian economic development, and condemning liquor and **peyote** use among Indians. The last LMC was held in 1929.

LAW. Indian nations, as sovereign bodies within the framework of the American legal system, make and enforce many of their own laws. However, Indian sovereignty is not absolute, and there are numerous limitations placed on Indians by federal statutes. In fact, Indian nations lack enforcement jurisdiction on **reservations** if a crime is committed by a non-Indian. This jurisdictional confusion leads to many crimes and other illegal offenses committed on reservations going unpunished. The easiest way to conceptualize Native American law is to focus on three distinct categories of Indian rights in the United States: the plenary power of Congress, the Doctrine of Diminished Sovereignty, and the Trust Doctrine.

The Plenary Power Doctrine can explain most of the limits to Indian sovereignty. This legal principle states that the U.S. Congress exercises decision-making authority over Indians. Congress can force Indian nations to obey the laws and statutes passed by the U.S. federal government. For example, the 1968 Civil Rights Act forced Indian tribes to extend to their members the same rights and guarantees granted to all Americans under the Bill of Rights. However, Congress has historically used its plenary power to limit the sovereignty of Indian tribes, as it did under the **Indian Reorganization Act (IRA)** of 1934. The Plenary Power Doctrine has been upheld in numerous court decisions. Despite these legal precedents, the principle of plenary power is rooted in the conquest theory, which states that Indian people, by right of discovery, are under the sovereign jurisdiction of the United States of America.

The conquest theory came to the New World with European colonists, but its history is generally rooted in the Middle Ages, specifically in the Crusades. During the Crusades, a just war was one that sought to expel non-Christians from Jerusalem and other holy sites in the Middle East. What developed was a legal theory that denied the rights of self-rule and property to non-Christians. The English used the same theory in their conquest of Catholic Ireland. When the Spanish first set foot in the Americas, they brought the conquest theory with them. Like the Moors before, Indians were seen as "heathens" and "infidels." Following the Spanish example, other colonial powers used the conquest theory when they established their plantations in the New World. Legal principles based on this theory, for example, plenary power, the domestic dependent status of tribes, and the federal trust responsibility, have been used by Congress and the courts throughout the nation's history to decide the scope and nature of Indian sovereignty.

More current problems of enforcement on reservations arise from the "checkerboard" jurisdiction pattern found on most reservations. The nature of the checkerboard can be traced directly to the programs of cultural assimilation that were prevalent throughout much of Indian history, specifically the **Dawes Severalty Act** of 1887. The act parceled out reservation lands and sold surplus lands to white settlers—in effect, severing Indian lands in smaller pieces and creating a number of non-Indian plots within tribal territory but not under tribal jurisdiction.

The Major Crimes Act of 1885 gave the federal government complete control over felonies committed on the nation's various Indian reservations. As a result, federal prosecution and investigation trumps tribal control and sovereignty over crimes committed by Indians and non-Indians alike. Policies like those already mentioned are based on the underlying principle that the majority possesses unchecked power over the lawmaking authority of Indian tribes. Not a single court in the Untied States has ever questioned this basic principle.

The unquestioned nature of the Plenary Power Doctrine leads directly to the second judicial principle: that tribal sovereignty is somehow diminished as a result of Euro-American contact and dominance. In a series of landmark cases, the Supreme Court has ruled that tribal jurisdiction is actually a privilege the federal government has given Indian peoples, even though it was actually destroyed by the conquest theory. In *Oliphant v. Suquamish Indian Tribe* (1979), the court stated that Indians no longer held inherent sovereignty and thus, could not punish non-Indians for crimes committed on Indian lands. Cited as precedent in the *Oliphant* decision was the 1832 John Marshall decision in *Johnson v. McIntosh* that stated that upon their incorporation into the United States, tribes lost their discretionary sovereignty, and the overriding authority of the federal government took precedence. Marshall's decision in the famous Cherokee Cases of the 1830s declared Indian tribes to be "domestic dependent nations."

Another major decision was handed down in 1989 in *Brendale v. Confederated Tribes and Bands of the Yakima Indian Nation*. The case involved the question of whether the Yakima Nation had the power to regulate land use on land owned by nonmembers within the allotted portions of the reservation. The Supreme Court held that Congress had divested the tribe of its sovereignty when the tribe was selected for allotment under the Dawes Severalty Act. Thus, as of 1887, the Yakima had lost the authority to regulate the lands under question in the case.

Finally, the Trust Doctrine evolved. The use and abuse of this doctrine is firmly rooted in the previous two principles, the Plenary

Power Doctrine and Limited Sovereignty. The Trust Doctrine states that federal officials possess broad authority over Indians, a relationship similar to that of guardian and child. The doctrine, presented by non-Indians as a sign of federal largess and protection, has historically stopped tribes from establishing their own schools and courts. It has only been in recent years that tribes have been able to circumvent the Trust Doctrine to establish their own reservation infrastructure. The **Cobell case** currently under adjudication is seeking to override the doctrine.

In short, Indians are sovereign nations, but that sovereignty is severely limited. As long as the conquest theory continues to guide federal law in the United States, the body of statutes known collectively as Indian law will remain limited, confusing, and undeniably racist.

LITTLE CROW (c. 1810–1863). A Mdewakanton Dakota leader, Little Crow was born near St. Paul, Minnesota, around 1810. His people, the Dakota, or Eastern Sioux, first engaged in fur trading with the French beginning in the mid-17th century. The United States later expanded into the region and built Fort Snelling after the War of 1812.

Not much in known about the early years of Little Crow. When his father, a tribal chief, died in 1846, leadership was passed to Little Crow's half-brother. Little Crow wanted to be the new chief, resulting in the two fighting and Little Crow winning, although he suffered serious wounds on both wrists. Treaties with the United States in the 1830s and 1850s, as well as Minnesota becoming a state in 1849 and more whites coming to the state, greatly impacted the Dakota people. **Reservation** life was not what was promised as government annuities and rations were not delivered on time or were reduced and more demands were placed on the Indians to sell more land and give up their Indian ways. In August 1862, a group of young Indians killed several whites, contributing to the short-lived Dakota Conflict, also called the Minnesota Uprising or Santee Sioux Uprising, of 1862.

Little Crow, who had angered whites for not strongly supporting assimilation and Indians for not becoming more aggressive against whites, was convinced by Indian warriors to lead them into battle. Although several hundred whites were killed during the conflict, Little Crow's forces were soon outnumbered and forced to surrender. Little Crow escaped to Canada but later returned to Minnesota. He was killed by a farmer on 3 July 1863 while he was picking berries. During his lifetime, Little Crow tried to help his people acculturate to a new way of life, but failed government policies and discontent among his people dictated otherwise.

LITTLE TURTLE (c. 1752–1812). Believed to be one of the greatest Algonquian war leaders of all time, Little Turtle grew up during the American Revolution and led an armed resistance against the American invasion of the Old Northwest. It was Little Turtle who assumed the leadership mantle of **Joseph Brant** after Brant developed the Western Confederacy. Little Turtle began as a supporter of peace with the Americans in the early years of the 19th century. As a result of this stance, he lost status among his Miami people and was identified as an "American chief."

After the Treaty of Paris in 1783, American officials attempted to force four treaties on the tribes of the Old Northwest. Each of the treaties was rooted in the conquest theory and stated that the Indians had lost their rights to the land by siding with the British during the American Revolution. Resistance by Indian people quickly developed into a full-scale border war, first in Kentucky where settlers flocked and later into the entire Ohio River Valley. Little Turtle protected the village of Kekionga, a large village of mixed tribal inhabitants.

President George Washington ordered an attack of Little Turtle's village in 1790. Under the cover of darkness, Little Turtle evacuated the village. When General Josiah Harmar sacked the village on 20 October, it was deserted. Little Turtle then struck at Harmar's force in a surprise ambush, and 183 Americans died. The following year, General Arthur St. Clair led another attack on Little Turtle's village. This time Little Turtle attacked directly, leading his force against St. Clair. When the smoke cleared, Little Turtle and his warriors had defeated almost the entire U.S. army. Indians killed more than 600 officers and men in what is considered the worst defeat of an American army to this day. In response, General Anthony Wayne was dispatched to put an end to hostilities. Little Turtle launched a series of small attacks on Wayne's force, probing for weaknesses. He concluded that the force was unbeatable and called for peace negotiations. Unable to convince his force of the indestructibility of Wayne's force, Little Turtle retired from the field, leaving leadership to Blue Jacket of the Shawnees. Wayne defeated the allied tribes with little loss on his side at Fallen Timbers on 20 August 1794.

Little Turtle returned to his leadership position to act as the spokesman for the 11 confederated tribes at Greenville in July 1795 to negotiate peace with the Americans. During negotiations, Little Turtle made an eloquent defense of Indian rights in the Old Northwest. He outlined what became known as "Little Turtle's Claim," which presented the case for Miami ownership of all of present-day Indiana and parts of Ohio, Illinois, and Michigan. At the end of negotiations, Little Turtle promised peace with the Americans.

Little Turtle lived out the rest of his life at his village west of Fort Wayne. He died peacefully on 14 July 1812. His fame rested on his abilities as a warrior and his diplomacy at Greenville. Although he lived his final days as a puppet of the Americans, he is still seen as a great chief.

LONGEST WALK. In February 1978, in San Francisco, California, **Dennis Banks**, one of the leaders of the **American Indian Movement (AIM)**, organized the Longest Walk to commemorate the organization's earlier **Trail of Broken Treaties** march on Washington, D.C., in 1972. During the Longest Walk march to the nation's capital, AIM held forums that provided information on Indian issues, and additional Indians joined in along the way. Arriving in the nation's capital on 25 July, several hundred Indians staged a major demonstration at the Washington National Monument. Their demands included the return of tribal lands taken illegally, recognition of tribal sovereignty, and recognition of civil rights for American Indians.

LORD DUNMORE'S WAR. This colonial conflict involved Indians of the Ohio River Valley and militia forces led by the last royal governor of Virginia, John Murry, earl of Dunmore. Dunmore and wealthy Virginians hoped to gain control of the Ohio Valley, taking the territory both from the Indian inhabitants and colonial rival Pennsylvania. The movement of a large number of settlers into Shawnee territories sparked rumors of a general Indian uprising in the Ohio River region. However, the war began when Virginians attacked two Indian hunting parties in April 1774. The victims of the initial raid responded by launching a **mourning war** against the colonists and matched the number of colonial dead with the number of Indians lost in the attack.

Hearing rumors of a large-scale Indian uprising, Dunmore gathered his force and marched west. Arriving in Pittsburg, Dunmore learned that he had been misled and that attacks on the frontier were grossly exaggerated. Undaunted, he pledged to continue his plan to take the war to the Shawnees. Dunmore called a council of Delawares, Iroquois, and Wyandot hoping to convince them to remain neutral and thus isolate the Shawnees.

With the Shawnees isolated, Dunmore marched his army into the Ohio Valley. The Shawnees launched a counterattack at Point Pleasant. In a full day of fighting, Indians battered many of the advancing columns but proved unable to overrun Dunmore's army. Unable to defeat Dunmore on the battlefield, the Indians sent an emissary seeking peace terms. The result of the peace negotiation was the Treaty of Camp Charlotte. According to the treaty, the Shawnees agreed to return all **captives** and stolen **horses** and remain north of the Ohio River, turning over Kentucky to Virginia.

Despite the terms of the treaty, the Shawnees continued to hunt south of the Ohio River, and their relationships with neighboring tribes seemed unaffected by the conflict. It is likely that the Shawnees never desired a full-scale war with Virginia and would have negotiated a similar peace without hostilities. However, the events of Lord Dunmore's War demonstrated a growing militancy among Indians living in the Ohio Valley.

LOYAL ORDER OF TECUMSEH. Arthur Parker, a Seneca, organized The Loyal Order of Tecumseh as a secret body inside the **Society of American Indians**. The purpose of the order was to provide common ground between those with lesser degrees of "Indian blood" and those who were more "pure." The members of the order held no voting privileges and therefore would not affect the policies of the parent organization. The Loyal Order of the Tecumseh, therefore, was far from active but is significant because it eventually evolved into other fraternal groups during the 1920s.

LYONS, OREN (1930–). Lyons was born in 1930 and raised on both the Seneca and Onondaga **reservations** in northern New York. After leaving the U.S. army, he enrolled in Syracuse University, pursuing a degree in fine arts. Lyons was also a member of the Syracuse **lacrosse** team. He and teammate, future NFL hall of famer Jim Brown, led the Orangemen to an undefeated season during Lyons's senior year. After graduation, Lyons pursued a career in commercial art in New York City.

In 1970, Lyons returned to Onondaga, was named a chief, and since has served as a leading advocate of American Indian causes. For more than 30 years, he has served on the Indigenous Peoples Council of the United Nations Human Rights Commission. He established the Working Group on Indigenous Populations in 1982, served on the executive committee of the Global Forum of Spiritual and Parliamentary Leaders on Human Survival, and is a prominent figure in the Traditional Circle of Indian Elders, an annual grassroots leadership council of North American Indian nations. He was the negotiator between the governments of Quebec, Canada, New York, and the Mohawks during the 1990 Oka Crisis. In 1991, Lyons led an Indian delegation that met with President George H. W. Bush at the White House. He is currently a tenured professor of American studies at the State University of New York, Buffalo.

– M –

MACDONALD, PETER (1928–). Born on 16 December 1928, at Teec Nos Pos, located on the Navajo Reservation in Arizona, MacDonald was raised in a traditional Navajo environment. At the age of two, he lost his father and later had to quit school after the seventh grade to herd sheep and work.

Before he turned 16 years old, MacDonald joined the U.S. marine corps during World War II and became one of the last members of the **Navajo Code Talkers**. After the war, he attended high school in Bacone, Oklahoma, received an associate of arts from Bacone College, and in 1957 earned his bachelor of science in electrical engineering from the University of Oklahoma. He worked for Hughes Aircraft Company in California until 1963, when he returned to Arizona to serve on the New Mexico Economic Development Advisory Board and become head of the Management, Methods, and Procedures Division of the Navajo tribal government.

In 1965, MacDonald accepted the directorship of the Office of Navajo Economic Opportunity, and he was extremely successful in obtaining millions of dollars in federal grants that established programs for reducing unemployment, improving medical and dental care, offering more legal services, constructing better roads, and providing more **educational** activities and opportunities for Navajo students. Such achievements increased MacDonald's popularity among Navajos but also created resentment among others, including federal officials who felt threatened by Navajos exercising and increasing their political, economic, and social sovereignty.

MacDonald was elected Navajo tribal chairman in 1970 and held the office from 1971 to 1982 and 1987 to 1989. Chairman MacDonald continued his efforts to improve **reservation** conditions and increase Navajo self-determination and sovereignty rights. He criticized the **Bureau of Indian Affairs**, Arizona officials, and big business for not recognizing and protecting Navajo rights. He renegotiated new and fairer leases of Navajo minerals—especially coal and uranium—with private businesses, demanded protection of Navajo land and water rights, and emphasized educational reform for Navajo children. In 1975, he helped establish the **Council of Energy Resource Tribes** and later served as its chairman.

As the years passed, MacDonald's enemies, both Navajo and non-Navajo, did not like his what they considered aggressive tactics, and they sought to remove him as tribal chairman. MacDonald, like other politicians, tended to play favorites and accepted questionable loans and gifts. Charges were brought against him, and in 1991, the U.S. District Court sentenced him to 14 years and seven months in prison for receiving kickbacks in a multimillion dollar tribal purchase of the Big Boquillas Ranch in Arizona and also for inciting a riot at the tribal headquarters in Window Rock, Arizona. In 1993, he began serving his sentence and served more than seven years. During those years, MacDonald suffered from diabetes and heart problems that included quadruple bypass surgery. While in prison, he apologized to the Navajo for any problems and suffering he had caused. Several appeals were filed for his release, and President Bill Clinton commuted MacDonald's sentence in 2001.

MacDonald continues to have loyal followers and has become a Navajo elder statesman. He remains outspoken on issues that threaten Navajo self-determination and sovereignty.

MANITOU. Manitou is the Algonquin belief, similar to the Iroquois **orenda** and the Sioux **wakonda**, that a great supernatural force flows through and unites the entire universe. *See also* RELIGION.

MANKILLER, WILMA (1945–). Born in Adair County, Oklahoma, in 1945, Mankiller's father was Cherokee and mother Dutch-Irish. She had 10 siblings and was raised in a home without running water or electricity. The Mankiller family moved to San Francisco in 1956 as part of the **Bureau of Indian Affairs** Relocation Program. Mankiller became involved with other Indian activists in the city and participated in the occupation of **Alcatraz** Island off the coast of San Francisco, California. After a failed marriage, Mankiller returned to Oklahoma in the late 1970s and became involved with the Cherokee Nation and its programs. She became the first woman principal chief of the Cherokee Nation in 1985 and held the position for 10 years. During her administration, she supported several programs that improved conditions among the Cherokee, including providing better employment opportunities and increasing health care services. In 1987, she was recognized as woman of the year by *Ms. Magazine*; in 1993, she was elected into the National Women's Hall of Fame; and in 1998, she was given the Medal of Freedom by President Bill Clinton. In 1993, Mankiller wrote her autobiography, *Mankiller: A Chief and Her People*, which detailed her remarkable accomplishments that are even more extraordinary because of major tragedies she endured, including almost dying in an automobile accident in 1979, having major nervous system complications in 1980, receiving a kidney transplant in 1990, and contracting cancer in 1996. *See also* WOMEN.

MASCOTS. The use of Native Americans as mascots and the use of Indian nicknames—some of them highly offensive—in sports is a controversial issue in Indian and white relations. The question that remains the focus of controversy is, Do such practices honor or dishonor Native Americans?

Mainstream America has used Indian images, ways, and symbols for many years, especially as the 20th century dawned. The Indian Head nickel, summer camp outdoor activities, and the rituals of the Boy Scouts and Girl Scouts are just a few examples. In college and professional sports, the University of Wisconsin called its teams the

Indians in 1909; in 1912, the Boston Braves was established; and in 1915, the Cleveland Indians was created. Other names of college, professional, and high school teams included braves, chiefs, and redskins.

Most Indians declare that they are not mascots and demand that teams that have Indian names or use Indian symbols change them. **Russell Means** and **Dennis Banks** of the **American Indian Movement**, **Vine Deloria Jr.** of the **Morning Star Institute**, and many others actively protested for changing team names and discontinuing such Indian practices as the "tomahawk chop" and other inappropriate actions that demeaned Indian people. Although teams have voluntarily changed their names, many have not, and among their arguments are that they are honoring Native Americans, that a name change would have a negative impact on the team's tradition, and finally, in some cases, that the costs to do so would be prohibitive.

In 2005, the National Collegiate Athletic Association (NCAA) ruled to ban teams that had "abusive" and "hostile" Indian names from playing in postseason games. Among the teams affected were college powerhouses the Florida State Seminoles and the University of Illinois Fighting Illini, the latter primarily because of its mascot, Chief Illiniwek. These teams and others appealed the NCAA ruling, and Florida State was allowed to continue calling itself the Seminoles because Seminole tribal leaders in Florida gave them permission to do so, while Illinois "retired" the 81 year old mascot, Chief Illiniwek, but retained the name Fighting Illini because it is a shortened version of Illinois. While some colleges like Dartmouth and Stanford have dropped their Indian names, numerous other colleges, public schools, and professional teams, including the Washington Redskins, Atlanta Braves, Kansas City Chiefs, and Cleveland Indians, continue to keep and resist efforts to change their Indian names and the portrayal of Indian customs during games, which most Indians consider highly offensive and extremely negative representations of their heritage and traditions.

MASHPEE REVOLT. *See* APESS, WILLIAM.

MCNICKLE, D'ARCY (1904–1977). Born on 18 January 1904, and raised on the Confederated Salish and Kootenai Tribes, or Flathead,

Reservation in Montana, McNickle was enrolled as a Flathead, but his father was Irish and his mother was Metis, or mixed Cree and French ancestry. They farmed on allotted **reservation** land. Although not much is known about his early years, McNickle's parents frowned on him playing with other Indians, and he attended federal boarding schools and later public school in Tacoma, Washington. He played the violin and loved to read. Although McNickle attended several universities, including the University of Montana and Oxford University, he never graduated with a degree. He moved to New York City in the 1920s and hoped to become a writer. In 1936, he published his first novel, *The Surrounded*, which is somewhat autobiographical and tells the tragic story of America's mistreatment of Indians and the problems encountered by the novel's mixed-blood leading character.

Shortly after the publication of his novel, McNickle gained employment with the Federal Writers Program of the Works Progress Administration in Washington, D.C. He became more interested in Indians and longed to work with commissioner of Indian affairs **John Collier** at the **Bureau of Indian Affairs (BIA)**. Collier hired him, and the two established a close working relationship and became good friends. McNickle developed an intense interest in anthropology and history, and many of his Indian New Deal assignments dealt with these areas. He and other anthropologists engaged in fieldwork among different tribes and held special workshops on contemporary Indian issues for tribal leaders. His writing skills allowed him to publish articles in BIA and nongovernmental publications. During his lifetime, McNickle published four novels and five nonfiction books, all based on his perspectives as a Native American writing about Native Americans.

McNickle also helped found the **National Congress of American Indians (NCAI)** in 1944 as a **Pan-Indian** movement to make the U.S. federal government aware of Indian issues. He resigned from the BIA in 1952 but remained involved in Indian affairs for the remainder of his life. He continued his work with the NCAI; helped direct community development projects, especially related to health and hygiene issues among Navajos in Crown Point, New Mexico; addressed the need for more Indian students to graduate from high school and college; and helped organize the **American Indian**

Chicago Conference in 1961. In 1966, he accepted an offer from the University of Saskatchewan in Canada to become chair of the Department of Anthropology. He had no college degree—although shortly before becoming chair he received an honorary doctorate of science from the University of Colorado—or formal teaching experience, but he was widely recognized as an expert in his field. McNickle held the position until 1971 when he moved to Albuquerque, New Mexico. Additional honors included membership on the Smithsonian Institution's editorial board for the revised multivolume *Handbook of North American Indians* and, in 1971, appointment as the first director of the Center for the History of the American Indian at the Newberry Library in Chicago, Illinois. In 1977, he was named distinguished research scholar at the Newberry Library, and in 1983, the center was renamed the D'Arcy McNickle Center for the History of the American Indian. McNickle died on 15 October 1977 in Albuquerque from a massive heart attack.

MEANS, RUSSELL (1939–). One of the most well-known Indian activists of the **Red Power Movement** and supporter of **Pan-Indianism**, Means was born on 10 November 1939, at the Pine Ridge Indian Reservation in South Dakota. In 1942, he moved with his family to Vallejo, California, where his father worked in a shipyard. Means attended public school and graduated from San Leandro High School in 1958, despite being a problem student who frequently fought, drank, and took and sold drugs. After graduation, he drifted from place to place and job to job, working as a ballroom dancer, a janitor, an accountant, and a rodeo hand. In 1961, he married the first of his four wives. He enrolled in several colleges but did not receive a degree. Means still engaged in criminal activities, including drunkenness, street scams, and assault with a deadly weapon. In 1964, he participated in his first demonstration, the initial and short-lived occupation of **Alcatraz** Island at the abandoned federal prison off the coast of San Francisco, California. Joining his father in the movement, Means later recalled that the experience instilled in him pride in being an Indian and motivated him to address issues affecting Indian conditions.

As the 1960s ended, Means again held several jobs that included designing personnel and financial reporting systems on the Rosebud

Reservation in South Dakota and moving to Cleveland, Ohio, where he helped in Indian relocation. He helped organize the Cleveland American Indian Center and served as its executive director in 1970. He also joined in movements to end using Indians as **mascots** and began a campaign to convince the Cleveland Indians baseball team to abandon their mascot, Chief Wahoo, a racist stereotype. Means joined the **American Indian Movement (AIM)** after meeting **Dennis Banks**, one of AIM's founders, and later established an AIM chapter in Cleveland. Banks was impressed with his speaking skills and believed Means could become an effective spokesman for the cause.

During the 1970s, Means engaged in many of the major AIM demonstrations throughout the United States. He was among the demonstrators who boarded the *Mayflower II* in Plymouth, Massachusetts, on Thanksgiving Day in 1970 to protest the mistreatment of Indians by colonial settlers and other Indian grievances. Wanting to learn more about his own Indian roots, Means participated in a **Sun Dance** at Pine Ridge in 1971. He and AIM continued their efforts assisting Indian people, both on and off **reservations**, throughout the 1970s. He was among those protesting the lack of attention given by white law enforcement officials to cases involving Indian murders, especially in South Dakota. He also helped plan the **Trail of Broken Treaties** caravan to Washington, D.C., and the subsequent Bureau of Indian Affairs takeover in 1972.

Because of deplorable conditions at Pine Ridge and demands to remove Tribal Chairman Richard Wilson, Means was among those who occupied the hamlet of Wounded Knee, the site of the 1890 tragedy, in 1973. The occupation, known as **Wounded Knee II**, lasted for 71 days and attracted media attention to Indian issues at Pine Ridge and nationwide. At a subsequent trial in 1974, in which the judge cited government officials for gross misconduct, Means and Banks were found not guilty of criminal conspiracy. Conditions at Pine Ridge did not improve, and Means failed in his attempt to defeat Wilson in the tribal chairman election in 1974.

During the last decades of the 20th century, Means continued his activism. He participated in the **Longest Walk**, fought for the rights of indigenous peoples in Latin America, demanded that the sacred Black Hills be returned to the Sioux Nation, supported the name change of the Custer Battlefield National Monument to the Little Bighorn Battlefield National Monument, and demonstrated against **Columbus Day** activities in Denver, Colorado. Means also began a career as an actor, appearing in television programs and in movies, most notably having a major role in the film *The Last of the Mohicans* in 1991. For the remainder of the 1990s and into the 21st century, Means continued accepting acting roles in Hollywood. Means and other AIM members, like **Clyde Bellecourt** and **Vernon Bellecourt**, eventually parted ways, each accusing the other of not truly representing the movement. In 2004, Means failed in his bid to become tribal president of the Oglala Nation, losing the election to **Cecilia Fire Thunder**, and he is currently involved in a case concerning a physical confrontation between him and an Omaha Indian relative on the Navajo Reservation in Arizona, in which he claims Navajo jurisdiction does not apply to him since he is a Lakota.

MEDICINE BUNDLE. A pouch, wrap, or bag that contained a sacred object or a collection of sacred objects. A medicine bundle provided special powers to help tribal members in life, hunting and battle, and curing illness. Many tribes had medicine bundles that held such items as remnants of small animals and birds, eagle feathers, bison horns, flora seeds, shells, and stones. The bundles were often associated with tribal origin tales and used in ceremonies. Specially trained individuals kept the medicine bundles, and if they were not handled properly, it was believed that harmful and evil results would occur. *See also* RELIGION.

MENOMINEE DRUMS. The Menominee in Wisconsin was one of several tribes terminated in the 1950s. **Termination** meant ending federal supervision, support, and the special status Indians held. Tribes that were deemed self-sufficient and "prosperous" could be terminated and come under state jurisdiction. The Menominee operated a tribal sawmill and lumbering operation. In addition, the Menominee had won a federal suit regarding mismanagement of their forests and wanted a per capita payment to tribal members. Utah Senator Arthur Watkins, a staunch supporter of termination, informed the Menominee that they could only have the payments if they accepted termination. Many Menominee did not comprehend the repercussions of such a vote.

The Menominee Termination Act of 1954 did not take effect immediately but was finalized in 1961. The Menominee created a corporation called Menominee Enterprises Incorporated (MEI), which replaced the tribal government and managed the lumbering business, and the **reservation** became a new county in the state. Termination devastated the Menominee, who no longer had federal services. They had to start paying taxes, their lumber industry collapsed, unemployment rose, health problems increased, and their hospital closed. Many Menominee had to sell their land to survive, and their county became the poorest in Wisconsin.

Menominee DRUMS, which stood for Determination of the Rights and Unity of Menominee Shareholders, was established in 1970 by **Ada Deer**, other Menominee, and non-Indians living in Milwaukee, Wisconsin, and Chicago, Illinois, to fight for restoration as a federally recognized tribe. DRUMS was able to gain control of MEI's board of directors, who had opposed the organization, and through Deer's tireless work as a lobbyist in Madison, Wisconsin, and Washington, D.C., state and federal officials were convinced of the failure of termination. President Richard M. Nixon signed the Menominee Restoration Act in 1973, which restored federal tribal status to the Menominee.

METACOM (c. 1639–1676). Also known as King Philip, Metacom personified resistance to the increasing power of Puritan New England over Indian peoples. Metacom was born in what is now southeast Massachusetts, aware of the increasing power of his white neighbors. He was born just 20 years after his father, Massasoit, made the first alliance with the Puritans and two years after his Wampanoag tribe rose to power by destroying the once-mighty Pequots.

In 1660, Massasoit died, and Metacom's brother, Wamsutta, became sachem of the Wampanoag. When the brothers appeared in Boston, their Puritan neighbors dubbed them "Alexander" and "Philip." Alarm rang out in Plymouth when Wamsutta (Alexander) began selling land to other colonies. In 1662, an armed party arrested Wamsutta and planned to force his testimony before an inquest; however, Wamsutta became sick and died before he could deliver his testimony. Metacom suspected his brother was poisoned, and after becoming sachem, he remained distrustful of the Puritans.

As sachem, Metacom attempted to maintain his power and protect the general welfare of the Wampanoags in the face of ever-growing Puritan power. The Puritans began a concerted effort to undermine Metacom's power and eventually fractured the Wampanoag Confederacy. The result of the undermining was the uprising known as **King Philip's War**.

MOHAWK BLOCKADE. In the 1950s, Canadian authorities began stopping the flow of Mohawk people across the International Bridge, a right they were guaranteed by Jay's Treaty of 1794. To protest Canada's regulation of the Mohawks, activists blocked all passage on the International Bridge in 1968. Although several Mohawk activists were arrested, neither New York nor Canadian authorities were able to prosecute, since the U.S. federal government had jurisdiction over the bridge. Eventually, the Mohawk Nation and Canada negotiated a settlement that guaranteed Mohawk rights of passage. In response to the blockade, the Mohawks began publication of *Akwesasne Notes*, a journal dedicated to Indian activism and militancy.

MONTAUK CONFEDERACY. Located along central and eastern Long Island, New York, the Montauk Confederacy was formed by island tribes to protect themselves from such mainland tribes as the Pequot. The Montauk were the most powerful tribe in the confederacy and thus gave their name to the entire organization. Confederacy members lived in individual villages but shared similar cultural patterns and even the same language. A trade network with Europeans developed early in the 16th century.

Each village was independent and ruled by a hereditary sachem. Sachems met as needed and never made independent decisions, always operating as a confederacy. The confederacy and its council were presided over by a Montauk sachem who served as grand sachem. The confederacy numbered around 6,000 in 1600, but because of the relationship with whites, **disease**, **alcoholism**, and warfare, there was a rapid population decline. In 1788, with only 100 members, the confederacy joined with the Brotherton Indians of New York and later moved to the Oneida Indian Reservation in Wisconsin. A handful of holdouts on Long Island retained their cultural traditions into the 19th century. The last hereditary sachem, David Pharaoh, died in 1875. The customs, traditions, and languages of the Montauk Confederacy were lost shortly after Pharaoh's death.

MONTEZUMA, CARLOS (c. 1866–1923). Born around 1866 and named Wassaja by his Yavapai parents, he was captured by Pima Indians in 1871 and sold for $30 to Carlos Gentile, a photographer, who renamed the boy Carlos Montezuma and moved back east. As the years passed, young Montezuma impressed his non-Indian benefactors, including William Steadman, a Baptist minister in Urbana, Illinois, with his thirst for knowledge. In 1884, Montezuma earned a bachelor of science from the University of Illinois, and he later obtained his medical degree from the Chicago Medical College in 1889.

Between 1889 and 1896, Montezuma worked for the **Bureau of Indian Affairs (BIA)** as a government physician, first at Fort Stevenson Indian School in North Dakota, then at the Western Shoshone Agency in Nevada, then at the Colville Agency in Washington, and finally at Carlisle Indian School in Pennsylvania. His years working among Indians convinced him that better federal Indian policies needed to be implemented to help Indian peoples adjust politically, economically, and socially. He later became a leading advocate of the movement to abolish the BIA. In 1896, Montezuma joined a private practice in Chicago, Illinois, working with a prominent non-Indian physician and specializing in internal and stomach problems. The experience was successful and allowed him to become more involved in Indian reform movements.

As an Indian reformer, Montezuma worked with other educated Native Americans to establish the **Society of American Indians** in 1911, an organization run by Native Americans and dedicated to identifying significant issues of Indian peoples. He also began publishing a newsletter, the *Wassaja*, in 1916. In the *Wassaja*, Montezuma expressed many of his views, which included abolition of the BIA, U.S. citizenship rights for Native Americans, and improvement of conditions and opportunities on Indian **reservations**. He initially believed reservations needed to be eliminated because of their confining ways and the manner in which Indians were treated, but he later changed his views, believing that Indian reservations had become new and important havens for Indian residents and, in turn, recognized and guaranteed their rights and sovereignty. Montezuma

fought hard to protect the land and water rights of his tribe, the Yava-
pai, who lived on the Fort McDowell Reservation in Arizona. On 31
January 1923, Montezuma died and, per his request, was buried at
Fort McDowell.

MOONEY, JAMES (1861–1921). Although not Native American,
Mooney's works, especially *Myths of the Cherokee* (1900) and *The
Ghost Dance Religion and the Sioux Outbreak of 1890* (1896), stand
as influential studies of some of the most important movements in the
history of Indian people. Born in 1861 to Irish immigrant parents,
Mooney was obsessed with Indian culture. In 1885 he moved to
Washington, D.C., and earned a job with the Bureau of American
Ethnology, which he held for the rest of his life. During his career, he
studied Cherokee mythology, the Kiowa, and the Sioux. One of his
most famous studies is his discussion of the **Ghost Dance** ritual
found among various Indian tribes.

Despite the fame of his work among the Sioux, Mooney's main interest was the Cherokee. He spent years living with the Cherokee in
North Carolina and was able to gain their acceptance and trust. His
dedication to the Cherokee people allowed him to write much of his
work from firsthand accounts. Mooney died in 1921 at his home in
Washington, D.C. A member of the first generation of professional
anthropologists, he left behind a wealth of ethnographic and historical data.

MORNING STAR INSTITUTE. Founded in 1984, the Morning Star
Institute was a national Indian rights organization dedicated to Native
peoples' traditional and cultural advocacy, arts promotion, and research. Suzan Shown Harjo, the institute's executive director and
president, organized an international effort to issue declarations of
tribal cultural property and achieve a Treaty Respecting the Property
Rights of Native Peoples. In 1992, the organization was a sponsoring
entity for the lawsuit *Harjo et al v. Pro Football, Inc.* regarding the
trademarks and name of the Washington Redskins.

MOUND BUILDERS. The term *Mound Builder* was first used in the
18th century as a catchall phrase for the makers of prominent earthworks found scattered across the lands west of the Appalachian

Mountains but east of the Mississippi River. Settlers in the region found themselves surrounded by these structures, and debate raged over the identity of the builders. The debate intensified in time as more and more settlers moved into the region.

The earthen mounds often consist of intentional placements of earthworks, including some impressively large structures, hilltop structures with circumvallation, and elaborate geometric embankments. The sophistication of the construction added fuel to the debate: Were they built by the ancestors of Indians or some other ancient people? Most white travelers in the region, including many Indian missionaries, quickly concluded that the mounds were the work of a race of people unrelated to the Ohio River Valley's current Indian population. They confirmed their notions by using white stereotypes about Indian people: indifference to labor, lack of engineering skill, and inability to plan and coordinate the workforce necessary to construct the giant mounds. Many other theories began to circulate about the "mound builders." Many focused on various "lost peoples." Only two of the numerous theories had strong popular support. One stated that the Mound Builders were the descendants of the lost tribes of Israel; the other maintained that people from the south—associated with the Mexican culture groups—migrated north and built the mounds. Although "lost race" theories were the most popular, a small contingent adhered to a third view that the mounds were built by the ancestors of modern Indians.

Many famous early Americans took up the Mound Builder debate, including Thomas Jefferson, Albert Gallatin, George Rogers Clark, and Henry Schoolcraft. The Smithsonian Institution made the Mound Builder controversy its primary field of study during its early years. Professional archaeology in America was born when interested parties began excavating the mounds.

The mounds that dot the Ohio Valley must be seen in their historical context, something early theories failed to do. The "Mound Builders" actually belong to a series of distinct periods. The earliest mounds were built in Louisiana around 4000 BCE, when groups formed in the lower Mississippi Valley. Most of the mounds from these earliest settlements are burial mounds, and while they can be quite large, they are actually isolated. One early variant to these burial mounds are the effigy mounds in the shape of animals. These mounds are most common in the Great Lakes region and date from 500 to 1000.

Another mound function is noted at Poverty Point in Louisiana. At this site, massive works were built in an area where various groups from different areas came together. At its height, Poverty Point covered more than 100 acres and consisted of six concentric ring earthworks.

Geometric earthworks, found in large river bottoms, offer another avenue of exploration, because of their precise geometric layouts and meticulous engineering. With the development of corn-based agriculture around 1000, flat-topped pyramid mounds came to dominate the landscape, particularly in the southeast. These mounds served as platforms for chief's homes as well as those of the priestly class who controlled special shrines. The largest mound in eastern North America is Monk's Mound at the Cahokia site in Illinois. The mound is 100 feet high and covers 13 acres at its base.

After 1300, mound construction ended in the American southeast. By the 16th century, when European settlers entered the region, mounds were still in use, but there was little work being done to add to them or alter them in any way. Because the mounds were still in use by historical peoples, it seems safe to assume that the Mound Builders were indeed the ancestors of present-day Indian people.

MOURNING WARS. Prominent among the member nations of the **Iroquois Confederacy**, the mourning war was a ceremony to restore the loss of a family member. If a family member was killed, a number of ceremonies occurred to ease the pain of the remaining members. If the condolence ceremony proved insufficient, a "requickening" ceremony was performed. In this ceremony, the deceased person's family adopted someone to replace the lost loved one. If the deceased was of high status, a person from a lower rank within the same clan would fill the vacated position. If the deceased was of lower status, the family would seek a replacement from outside of the Iroquois Confederacy. The practice of looking beyond tribal borders led to the development of the mourning war. During these wars, Iroquois raiding parties waged war with the objective of taking **captives**. Sometimes captives were killed to allow the bereaved family to display its grief. More often, however, the captives were adopted into the clan and given the name and social rank of the deceased.

– N –

NATIONAL AMERICAN INDIAN COURT JUDGES ASSOCIATION (NAICJA).

In 1968, **Arrow, Inc.**—in partnership with the University of New Mexico—sponsored a Management Training Institute for Indian court judges. After the conference, the judges asked Arrow, Inc., to help establish a permanent body for improving tribal courts and providing judges with basic legal training. In 1969, Arrow, Inc., and the University of New Mexico cosponsored another workshop, and the product of these two meetings was the NAICJA, established in 1970.

The group is a nonprofit, Indian-controlled body designed to improve the American Indian court system. In recent years, the NAICJA has trained tribal judges in such areas as courtroom procedure; criminal, civil, and family law; and rules of evidence. The NAICJA and its advisors have developed all the teaching materials and texts used at the training sessions, making the association the leading contributor to the literature of the Indian judiciary. The association has also compiled the first collection of tribal codes, with more than 71 codes totaling 10,000 pages.

In 1978, the association established a reference library for tribal court clerks and assisted more than 10 tribes in establishing a modern court system and developed a Model Code of Judicial Ethics directed toward tribal judges. In recent years, the NAICJA has begun to concern itself with the relationship between state and local courts and tribal courts and governments and with improving tribal services to minors.

NATIONAL AMERICAN INDIAN MEMORIAL ASSOCIATION (NAIMA).

Founded in 1911 by Rodman Wanamaker, a wealthy businessman in Philadelphia, Pennsylvania, the NAIMA was established to preserve and honor the role Native Americans have played in American history. Wanamaker and other non-Indians had a romantic view of Native Americans and believed, like many people of the time, that Indians were "vanishing Americans" and that their contributions must be preserved. To honor the "noble race," the NAIMA wanted to build a bronze Indian statue on Staten Island in New York harbor larger than the Statue of Liberty. Congress gave permission for the land use, and an elaborate groundbreaking ceremony was held in 1913. President William Howard Taft, more than 30 Indian chiefs, and other dignitaries attended the event. The statue memorializing Native Americans was never completed because bronze was in short supply during World War I and because of a general lack of interest in the project at war's end.

Wanamaker and the NAIMA supported such other projects as the recruitment of Native American regiments to fight in World War I and the production of two films, one on Indian leaders in council and the other on **Hiawatha**. Regarding the former, the NAIMA suggested that U.S. citizenship be granted to those Indians who fought in the war. The NAIMA membership of wealthy non-Indians believed in assimilation policies and the evolution of mankind to a higher level of civilization. The demise of the NAIMA cannot be easily determined, but it most likely disappeared sometime after World War I.

NATIONAL CENTER FOR AMERICAN INDIAN ENTERPRISE DEVELOPMENT (NCAIED). The NCAIED, founded in 1969, is a nonprofit organization designed to facilitate the involvement of American Indians in business. Dedicated to the principles of business ownership and entrepreneurship, the center is the first organization by and for Indians dedicated to integrating American Indian people into the business world. The organization's goals are to expand the private sector that employs Indian people, increase the number of successful tribal and individual Indian businesses, and boost the economic productivity of Indian **reservations** by establishing partnerships between Indian nations and the surrounding business community.

NATIONAL CONGRESS OF AMERICAN INDIANS (NCAI). The NCAI was founded in Denver, Colorado, in 1944. **D'Arcy Mc-Nickle**, a Metis-Flathead, and Napoleon Johnson, a Cherokee, organized the event, and representatives of approximately 50 Indian tribes attended the meeting. Initially, only Indians could be members, but later non-Indians could become associate members. The NCAI lobbies in Washington, D. C., on behalf of American Indian tribes regarding major issues affecting them. The congress helped organize the **American Indian Chicago Conference** in 1961.

From its inception, the NCAI has stressed the importance of Indian cultures to non-Indians, supported the voting rights of Indians in New

Mexico and Arizona, fought against the federal policy of **termination** of Indian treaties, and advocated many Indian self-determination and sovereignty issues, including economic development projects and repatriation of Native American artifacts and remains. The NCAI remains a highly visible, respected national **Pan-Indian** organization.

NATIONAL COUNCIL OF AMERICAN INDIANS. The National Council of American Indians was organized in 1926, by **Gertrude Bonnin** in response to the Indian Citizenship Act of 1924. The council was established to aid in organizing Indians politically for the protection of their rights. Bonnin's diverse reform activities doomed the council to failure as important Indian leaders and tribal officials ignored the organization in preference for Bonnin's more well-known ventures, like the **Society of American Indians**. The council was unable to outlast its founder and closed its doors upon Bonnin's death in 1938.

NATIONAL INDIAN DEFENCE ASSOCIATION (NIDA). Founded in 1885 in Washington, D.C., by Dr. Thomas A. Bland, the NIDA was another example of organizations established by white Indian reformers to solve the "Indian problem" and improve Indian conditions on **reservations**. Bland, like many white reformers, supported land allotments on Indian reservations; however, he nearly stood alone in advocating that Indians, not the U.S. federal government, should decide if they wanted their communal holdings on reservations changed to individual land allotments. He thus formed the NIDA and further campaigned for a more cultural pluralism approach to Indian and white relations, one in which Indian cultures should not be totally considered pagan and instead be recognized for their positive contributions. Needless to say, Bland and the NIDA were in the minority of white Indian reform movements that demanded assimilation and rejection of Indian ways and land allotments on reservations regardless of Indian consent. Bland expressed many of his views in *The Council Fire*, also called *The Council Fire and Arbitrator*, a newsletter he edited after the death of his friend, Alfred Meacham, another Indian reformer.

NATIONAL INDIAN EDUCATION ASSOCIATION (NIEA). The NIEA is the oldest membership-based organization dedicated to increasing the educational opportunities and resources for Indian people while protecting Indian cultural and linguistic traditions. Founded in 1969, the NIEA is the largest Indian education organization in the nation and strives to keep moving Indian nations toward educational equality. A board of directors oversees operations and ensures that Indian people are represented at the various educational institutions and conferences across the nation. The association holds annual conferences, and among its publications is a newsletter entitled *Indian Education*.

NATIONAL INDIAN GAMING ASSOCIATION (NIGA). The NIGA is a nonprofit organization comprised of almost 200 Indian tribes and nonvoting associate members engaged in tribal gaming enterprises across the United States. Established in 1985, the NIGA's purpose was to advance the lives of Indian people economically, socially, and politically. To fulfill its purpose, the association sought to protect and preserve the general welfare of Indian tribes striving for sovereignty through a casino. Thus, the NIGA worked closely with members of Congress to develop sound policies and practices. The organization also operated as a "clearing house" for educational, legislative, and public policy resources for the nation's Indian tribes and the public on issues of tribal community development and Indian gaming. *See also* GAMING; NATIONAL INDIAN GAMING COMMISSION (NIGC).

NATIONAL INDIAN GAMING COMMISSION (NIGC). An independent federal agency, the NIGC was established in 1988 as part of the Indian Gaming Regulatory Act. The NIGC's primary responsibility is regulating gaming activities on Indian land. The purpose of the commission's oversight is to protect Indian nations from the influences of organized crime, ensure that tribes are the beneficiaries of gaming proceeds; and establish and monitor casino operations. *See also* GAMING; NATIONAL INDIAN GAMING ASSOCIATION (NIGA).

NATIONAL INDIAN YOUTH COUNCIL (NIYC). Established in Gallup, New Mexico, in August 1961, shortly after the **American Indian Chicago Conference** ended, the NIYC represented a more active, aggressive approach to seeking federal Indian policy reforms than the older, more conservative **National Congress of American Indians**. Mel Thom, a Paiute, **Clyde Warrior**, a Ponca, and Shirley Witt, a Mohawk, were elected to leadership positions in the new movement, and Albuquerque, New Mexico, was chosen as the national headquarters.

The NIYC held demonstrations for **fishing** and **hunting rights**, holding fish-ins and demanding recognition of Indians' hunting privileges. Other areas of council involvement concern environmental issues, Indian self-determination, civil and human rights issues, and the need for more Indian participation in federal and state elections. The NIYC has also become involved in supporting the needs of indigenous peoples throughout the world.

NATIONAL LEAGUE FOR JUSTICE TO AMERICAN INDIANS (NLJAI). The NLJAI was formed in 1933 by Marion Campbell of Los Angeles, California. The organization had one single purpose: the abolition of the **Bureau of Indian Affairs (BIA)**. The NLJAI argued that Indian affairs should be made the province of the states, the BIA budget should be allocated to the states, and tribal property be placed in separate trusts devoid of the political infighting they believed corrupted the BIA. The information detailing the NLJAI's rise and fall during World War II has vanished, and only scant references in the papers of the Indian Rights Association remind us of its existence.

NATIONAL SOCIETY OF INDIAN WOMEN. Founded in Spokane, Washington, in 1926, the National Society of Indian Women was another example of a fraternal **Pan-Indian** movement that was more regional or local in nature than its title suggested. Although not much is known about the organization, it was also called the Eagle Feathers Club and apparently had chapters that were sponsored by white women. The society held a romantic view of Indian culture and used, like similar organizations, Indian names for certain membership positions and events. *See also* WOMEN.

NATIONAL TRIBAL CHAIRMEN'S ASSOCIATION. Developed in the early 1970s as a reaction against the U.S. federal government's

termination policy, a group of tribal leaders established a tribal chairmen's association to serve as a liaison between Indian tribes and the **Bureau of Indian Affairs**. The National Tribal Chairmen's Association lobbied for self-determination and protection of Indian land holdings and operated as a **Pan-Indian** organization speaking with one voice to increase Indian political power. The association represents more than 100 tribes and remains active in national Indian affairs.

NATIVE AMERICAN CHURCH. Founded in 1918, the Native American Church has faced many attempts by federal, state, and local governments to ban the use of **peyote** in its ceremonies. Peyote existed in Mexico before the Spaniards arrived and spread northward to other tribes. Indians used peyote as a means to achieve harmony and self-worth. Generally, peyote rituals began on Saturday evening and continued into Sunday morning. A special tent was erected for the ceremony, and inside was a crescent-shaped peyote altar. Peyote eaters used fans, rattles, and drums and smoked cornhusk-rolled peyote cigarettes. The worshippers sang songs and prayed to God. During the morning hours, they held a feast. Peyote rituals vary, and one of the key differences is the degree of Christian elements incorporated in the rites.

Comanche leader **Quanah Parker** was a leading advocate of peyote in the late 19th century and helped spread its use to other tribes in **Indian Territory**. Many Indians used peyote as a way to deal with assaults on their cultural ways, **reservation** life, and assimilation policies. The **Bureau of Indian Affairs** vehemently opposed peyote and believed it had the same devastating effects as liquor, while Indian opponents of peyote use also saw it as a challenge to other traditional tribal religious ceremonies. However, the increasing numbers of peyote celebrants continued to practice the religion and developed the concept of the Peyote Road, which was an ethical code of conduct for practitioners based heavily on Christian teachings.

In 1918, the Native American Church was established to provide a major organization for peyote users and combat attacks against their religious and constitutional right to practice peyotism. As the 20th century continued, peyote use continued to grow, resulting in several court battles to outlaw its use. In *People v. Woody* (1964), the California Supreme Court declared that peyote was a religious sacrament not unlike the use of bread and wine in Christian ceremonies, and with the passage of the American Indian Religious Freedom Act in 1978, peyote use by worshippers has been further strengthened by First Amendment rights. *See also* RELIGION.

NATIVE AMERICAN RIGHTS FUND (NARF). Becoming its own entity in 1971, NARF was a project financed by a Ford Foundation grant given to the California Indian Legal Services in 1970 to create a national program that protected the legal rights of Native Americans. As a separate body, NARF set up headquarters in Boulder, Colorado, and established a branch office in Washington, D.C. These offices, plus a third opened in Anchorage, Alaska, in 1984, still function.

Native Americans needed an organization like NARF because of the numerous legal challenges they faced in post–World War II America. The fund provides consultation and legal assistance to tribes concerning such areas as treaties, court decisions, legislation, and special status issues. In 1972, NARF secured a Carnegie Foundation grant to establish the National Indian Law Library.

Currently, 13 Native Americans from several tribes serve on the NARF board of directors, which governs the body. Fifteen attorneys handle heavy case loads, and many of the cases take years to resolve. The fund concentrates on preserving tribal existence; protecting tribal natural resources; promoting Native American human rights; developing Indian **law**; educating the public about Indian rights, laws, and issues; and ensuring that all governments are accountable in enforcing proper laws regarding Native American affairs. Examples of legal assistance provided by NARF include aiding the Menominee in their efforts to reverse **termination**, defending Native American **fishing rights**, strengthening provisions of the 1978 American Religious Freedom Act, helping such Indian tribes as the Penobscot and Passamaquoddy win their land claims case, assisting nonfederally recognized tribes gain federal recognition, and helping Indian plaintiffs in the **Cobell case**. The fund operates on donations and federal and other funding and is recognized for its efforts to defend Indian rights.

NATIVE AMERICAN STUDIES. A rather tongue-in-cheek argument can made for Native American studies being the first academic discipline found in the New World. Mothers, fathers, clan leaders, elders, and chiefs taught classes in agriculture, zoology, botany, medicine, engineering, and psychology. This course of study was also the first experiment in bilingual education. Instructors were sure that their pupils would come into contact with their neighbors at some point; these neighbors would likely speak a foreign language since they always had. No degrees were issued, but Native American studies was taught well before the Europeans arrived in the New World. During the colonial era, nonnatives became interested in Native American studies, but their ancestors quickly dismissed the mode of study for one they found more "civilized."

More specifically, American Indian activists, as part of the **Red Power Movement**, revived interest in Native American studies as an academic discipline. Both Indian and non-Indian students pressured higher learning institutions to offer courses that focused on Indian peoples. Responding to these requests, colleges and universities created a specific discipline called Native American studies. These programs faced numerous obstacles, but none were more crucial than the focus of the program: Should the program foster American Indian identity and focus on Native American students or provide a more generalized education for all students? Secondly, almost across the board, Native American studies programs did not receive adequate funding or academic support from the administration or faculty.

Overcoming these obstacles, departments emerged at numerous prestigious colleges, including the universities of Arizona, California, Wisconsin, Minnesota, Montana, Oklahoma, North Dakota, South Dakota, and Washington. When these departments formed in the early 1970s, both Indian and non-Indian students showed a surprising amount of interest in them. By the 1980s, 107 colleges and universities offered courses in Native American studies, but only a few of these were offered through a Native American studies department. The discipline was frequently combined with some other department, most often **anthropology**. In these departments, Native American studies was seen as secondary to the faculty's more traditional offerings.

Native American studies, however, has always been an interdisciplinary discipline. For example, historians of Native America use methods from anthropology, literature, oral interviews, political science, and other disciplines in an effort to recreate a fuller picture of Indian life. The interdisciplinary approach has sparked many academic problems. First, older scholars argue that Native American studies remains a "corrupted" discipline and have derided the approach. Another problem is that of scholarly acceptance and publication. Because traditional history, anthropology, and sociology journals have shunned the interdisciplinary approach, scholars of Native American studies were forced to create their own publishing outlets. As a result, such academic journals as *American Indian Quarterly*, *American Indian Culture and Research Journal*, and *Ethnohistory* were formed to reach a new audience and present the findings of these pioneering scholars. So important has the research of Native American studies scholars become that older journals, like *Western Historical Quarterly*, have begun to accept interdisciplinary offerings.

Native American studies, as an academic discipline, remains the most widely accepted at the nation's tribally operated colleges. Today, there are more than 40 of these institutions, and all offer courses in Native American studies. At these colleges, there is no question about the role of the courses or the program. Rather, all encourage Indian students to pursue higher education while maintaining their Indian identity. Perhaps the "tongue-in-cheek" argument referred to earlier holds an element of truth.

NAVAJO CODE TALKERS. Native Americans have served in every major U.S. war. During World War II, the U.S. marine corps created a special unit known as the Navajo Code Talkers to send and receive messages that the Japanese could not decipher.

Philip Johnston, a non-Indian World War I veteran and son of a missionary who grew up among the Navajo, proposed the idea of using the Navajo language as code in February 1942. He reminded the marine corps that the Choctaw language was sparingly used to send messages during World War I and that the Germans failed to break the code. Marine corps officials agreed to hold a demonstration at the Los Angeles Coliseum in California, and the Navajos brilliantly performed the tasks of translating military terms into Navajo words and transmitting them effectively. The corps accepted the proposal, and in

May 1942, thirty Navajos, who could speak both their native language and English, began their training in San Diego, California, as the original Code Talkers (one did not complete the program). Approximately 400 men became members of the Code Talkers, which included a future tribal chairman, **Peter MacDonald**, who did not engage in combat.

Adjusting to some of the military rules was not easy, but the Navajos adapted and performed extremely well on the rifle range. More importantly, they played a major role in designing the initial Navajo code of 211 words, later expanded to more than 400, that even other Navajos had a difficult time deciphering. A bomber plane was called a buzzard, a submarine was termed a whale, Britain became known as between the waters, and Germany was referred to as iron hat. They also used Navajo words for each of the 26 letters of the alphabet: The Navajo word for ant usually stood for the letter A, but alternate Navajo words for apple and axe could also be substituted for the letter. The Japanese never broke the Navajo code.

By April 1943, approximately 200 Navajos had become Code Talkers. In major battles in the Pacific, including Guadalcanal, Okinawa, and Iwo Jima, they performed courageously and made few errors in their transmissions. During the landing at Iwo Jima, for example, the Code Talkers sent 800 errorless messages in 48 hours.

Because of the necessity to keep the Navajo Code Talkers unit classified, little was known about their accomplishments until 1968, except by the Navajo people who knew and honored their achievements. Long overdue recognition finally came in July 2001, when the original 29 Code Talkers, of whom only five were still alive, received Congressional Gold Medals of Honor in the nation's capital. In November 2001, Congressional Silver Medals of Honor were awarded to the other Navajo Code Talkers at Window Rock in Arizona. Several books, documentaries, and a major Hollywood film, *Windtalkers* (2002), are among the other accolades honoring their service to America.

The Navajo Code Talkers distinguished themselves as patriotic Americans, as did many other Indians fighting in the nation's wars. They believed that their participation would contribute to Native American reform movements that would improve their political, economic, and social conditions.

NEOLIN. Neolin, a Delaware, was the foremost of a number of prophets of the 18th century who attributed the decline of Indian societies to the corrupting influence of white Europeans. He preached a message of returning to Indian traditions, beliefs, and practices. Neolin's influence was important to the general Indian uprising of 1763, known as "Pontiac's War."

During Neolin's time, his Delaware society was forced to continually adjust to white encroachment. The Delawares routinely gave ground, first surrendering areas of eastern Pennsylvania to the Susquehanna Valley, then retreating farther west to the Allegheny and Muskingum valleys of Pennsylvania and Ohio. In their retreat, European diseases ravaged them, and their relationships with Christian missionaries, specifically Moravians, undermined Delaware theology.

In the mid-18th century, numerous Indian prophets preached a nativist message identifying whites as the source of Indian misfortune. Divine favor, these prophets assured their followers, could only be restored by rejecting European influences. Around 1760, Neolin claimed that a vision showed him the consequences of continual Indian degradation. By 1762, he was preaching from a base on the Cuyahoga River calling upon Indians to end their association with whites. According to Neolin's teachings, whites placed numerous obstacles on the route to heaven. Indians, he proclaimed, neglected their old traditions, abandoned the customs that made them distinct, drank **alcohol**, wore European clothes, used European tools, and most damning, permitted the British to live in their territory.

Neolin received widespread acclaim for spreading his message among the various tribes of the Great Lakes region. He provided elaborate diagrams for his message, which reached as far west as the Illinois River, where Potawatomies, Ojibwas, Wyandots, and Ottawas—especially those under the leadership of **Pontiac**—readily adopted his antiwhite sentiments. Pontiac used Neolin's message as part of his plan to attack the British, who were in command of Fort Detroit, in 1763. After Pontiac's War, Neolin lost many followers.

In 1764, Neolin lived among the Shawnee at their Muskingum River village, Wakatomica. Two years later, he was back among the Delawares living in the village of the powerful chief, Newcomer. Among the Delawares were two Presbyterian missionaries whose reports detail long conversations with Neolin about religion. There are no references to Neolin after 1766; however, in 1770, sickness in Newcomer's village led a prophet to predict annihilation if Indians did not stop the progress of the Moravian missionaries and subsist on a diet of corn and water. Neolin may have disappeared into the mists of history, but he was the most noted prophet of the nativist sentiments who periodically influenced Indian history during the Colonial Era and afterward. *See also* RELIGION.

– O –

OAKES, RICHARD (1942–1972). Oakes, a member of the Mohawk Nation, is best known for his leadership during the occupation of **Alcatraz** Island off the coast of San Francisco, California, from 1969 to 1971. Born in New York, he attended school until he was 16 years old, when he dropped out. Oakes bounced around New York and finally decided to travel west to California. On his journey west, he traveled to numerous Indian **reservations** and became increasingly aware of the political and economic situation prevalent in Indian Country.

Oakes worked odd-jobs in San Francisco until he enrolled at San Francisco State University in February 1969, the result of a government economic opportunity program. During this time, he met Annie Marufo, a Kashia Pomo Indian from northern California.

Oakes was at the helm in November 1969, when Indian activists from nearby San Francisco took over Alcatraz Island and named themselves "**Indians of All Tribes**." The occupation was an attempt to raise awareness of the plight of American Indian people in the United States. The media and many of the occupiers recognized Oakes as the leader of their movement, even though he never claimed the position for himself. He left Alcatraz when his stepdaughter fell down a stairwell at the vacant prison and suffered a head injury.

After leaving Alcatraz, Oakes remained active in Indian movements and was important to the Pomo and Pit River Indian attempts to regain their ancestral lands in northern California. He was the leader of numerous occupations of federal lands in northern California, occupations that led to the return of many acres to the Pomo and Pit River Indians.

Oakes was shot and killed on 21 September 1972. His murder produced an increased sense of urgency among the Indian activists then organizing the **Trail of Broken Treaties** march, which was being planned on the Rosebud Reservation in South Dakota and was designed to reach Washington, D.C., in time for the 1972 presidential election.

OGLALA SIOUX CIVIL RIGHTS ORGANIZATION (OSCRO). Established by mainly traditional Oglala Lakota on the Pine Ridge Indian Reservation in South Dakota in 1973, the OSCRO demanded the removal of Tribal Chairman Richard Wilson. The organization accused his administration of corruption and graft, nepotism, violent actions against those who opposed him, and failure to improve deplorable **reservation** conditions. The OSCRO invited the **American Indian Movement** to meet with them on the reservation to plan an action that later resulted in the occupation of Wounded Knee, known as **Wounded Knee II**.

ORENDA. Among the Iroquois, orenda is the source of supernatural power. Orenda is a great invisible force that flows through the universe and can be tapped by individuals during their dreams. It is similar to the Algonquin **manitou** and the Siouan **wakonda**. *See also* RELIGION.

– P –

PAN-INDIANISM. Native American movements in which individual tribes came together in an effort to combat political, economic, and social threats to their tribal sovereignty and existence are referred to as Pan-Indianism. Creating a unified Indian identity that addressed common issues affecting all Indians instead of focusing on purely tribal interests, Pan-Indian movements included those led by **Pontiac** in 1763, **Tecumseh** in the early 1800s, and **Wovoka** in the late 1880s. Such 20th-century organizations as the **Society of American Indians** and the **National Congress of American Indians** are examples of major bodies that embraced Pan-Indianism.

PARKER, ARTHUR CASWELL (1881–1955). Born on 5 April 1881, on the Cattaraugus Reservation in New York to a Seneca father and white mother, Arthur Parker was a member of an influential Seneca family that included **Ely Parker**, a brigadier general and military staff aide to General Ulysses S. Grant during the Civil War and the first Indian to serve as commissioner of Indian affairs. Parker's grandfather, Nicholas Parker, a Seneca leader and Ely's brother, served as a major role model for his grandson.

Arthur Parker first attended school on the **reservation** and later went to public school in White Plains, New York. After graduating from high school in 1897, he later enrolled at Dickinson Seminary in Williamsport, Pennsylvania, in 1900 but did not graduate. He returned to New York and briefly worked as a reporter before deciding to become an anthropologist. He had developed an interest in **anthropology** in the late 1890s and spent a great deal of time at the American Museum of Natural History in New York City, where he established a close friendship with Frederick W. Putnam, a noted anthropologist who introduced him to such important figures in the field as Frank Speck and Franz Boaz.

In 1904, Parker secured a position at the New York State Library, where he researched and collected materials on Iroquois culture. In 1906, he became an archaeologist at the New York State Museum, a position he held until 1925, when he accepted appointment as director of the Rochester Museum of Arts and Sciences in New York. Although Parker lacked formal academic credentials, his research and publications were impressive. By the time he retired from his directorship at the Rochester Museum in 1946, he had written hundreds of articles, several significant books on the Iroquois, and even a few children's books. His collections of items on the Iroquois both at the New York State Museum and the Rochester Museum are also noteworthy. Parker received honorary degrees for his many contributions to the field, including a master of science from the University of Rochester in 1922, a doctorate in science from Union College in 1940, and a doctorate of humane laws from Keuka College in 1945.

Aside from his contributions in the field of anthropology, Parker was a major figure in Indian reform movements. He was among the educated Native Americans who founded the **Society of American Indians (SAI)** in 1911 and later served as editor of its quarterly journal, SAI secretary, and SAI president. He favored Indian participation in World War I as a way of convincing non-Indians to accept Indians into mainstream America. After the demise of the SAI in the 1920s, Parker supported Indian New Deal programs in the 1930s to help Indians secure employment, and in 1944, he helped found the **National Congress of American Indians**. He died on 1 January 1955.

PARKER, ELY SAMUEL (1828–1895). Born in 1828 on the Tonawanda Indian Reservation in New York into a prominent Seneca family and related to such important Iroquois figures as Red Jacket, **Handsome Lake**, and **Arthur Parker**, Ely Parker was educated at a nearby Baptist missionary school and two private academies, Yates Academy and Cayuga Academy, both in New York. He hoped to become a lawyer but was denied entry to the New York bar because he was not a citizen. Instead, he worked as a state engineer in New York in 1849 and later as a civil engineer for the U.S. federal government. He became well-known for his engineering skills and worked on canal and other projects in New York, Virginia, North Carolina, Michigan, Iowa, and Illinois. It was in Galena, Illinois, that Parker met Ulysses S. Grant in the late 1850s, and he would later serve on Grant's personal military staff during the Civil War and as a federal employee during Grant's presidency.

Like his relatives, Parker assumed leadership roles in his tribe. He became one of the 50 principal sachems of the **Iroquois Confederacy** in 1851 and represented the Tonawanda Seneca in **reservation** land disputes in both New York and in Washington, D.C. In 1857, he assisted in negotiating a treaty that kept most of the Tonawanda Reservation in tact. During these years, he met with President James K. Polk, President Franklin Pierce, and President James Buchanan. Parker also supplied valuable information on the Iroquois for works published by Henry Rowe Schoolcraft and Lewis Henry Morgan.

When the Civil War broke out, Parker attempted to join the Army Corps of Engineers but was denied because of racial issues. However, in 1863, he became a captain of engineers in one of General Grant's divisions and later joined the general's personal military staff, serving as a valuable aide to Grant. He rose through the ranks and was brevetted as a brigadier general. In 1865, Parker wrote the final copy of the surrender terms at the Appomattox Court House meeting between General Grant and General Robert E. Lee that ended the Civil War.

In 1869, Parker became the commissioner of Indian affairs under President Grant. As the first Indian to ever hold the position as head of the **Bureau of Indian Affairs (BIA)**, Parker worked zealously to implement Grant's policies of assimilation and expose fraud and corruption in BIA operations. Ironically, he was accused of corruption but later cleared of all charges. As a result, an angry Parker resigned in 1871.

After his resignation, Parker had several unsuccessful investments. In 1876, he found employment in the Buildings and Supplies Division of the New York City Police Department, a position he held for 19 years. Proud of his military service, he was active in veterans' organizations. He also presented lectures on the Iroquois at public forums. Parker died on 30 August 1895 in Fairfield, Connecticut.

PARKER, QUANAH (c. 1853–1911). Born in the 1850s, Quanah Parker was the son of Cynthia Ann Parker, a white captive, and Peta Nocona, a Comanche warrior. Little is known about his early years, but by the mid-1870s, Parker was recognized by his people as a leader for his fighting and hunting skills. His band, the Quahadas, agreed to accept **reservation** life in Indian Territory in 1875, and the United States would later recognize him as the primary chief of the Comanche Indians.

Parker supported assimilation policies, although he really advocated an acculturated approach that adopted selective white ways while retaining certain Indian traditions. He refused to cut his hair and continued to practice polygamy. Parker was also was an advocate of **peyote** use among Indians. Nevertheless, government officials continued to work with him and recognized his accommodation abilities. Parker accepted the leasing of reservation land to Texas cattlemen, which brought income to his people. A skilled negotiator, he delayed the application of land allotments on his reservation for several years and fought to get the best lands and deals for his people.

Parker was wined and dined by influential whites, and he lived well, with an impressive home on the reservation, with large cattle and horse herds, and receiving such lavish gifts as a diamond brooch and an ivory-handled pistol. Although he fell on hard financial times in later years, Parker still had powerful white friends, including President Theodore Roosevelt, whose 1905 presidential inauguration parade he rode in. A clever political and religious leader, Parker died on 23 February 1911.

PELTIER, LEONARD (1944–). Born on 12 September 1944, in Grand Forks, North Dakota, Peltier, an Ojibwa-Sioux, joined the **American Indian Movement (AIM)** in the 1960s and participated in a number of demonstrations, including the **Trail of Broken Treaties** march on Washington, D.C., in November 1972. More than 500 protesters demanded recognition of Indian rights and a redress of grievances, and they later occupied the **Bureau of Indian Affairs** building for several days. In the end, federal officials agreed to study the Indians' demands and provided funds to allow the protesters to return home.

Indian activism during the 1960s and 1970s caused the Richard M. Nixon administration to direct the Federal Bureau of Investigation (FBI) and its Counterintelligence Program (COINTELPRO) to increase surveillance of such activities, especially those of AIM on the Pine Ridge Indian Reservation in South Dakota, where Peltier resided. This federal involvement heightened tensions and sometimes resulted in physical confrontations and questionable activities by COINTELPRO, for example, Indian activists' claims that COINTELPRO created false charges and fabricated evidence against them.

Conditions at Pine Ridge were explosive due to the presence of federal agents, AIM, and the tribal government, which AIM and other Indians declared was extremely corrupt. On 26 June 1975, two FBI agents were shot, and after a massive manhunt for the murderers, the FBI finally indicted four Indians for the crime, including Peltier, who was the only one of the four found guilty of aiding and abetting in the deaths of the FBI agents. In June 1977, he received two consecutive life sentences.

Several international and national organizations and leaders proclaim that the United States committed a gross injustice in finding Peltier guilty. They and others claim that Peltier was convicted on circumstantial evidence and that the FBI manufactured and suppressed evidence. Peltier has been denied a new trial or parole on several occasions. He remains incarcerated and represents to his supporters a symbol of injustice and racial discrimination toward minority people by a powerful central government.

PETERSON, HELEN (1915–2000). Born on 2 August 1915, on the Pine Ridge Indian Reservation in South Dakota, Peterson, a Cheyenne and enrolled Oglala Sioux, lived in poverty as a child but graduated from high school in Hay Springs, Nebraska, in 1932. She attended Chadron State College in Nebraska, hoping to become a teacher. Peterson moved to Colorado in 1937 and later worked at Colorado State College, where she became interested in minority group issues.

In 1942, Peterson became executive director of the Rocky Mountain Council of Inter-American Affairs at the University of Denver, and in 1948, she accepted a position with the Chicano Rights Movement of the Commission on Community Relations to promote racial equality in Denver. The following year, she attended the Second Inter-American Indian Conference in Peru and proposed a resolution on Indian **education** that was adopted. Peterson began to focus more on issues affecting Native Americans, and in 1953 she became executive director of the **National Congress of American Indians (NCAI)**, a position she held until 1962.

Under her direction, the NCAI increased its involvement in international conferences and in Native American issues and reform movements. Peterson spoke out against the 1950s federal policy of **termination** that threatened the special status that Indians held and sponsored publications concerning Indian-related topics. In 1961, Peterson was among those in attendance at the **American Indian Chicago Conference**, where she played a major role in identifying issues important to Native Americans that resulted in the "Declaration of Indian Purpose" proposal, which was submitted to the John F. Kennedy administration.

After leaving the NCAI executive directorship, Peterson remained active. She became director of the Denver Commission on Community Relations, and in 1978, she moved to Portland, Oregon, and began working with Native Americans in the state. She served on many advisory boards, committees, and organizations, including the American Indian Civil Liberties Trust, National Association for the Advancement of Colored People, Latin American Education Foundation, Japanese American Citizens League, and Girl Scouts of America.

Peterson worked tirelessly throughout her career to protect Indian rights and improve Indian conditions. She died on 10 July 2000. *See also* WOMEN.

PEYOTE. Native Americans in Mexico used *Lophophora williamsii*, or peyote, for many centuries before the coming of Europeans to the region. A small, often carrotlike cactus, peyote spread northward and was adopted by several tribes in the United States, including the Lipan Apaches, Mescalero Apaches, Kiowas, and Comanches. Indians cut the top of the peyote cactus and ate these "peyote buttons" in ceremonies. The eaters believed that peyote provided them with medical and spiritual enhancements. Nonbelievers advocated banning peyote, and use became more controversial with the creation of the **Native American Church** in 1918 and its belief in peyotism. *See also* RELIGION.

POCAHONTAS (c. 1596–1617). A favorite daughter of Powhatan, who headed the powerful **Powhatan Confederacy**, Pocahontas is closely associated with the first permanent English settlement in America at Jamestown, located in present-day Virginia and founded in 1607. Both the English and the Powhatans thought highly of Pocahontas, admiring her wisdom, personality, and abilities as a peacemaker.

Pocahontas became fascinated with the Jamestown colonists after their arrival in the New World. She supplied them with food when they were starving and tried to maintain peaceful relations between her people and the English settlers. The well-known story of her saving the life of Captain John Smith has been romanticized but probably did happen, as it was a Powhatan ritual, which apparently Smith did not comprehend. During the ritual, a **captive** is threatened with death but later saved, symbolizing the adoption of Smith into the tribe and control over him by Chief Powhatan.

Because of the influx of English settlers to the region and the conflicts that occurred, war broke out in 1610. During the war, Pocahontas was captured in 1613 and forced to live at Jamestown, where she was treated well. During her captivity, she became an Anglican, was baptized, and agreed to marry John Rolfe and live in Jamestown. The marriage represented a diplomatic union that helped terminate the warfare between the two sides. The couple had a son in 1615.

While visiting England with her husband and son, Pocahontas died on 2 March 1617. Her immune system failed to protect her from foreign diseases. After her passing, relations worsened between the English and the Powhatan Confederacy, and the confederacy was decimated by the mid-17th century.

The role Pocahontas played as a peacekeeper is often overlooked. She was among the first Native Americans to promote cordial relations between Indian and non-Indian peoples. *See also* WOMEN.

PONTIAC (c. 1720–1769). Pontiac was an Ottawa war leader involved in the growing anti-British sentiment prevalent in the American interior after the French and Indian War. While speaking out against the new British policies of limited gift exchange, Pontiac came under the influence of **Neolin**, the Delaware prophet who preached a nativist message of Indian renewal. Pontiac adopted Neolin's message but adapted it to fit his unique circumstance. Pontiac stripped the prophet's message of its renunciation of European technology and turned it into a renunciation of all things British.

By 1763, Pontiac was the most powerful Indian in Detroit. That spring he attempted to take the fort in a surprise attack but was unsuccessful, the result of his plan being somehow discovered. The British regiment was prepared for battle when Pontiac and his council party entered the fort. When the attempt to take the fort failed, Pontiac turned to more conventional means and led both the French and Indians in a siege of Detroit. Pontiac expected his actions to reinvigorate the French king and that French troops would soon arrive to increase the number at the siege lines.

The siege of Fort Detroit became the centerpiece in a larger movement that Europeans mistakenly refer to as "Pontiac's Rebellion." The attack on Detroit was only one aspect of a loosely organized series of attacks that swept across the Great Lakes region and through the Ohio River Valley. British forces eventually broke the siege at Detroit and eliminated resistance along the Ohio Valley frontier. However, the combined Indian forces had successfully pushed British settlers east across the Appalachian Mountains as far as

Carlisle, Pennsylvania. His siege broken, Pontiac left the Detroit area to avoid capture. He retained a following among the Ottawas along the Maumee River but chose to move west to Illinois. In the Illinois Country, he became more than a storied war chief; he rose to prominence among the towns of the Wabash and Illinois River valleys and continued to denounce the British.

Pontiac's influence continued to grow, even as the Indian confederacy his name was associated with fell apart. In 1764, the Shawnees made peace with the British. Pontiac used this opportunity to increase his standing and began to seriously consider British peace offerings, an effort to distance himself from leaders that were more militant. However, Pontiac made a fatal mistake when he began to see himself as the leader of an Indian confederacy that dominated the British interior. From a simple Ottawa war chief seeking to restore French authority, Pontiac transformed himself into the leader of a vast Indian empire.

By 1766, Pontiac was consumed with his own position. Returning to Detroit, he stabbed a rival and lost almost all support among the Ottawas, both those at Detroit and those along the Maumee River. By 1768, after sustaining a beating at the hands of young Ottawa warriors, he—the most famous Indian east of the Mississippi River—was a man without a home. He was forced into exile and returned to the Illinois Country, where his actions only secured him more enemies. On 20 April 1769, the nephew of Peoria chief, Makatchinga, killed Pontiac on the outskirts of the French settlement of Cahokia.

In the end, Pontiac pursued power that was never possible in Indian cultures. It was only after the misnamed "Pontiac's Rebellion" that he attempted to construct the Indian empire of the Woodlands that Europeans credited him with having already established. Historians and playwrights alike have looked back on Pontiac and constructed a noble savage who symbolized the ideals of a vanishing race. However, Pontiac and the rebellion that bore his name are much more; they show the contests for control that raged in colonial America in the years before the American Revolution.

POPE (PO'PAY) [c. 1630–?]. Pope was a Pueblo religious and political leader born around 1630 in a village that today is San Juan Pueblo in New Mexico. Pope's upbringing was unremarkable, and there is no reason to assume that he did not grow up following the strict rules of Pueblo childhood. As a child, he would have been engrained in the vigorous religious practices of his people.

As he grew up, Pope became an assistant to the tribal war captain, helping plan the dances and ceremonies his clan was responsible for. After serving in this position, Pope was named tribal war captain by the village leaders, a post that carried with it great responsibility and prestige. In this new position, Pope learned for the first time the pressures the Spanish were putting on the Tewa and other Pueblo people. As he grew to adulthood, the Spanish established themselves in Santa Fe, setting up a colonial government and beginning numerous missions to the Indians. The Spaniards told the Pueblos to stop performing their traditional dances and practicing their ancient customs because they amounted to "idolatry" at best and "worship of the devil" at worst.

During the initial phases of colonization, the Pueblos passively resisted these attempts to eradicate their culture. But Spanish pressure continued, and in the arid country of the Rio Arriba, the situation worsened. Conditions for family farming were never favorable in the region. The Spaniards demanded that the Pueblos give a portion of their crops to their colonizers, a practice the Spanish referred to as *encomienda*. The Pueblo people were further required to "donate" their labor to the Spanish hacendados through a system known as *repartimiento*. These colonial policies were designed to aid the Spanish settlers in "civilizing" the new country. Spanish priests also continued to harass the Pueblo people, often violating the sanctity of their **kivas** in the name of their Catholic faith.

The failure of the Pueblos to adopt Christianity led to an incident that forever altered their relationship with the Spaniards. In 1675, 47 Pueblo leaders were charged with sorcery and brought to Santa Fe to stand trial. To the Pueblos, the reason for the arrest was that the individuals refused to submit to Christianity. The trial was quick, and the sentence was handed down even faster. Four of the offenders were condemned to hang, and the others were ordered whipped; Pope was one of those whipped.

In this increasingly volatile atmosphere, Pope returned to his village and began considering uniting the Pueblos against the Spanish colonizers. He started calling meetings, and over time the meetings grew and included an ever-increasing number of disgruntled Pueblos. Pope organized the Pueblos into an anti-Spanish confederation. During a 1680 meeting at Tesuque Pueblo, it was decided that messengers would be sent to all Pueblo villages to facilitate planning a decisive assault against the colonizers. The event would take place at a date and time of Pope's choosing. The desired outcome was the expulsion of the Spanish from Pueblo lands.

Like many movements, this one was almost thwarted by pro-Spanish Pueblos, who on three separate occasions informed their padres of the plan. Colonial governor Antonio de Otermin learned of the plan and captured the messengers and ordered them hanged for treason. The governor's action caused the Pueblos to raise a general alarm, fearing they too would be killed. On 10 August 1680, in a pre-emptive strike, the Pueblos killed a Spaniard in one of their villages. The next morning, when the priest arrived to say Mass, Fray Juan Baptisto Pio was killed.

A general revolt was now underway throughout Pueblo country. Surviving Spaniards were forced to seek shelter in Santa Fe. As the colonial capital became a refugee camp, Pueblo warriors closed in and placed the city under siege on 15 August. The warriors later blocked the only water supply to the city and waited out the Spaniards. For two days, the Spanish suffered inside the city; people and animals succumbed to the lack of water. Left with no choice, the Spanish fought their way out of the city on 21 August.

The Spanish had been driven out of New Mexico. For Pope and the other "rebels," life returned to normal. In the years following the Pueblo Revolt, Pope lost his position to Luis Tupatu of Picuris Pueblo. There is no information on when or where Pope died.

POTLATCH. Pacific Northwest Indians held potlatches, or major gift-giving ceremonies, which often related to the political, social, and economic powers of the hosts of the events. Although the giving of gifts has always been a major practice among Indian peoples, such Indian tribes as the Haidas, Makahs, and Tlingits used potlatches as a way to redistribute wealth among tribal members and to counter rivals, who had to hold a larger potlatch to demonstrate their wealth and power. Although Canada and the United States outlawed potlatches, both countries later passed legislation that allowed Indians to hold the event. Among the gifts given at potlatches over the centuries were furs, pelts, weapons, slaves, blankets, ornaments, cash, and appliances.

POWHATAN CONFEDERACY. The term *Powhatan* was applied to the numerous 17th century Indian towns along the James River in Virginia. The Indian leader of these towns was also known as "Powhatan," as were the 30 chiefdoms he ruled, and the same name applied to the Algonquian-related language spoken by the Indians.

Powhatan, the man, established control over the other Virginia tribes by conquest and threats of violence. He ruled the resulting organization with an iron fist; confederacy is very much a misnomer in this regard. However, Powhatan was a paramount chief, not a king. He held absolute power over his subjects in many circumstances, but priests and councils of warriors acted as advisory groups. Powhatan lacked the authority to make laws that interfered with the private life of his subjects. As villages moved farther from the "capital" on the York River, Powhatan's control weakened.

Chiefs among the Powhatans occupied special positions for ceremonial occasions in their towns. Their duties were to receive guests and host the many feasts, all of which was accomplished while the chiefs remained surrounded by their many wives, councilors, and bodyguards. It was primarily on these occasions when the English settlers saw the interworkings of the "confederacy." Supported by tribute of corn, skins, and decorative ornaments, chiefs remained working people. There was no occupational specialization among the Powhatan Indians. All men hunted, fished, and made war, while **women** farmed, gathered food, cooked, cleaned, and made household items. Chiefs were guardians of tribal lands, which any tribal member could claim for farming.

English settlement, expanding from the 1607 colony at Jamestown, sparked three wars with the Powhatan Indians from 1610 to 1614, 1622 to 1632, and 1644 to 1646. The last war resulted in a treaty, but Indian people had been driven from much of the territory by 1670. Following Bacon's Rebellion in 1675 through 1676, the English settlers made another treaty with the Indians. The 1676 treaty established civil rights for Virginia's Indians. The treaty remains the basis for the Pamunkey and Mattaponi **reservations** today.

Powhatan culture changed dramatically as English colonization became permanent. The paramount chieftaincy evaporated after 1649; hereditary chiefs were relics by 1710. Tribal communities continued to lose members, and language use nearly disappeared. By the early 1700s, many young Powhatan Indians were monolingual in English. By the 18th century, the tribal priesthood and the vestiges of traditional **religion** were also gone.

Only community politics continued to hold the people who realized they were Indians together. Demonstrating the amalgamation of the Powhatan Indians, there were no 19th-century attempts to remove them across the Mississippi River. Rather, efforts were made to make Indians disappear by referring to them as "people of color" and grouping them with African-Americans for legislative purposes. Since 1980, the Powhatan tribe has been instrumental in the creation of the Virginia Council on Indians and the United Indians of Virginia, both designed to aid in community development and **education** for a now-recognized Indian population in the Old Dominion.

POWWOW. The term *powwow* has come to mean a secular gathering featuring singing and dancing by Indian and non-Indian people of all ages. The modern powwow has it roots in the dances, ceremonies, and social gatherings of the Prairie and Plains tribes and has developed into a larger expression of Indian identity and pride. Most powwows are no longer tribally exclusive, as members of other Indian tribes and even non-Indians frequently take part in the festivities. All powwows, except the large urban events, are sponsored by members of a particular community and have the explicit identification of that group.

Powwows range in size from smaller local events to three-day weekend affairs to huge urban gatherings lasting an entire week. The large, urban powwows are commercial events that do not focus as much on the community but rather on a generalized understanding of "Indian" identity often for a paying, non-Indian audience. Powwows of this nature include the Red Earth in Oklahoma City and the Gathering of Nations in Albuquerque.

Powwows vary from region to region, but most follow the general form of the Oklahoma-style gathering. Many different dances are performed, including the round dance, where the dancers hold hands and side-step left; the two-step, where a couple holds hands and follows the lead dancers through various figures; the gourd dance, whose name comes from the rattle carried by the dancers; and such solo presentations as the hoop, eagle, or spear-and-shield dances. The war dance, with origins in the warrior society rituals of the Prairie tribes, is the longest dance and takes up the most time during a powwow.

Women's dances were traditionally supportive, offering a rhythmic counterpart to the flashy men's styles. However, in the late 1960s, women began participating and winning competitions in which they competed against men in the fancy dance styles. While female fancy dancing has declined, two forms, the shawl and jingle dress, have gained popularity.

The major participants of any powwow are the head singers, head dancers, and the master of ceremonies or MC. The head singer is responsible for a variety of songs, including any special requests by the sponsoring group. The head dancers, both male and female, lead the dancing and all others follow. The MC keeps the affair operating smoothly. Interactions among dancers and spectators are often very important.

PRAYER STICK. Prayers to bring rains or good health to the Pueblos are often accompanied by offerings of decorated sticks referred to as prayer sticks. The sticks are carved or decorated according to which spirits they will be offered to. After the prayers have been "placed" on the stick, it is deposited in shrines so that the spirit may see and honor the prayer. *See also* RELIGION.

PRAYING INDIANS. During the 17th century, Puritan missionary John Eliot established "praying towns" in Massachusetts for Indians converting to Christianity. In 1651, Natick, Massachusetts, was the first of approximately 14 such settlements founded. With the valuable assistance of Christianized Indians, Eliot translated the Bible into the Algonquian language. The Puritans demanded that praying Indians in the towns give up their traditional ways and live like the English settlers. More than 1,000 Indian converts lived in the praying towns, and the praying Indians were to serve as models in the towns for unconverted Indians to emulate.

The New England Indians who converted to Christianity did so for various reasons, including the hope that the new **religion** would lessen the devastating effects of **alcohol**, disease, and other upheavals in their lives. A number of converted Indians blended Christianity with their traditional religious beliefs as a survival strategy. During **King Philip's War** in 1675, the Wampanoag and other Indians attacked English settlements and the praying towns. Moreover, the English suspected, arrested, and killed many praying Indians, and only about four praying towns remained by the 1680s.

PUEBLO REVOLT. *See* POPE (PO'PAY).

– R –

RED POWER MOVEMENT. By the 1960s, such federal Indian policies as **termination** and relocation had caused Native Americans to stage major demonstrations across the United States in an effort to force the U.S. federal government to recognize and address Indian civil rights issues and violation of treaty rights. The Red Power Movement was part of other protest movements in the United States by minority groups, students, **women**, and opponents of the Vietnam War. The **American Indian Chicago Conference** in 1961 is considered to be the beginning of the Red Power Movement, and organizations like the **National Indian Youth Council**, established in 1961, became more militant in demanding Indian rights. Red Power demonstrations included fish-ins, the occupation of **Alcatraz** Island, the **Trail of Broken Treaties**, the Bureau of Indian Affairs takeover, and **Wounded Knee II**.

From the last decades of the 20th century and into the 21st century, Red Power advocates have focused on political, economic, and social self-determination issues. They demand more control over government programs concerning Indians and retention of their special status with the federal government.

RED PROGRESSIVISM. As a result of failed federal Indian policies of the late 19th century, several prominent and educated Native Americans called for major reforms to address such issues as the reduction of **reservation** lands, the decline of the Indian population, and poverty and health issues among Indians. Known as red progressives because of the larger Progressive Movement of the early 1900s that sought to improve political, economic, and social conditions, **Arthur Parker**, a Seneca, Thomas Sloan, an Omaha, Dr. **Charles A. Eastman**, a Santee Sioux, **Carlos Montezuma**, a Yavapai, and other Indian progressives demanded better treatment of Native Americans and supported the creation the **Society of American Indians**, the first major **Pan-Indian** organization, in 1911. Many red progressives called for either a major reorganization of the **Bureau of Indian Affairs** or its abolition as a first step to improve conditions among Native Americans. Red progressivism helped strengthen the concept of increased Indian participation and input in issues affecting their lives.

RED STICK WAR. Around the time of the War of 1812, a group of young warriors inspired by political allegiance and religious devotion emerged within the Creek Nation to oppose the United States. Influenced by the teachings of the **Shawnee Prophet** and the work of his brother **Tecumseh**, this group, called Red Sticks by whites, advocated military action against the United States.

In August 1813, with promises of assistance from the Spanish and British and with American intrusions on the rise, the Red Sticks attacked Fort Mims, an American outpost near modern Mobile, Alabama. By taking the offensive, the Red Sticks gave the Americans a reason to launch a full-scale military assault on the entire Creek Nation. As the fighting commenced, the U.S. army, headed by General Andrew Jackson and allied with neighboring Indian nations, dealt crushing defeat after crushing defeat to the severely outnumbered Red Sticks. The final battle of the Red Stick War came at Horseshoe Bend on the Tallapoosa River on 27 March 1814. With the help of his Cherokee allies, General Jackson scored a stunning victory and ended resistance among the Creeks.

The Treaty of Fort Jackson ended the Red Stick War. The Creeks were forced to give up 14 million acres of land to the United States. In the final analysis, the Treaty of Fort Jackson laid the foundation for the removal treaties that would be signed by all of the southeastern tribes in the 1830s.

RELIGION. The various movements commonly referred to as Native American religions present a complex problem of description and interpretation. Euro-Americans have misinterpreted, misunderstood, derided, romanticized, and misappropriated these movements at almost every juncture. Until recently, the authoritative voice in all works dealing with Indian religious traditions was predominantly nonnative. Because these explanations were constructed by outsiders, the complex nature of Indian ritual life has been mislabeled and misrepresented since the early colonial period.

It has become clear that Native American religion is complex and affects the lives of its adherents socially, culturally, psychologically, and sociologically. Thus, it is not easy to describe Indian religions through a series of easily identifiable categories or Hollywood-style representations. The followers of traditional Native American "religions" insist that their entire culture was and is a vast expression of their spirituality and cannot be separated from the context in which it developed. The nature of these religions is often disconcerting to Euro-Americans. Outsiders were quick to identify particular rituals as "religion" for specific tribes, but Indian peoples saw the ritual as an expression of a larger ritual-complex that was intricately tied to the tribal social structure. Thus, cultural traditions and tribal structures were and are infused with a spiritual nature that cannot be separated from other aspects of day-to-day life. Nearly every human act required some type of religious thinking or habit. Thus, there is no such thing as Native American religion; rather, there are more than 500 distinct cultural traditions that can be identified north of Mexico and south of the Canadian border. These traditions cannot be separated from their cultural context.

However, there are some striking similarities among American Indian religious traditions. Almost without exception, the practices are entirely community-based and have no meaning outside of the context in which stories are told, songs are sung, or dances are preformed. Among the Lakota, the phrase "that the people may live!" is the most commonly used saying during any religious exercise. The sentiment of sacrifice for the community becomes the reason for the ceremony. A violation of specified rituals, therefore, also affects the entire community, not just the individual transgressor. The communal nature of Indian religions makes them distinct from Christian traditions, which stress an individual relationship with the divine.

For example, the **vision quest** requires personal sacrifice that includes fasting, several days of prayer, and removal from the community for a specified period of time. Many people have argued that because the practitioner separates from the community, the ritual is a sign of individualism. However, the entire village takes part in preparing an individual for the ritual, and family members remain at prayer until the seeker returns. Thus, even when an individual seeks personal power, the entire community has a vested interest in the person's success. In recent years, and since Indians are more closely associated with their white neighbors, the community aspects of many rituals have been removed, making them entirely individualistic. Indian peoples now spend time and resources ensuring that the followers of traditional practices understand the spiritual and social aspects of the community in which the traditions must be understood.

Another distinctive aspect of Indian religion is the concept of space. The spatial layout of a ceremony is of the utmost importance to the followers of Indian traditions. The structure of a **Green Corn Ceremony**, the location of a **kiva**, the shape of a **sweat lodge**, or the direction one turns during the **Ghost Dance** all have tribally specified values that reflect the relationship of Indian peoples to the space around them. Most tribes also have some manner of sacred space: The Black Hills for the Sioux, Blue Lake for some of the Pueblo people, Bear Butte for the Cheyenne, and the four mountains that ring the boundaries of the Navajo nation are but a few examples. The relationship between religious practice and space is distinctly different from European traditions that stress time. Christian rituals take place on a particular day or during a specific season.

Finally, Indian religious traditions are experienced as part of a lived tradition. The power of a place is a living entity. The entire created world is seen as alive and filled with sentient beings. Thus, a sense of interrelationship exists in Indian traditions where two-legged, four-legged, winged, and other living things all have a particular role.

Because of misappropriations of rituals, distortions now threaten to overshadow Indian religious traditions. Many Indian traditions are undergoing major transformations as a result of the various New Age movements that use the rituals outside of their cultural context. Indian peoples have very little legal recourse to protect and preserve their sacred spaces, places, and rituals, yet the traditions and their integral cultural contexts continue. *See also* MANITOU; NEOLIN; ORENDA; SHAWNEE PROPHET; WAKONDA; WOVOKA.

REPATRIATION. During the 1970s, advocates of **Red Power** launched a series of complaints aimed at federal, state, and local museums that held the remains of dead Indians or displayed important cultural and sacred artifacts. Scholars contended that various museums across the United States held the remains of 600,000 Indians. Activists demanded the repatriation of these artifacts, returning them to the tribes who had control over them. Anthropologists and archaeologists protested, stating that the items, including human remains, were vital to scientific research.

In 1989, the state of Nebraska responded to the demands of the Indian activists. That year, the legislature passed the Unmarked Human Burial Sites and Skeletal Remains Protection Act, which established legal protection for unmarked gravesites and ordered the return of all human remains and burial artifacts held by state agencies. Other states with large Indian populations quickly followed. That same year, the U.S. federal government moved on the issue of Indian remains when it passed the National Museum of the American Indian Act, which established a special museum for Indians and directed the Smithsonian Institution to begin the repatriation process. The act further established the Repatriation Review Committee to monitor the procedure. In 1990, Congress passed the Native American Graves Protection and Repatriation Act to protect all Indian burial sites on federal lands, and the act dictated that all federally funded agencies begin repatriation, a slow process with which many tribes still contend.

RESERVATIONS. The creation of reservations can be traced back to 17th century Colonial America when Indian tribes were forced to live on limited land areas that might or might not be the original lands the tribes occupied. Some tribes had to share reservations with other Native American tribes. By placing Indians on reservations, non-Indians believed it would be much easier to assimilate them into mainstream society; however, the insatiable thirst for acquiring Indian lands was the primary motive for restricting tribes to limited territories.

After achieving independence, the United States continued the practice of establishing reservations first by treaty negotiation and later by executive order or congressional legislation. For treaty-making practices, federal officials often used such unscrupulous tactics as deception, fraud, and liquor to convince Indians to sell their lands. The Department of War was initially in charge of Indian affairs, and through an agency that became known as the **Bureau of Indian Affairs (BIA)**, federal policies on reservations were enforced.

More reservations were established, resulting from the passage of the **Indian Removal Act** of 1830, the settlement of western lands by the United States, and successful U.S. military campaigns against Indian tribes who tried in vain to protect their homelands. Following the Civil War, assimilation efforts on reservations intensified. Indian agents withheld or selectively distributed payments of **annuities** and appointed Indians who accepted assimilation to leadership roles to pressure other reservation inhabitants to abandon their native ways. Missionaries also had a major impact on reservations by challenging Indian religious beliefs and causing further schisms among tribal members.

Many reformers believed reservations retarded assimilation efforts and demanded the dividing of reservation lands into individual Indian homesteads. In 1887, passage of the **Dawes Severalty Act** attempted to achieve this objective. The land allotment program, which lasted until 1934, caused undue hardships that included the loss of tens of millions of acres of reservation land being purchased by non-Indians and the weakening of what tribal sovereignty existed. At the beginning of the 20th century, conditions continued to deteriorate for most Native Americans living on allotted lands or still resided on reservations that were not selected for land allotments.

In 1933, **John Collier** became commissioner of Indian affairs and began Indian New Deal programs that included Congress passing the **Indian Reorganization Act (IRA)** of 1934, which, among other things, ended land allotments, allocated funds to repurchase land, allowed tribes to establish tribal governments on reservations, and encouraged economic development projects. Approximately half of the reservations formed IRA tribal governments, while others took advantage of additional IRA programs. Such issues as poverty, health concerns, and inadequate housing on reservations still remained major problems, however.

After World War II, reservations were again threatened by federal assimilation policies. **Termination** was designed to end the special status and relationship reservation Indians had with the U.S. federal government, while the relocation program offered reservation Indians job opportunities in large urban areas like Los Angeles, California, Dallas, Texas, and Cleveland, Ohio. Again, both policies had devastating effects on Native Americans and caused them to organize such movements as the **American Indian Movement** and **Menominee Drums** to demand a reversal of these policies; recognition of Indian treaty rights; and major political, economic, and social reforms on reservations.

During the last decades of the 20th century, federal officials began to support more programs and pass legislation that allowed tribal governments increased control over several services and programs on reservations that the BIA formerly directed. Tribes also applied for grants to establish economic development programs on reservations. After the passage of the Indian Gaming Regulatory Act in 1988, a number of tribes built casinos and used the profits from **gaming** for improving reservation conditions and opportunities.

According to recent census figures, there are more Indians living off than on reservations. In spite of some gains, there are still many urgent problems on most reservations that need immediate attention. These include jurisdictional issues regarding **law** enforcement on reservation lands; high rates of unemployment; **alcohol** and **alcoholism**; substandard housing; violence against Indian **women**; the rise of teenage gangs; and mismanagement of hundreds of thousands of individual Indian trust land accounts, as reflected in a major lawsuit against the federal government known as the **Cobell case**. Indeed, many reservations can still be regarded as "ghettos in the wilderness."

REVITALIZATION MOVEMENTS. Revitalization movements are a special kind of religious movement, usually occurring when people are oppressed. A major aspect of the revitalization movement is an attempt to recreate a mythic golden age of the past. Many of these movements developed among Indian people when they experienced dispossession, removal, and assaults on their culture. Spiritual leaders like **Neolin**, Tenskwatawa (the **Shawnee Prophet**), and **Wovoka** preached a return to native traditions and a rejection of white ways, especially **alcohol** consumption. After communing with the spirits, Indian prophets developed new rituals, ceremonies, and songs in an effort to restore the traditions of the past. Leaders of revitalization movements were often instrumental in Indian resistance efforts. *See also* RELIGION.

– S –

SACAJAWEA (c. mid-1780s–1812/1884). The exact birth date and death of Sacajawea, a Northern Shoshone, are not conclusively known. Two alternate spellings of her name—Sacagawea and Sakakawea—are also used. Sacajawea was born in the mid-1780s in the Lemhi Valley in present-day Idaho, and at the age of 10, a Hidatsa raiding party kidnapped her and returned to their village near present-day Mandan, North Dakota. In 1804, Toussaint Charbonneau, a French-Canadian fur trader, acquired Sacajawea from the Hidatsa. During the winter of 1804 and 1805, Captain Meriwether Lewis and Captain William Clark, while leading their famous expedition of the Louisiana Purchase, met Sacajawea and Charbonneau at Fort Mandan in present-day North Dakota and hired Charbonneau as an interpreter in April 1805. Lewis and Clark asked him to bring one of his Shoshone "wives" with him because she might prove useful to the expedition. Sacajawea, who had just given birth to a baby boy in February 1805, accompanied Charbonneau, often carrying her newborn in a cradle on her back.

The contributions of Sacajawea to the Lewis and Clark Expedition are significant. Although not a major guide, she helped them travel through regions she was familiar with, suggesting routes and identifying landmarks. On one occasion, she rescued important records and instruments when a boat capsized. Her knowledge of edible wild foods improved the diets of the explorers. Moreover, Sacajawea provided valuable service as an interpreter, speaking several languages and using sign language.

In August 1805, the expedition met a party of Shoshone in present-day Montana, and the leader of the Indians happened to be Sacajawea's brother, who agreed to provide **horses** and guides to the expedition as it moved westward. Instead of remaining with her tribe, Sacajawea accompanied Lewis and Clark to the Pacific Ocean. She continued to help the expedition on their return eastward, and on 17 August 1806, Sacajawea and Charbonneau finished their service with the expedition at Fort Mandan. Sacajawea received no pay for her services, although Charbonneau did. Sacajawea was well-liked by her comrades, especially Clark, who praised her services in his journal entries.

The remaining years of Sacajawea's life are not well-documented, and historians disagree on when she died. Most contend she died on 20 December 1812 at Fort Manuel in present-day South Dakota because of journal entries made by two individuals, one mentioning that Charbonneau's wife was ill in April 1811 and the other noting in December 1812 that his wife died at Fort Manuel. In the mid-1820s, Clark, who was researching members of the expedition, wrote dead by her name.

Other historians—as reflected by the oral traditions of the Shoshone, Hidatsa, Comanche, and other tribes—believe that Sacajawea died on 9 April 1884, passing in her late nineties. The oral traditions tell of her leaving Charbonneau around 1810, wandering from tribe to tribe, and finally living with her son and the Shoshone on the Wind River Indian Reservation in Wyoming, where she helped her people and was honored. Furthermore, those supporting the 1884 date of death maintain that the two journal entries dictating the 1812 death do not mention Sacajawea by name, that it was a well-known fact that Charbonneau had more than one Indian wife; and, finally, that Clark was misinformed in his one-word death notation inscribed next to her name. In the 1920s, noted Indian author and reformer Dr. **Charles A. Eastman**, who was working as an Indian inspector for the **Bureau of Indian Affairs**, had as one of his assignments finding her gravesite and determining when she died. He relied on the research of Professor Grace Hebard, who was writing a book on Sacajawea and supported the 1884 passing and reported that she died in 1884.

Regardless of the exact date of her passing, Sacajawea supplied valuable services to the Lewis and Clark Expedition, and she is revered in the oral traditions of several tribes. She, like **Pocahontas**, has become a significant and romanticized figure in the nation's history. *See also* WOMEN.

SAINTE-MARIE, BUFFY (1941–). Born on 20 February 1941, on a Cree reserve in Qu'Appelle Valley in Saskatchewan, Canada, Sainte-Marie was later adopted and raised in New England. As a college student in the 1960s, she became famous as a composer of songs for protest movements. Her songs were performed by some of the leading artists of the time, as well as by legendary artists like Elvis Presley. She later used her fame to expand her horizons and wrote essays, established a scholarship foundation to fund Native American study, and traveled the world exploring indigenous people.

In 1976, she quit recording and became a full-time mom and fine artist. Sainte-Marie and her son, Dakota, embarked on a series of appearances on Sesame Street, where they taught the characters—and millions of children around the world—that Indians still exist. In 1982, Sainte-Marie won an Oscar for her song "Up Where We Belong" recorded by Joe Cocker and Jennifer Warnes for the film *An Officer and a Gentleman*. Sainte-Marie returned to music in 1993 with her album *Coincidence and Likely Stories*.

In addition to her musical appearances, Sainte-Marie gives lectures at colleges and civic venues covering topics from American Indian issues to songwriting and works on her own Cradleboard Teaching Project, which works to provide information about Native American culture to students in public education. She serves as an adjunct professor at York University in Toronto and at Saskatchewan Indian Federated College in Regina. She has also taught at the **Institute of American Indian Arts** in Santa Fe, New Mexico. *See also* WOMEN.

SHAMAN. Shamans are men and **women** who directly experience the presence of spirits, whether in dreams, through illness, or in visions. The experience with the spirits gives the shaman access to sacred knowledge. Shamans who recover from an illness that brings them close to death are often believed to be possessed with unique powers. Shamans are also capable of altered states in which they can travel between this world and that of the dead, see long distances, and otherwise circumvent human experience.

Shamans often utilize their powers through the use of songs and trances. Because the shaman possesses great powers, he or she is often feared as a witch just as often as they are thanked for their works as medical practitioners. The rituals of shaman differ from tribe to tribe, and tribal names for this individual vary. Shaman is not a term often used by tribal people. *See also* RELIGION.

SHAWNEE PROPHET (1775–1836). The Shawnee Prophet was born to a Creek woman and a Shawnee war chief in 1775, in a village on the banks of the Mad River in western Ohio. In 1779, the prophet's mother left Ohio, leaving not only Mad River Country but her two children, the future prophet and his older brother, **Tecumseh**. Tecumseh was an athletic boy and an active participant in the games and contests popular among Shawnee youths. By contrast, the future prophet was an awkward and plump youth who accidentally took out his own eye by mishandling a bow and arrow. Because he often complained, the youngest brother was known as Lalawethika (the Noisemaker), a name he despised. Unlike his older brother, Lalawethika did not take part in the Indian battles against General Josiah Harmar in 1790 or General Arthur St. Clair in 1791, but he did join a war party led by his brother at the Battle of Fallen Timbers. In 1798, Tecumseh and Lalawethika moved to Indiana Territory, where Lalawethika attempted to become a **shaman**. Unable to succeed as a healer, he became an alcoholic.

In the years after the Treaty of Greenville in 1795, game and fur-bearing animals declined, and large numbers of white frontiersmen moved into Indian territories; new settlements were established, and white hunters poached what animals remained in the area. White juries routinely protected squatters while systematically prosecuting Indians for crimes against whites. Under stress, Indians increasingly turned to **alcohol**. The belief that witches were present within the tribe was prevalent among the Shawnees. The time was right for a **revitalization movement**.

In April 1805, Lalawethika fell into a trance. After a few hours, he awoke and informed his family that he had died, had been taken to a spot where he could see both heaven and hell, and had been given instruction on how to return the Shawnees to their former glory. He preached a new **religion**, one that demanded the Shawnees limit their contact with whites, give up American food and clothing, relinquish manufactured goods, and abstain from alcohol. Guns and ammunition could be used only for defense, and hunting must be done with bow and arrow. If the Shawnees followed this doctrine, he claimed that their dead relatives would return and game would be plentiful. If they refused, he professed that hell awaited them. Finally, Lalawethika announced that from that point onward, he would be known as Tenskwatawa (the Open Door), a name more befitting a prophet.

By 1807, Tenskwatawa's message was so popular that many Indians traveled to his village to meet him. White officials became alarmed at their numbers and the rate at which the Indians exhausted regional food supplies. One year later, the Shawnee Prophet moved his village to the confluence of the Tippecanoe and Wabash rivers. Prophetstown, the Shawnee Prophet's new village, sat on the site of present-day Lafayette, Indiana. In 1809, after the Treaty of Fort Wayne, Tecumseh attempted to capitalize on his brother's success and turn a religious movement into a centralized alliance designed to retain Indian lands in the West.

In November 1811, while Tecumseh was away gathering allies in the South, William Henry Harrison, governor of Indiana Territory, led an expedition against Prophetstown. Determined to protect his village, Tenskwatawa promised his followers that they would be immune from American attacks and ordered an offensive against Governor Harrison's camp. Although both sides suffered losses, the Battle of Tippecanoe crushed the influence of the Shawnee Prophet. In December 1812, Tenskwatawa fled to Canada. On 5 October 1813, he accompanied his brother Tecumseh to the Battle of the Thames. Tenskwatawa fled when the fighting began and did not see his brother fall to American bullets.

Following the War of 1812, Tenskwatawa remained in Canada for 10 years, attempting to reestablish his leadership position. In 1825, at the invitation of Michigan governor Lewis Cass, the Shawnee Prophet returned to the United States and used his influence to promote Indian removal. The prophet finally settled near present-day Kansas City, Kansas, where he sat for George Catlin in 1832. He died with little public notice in 1836. Although historians and contemporaries credit Tecumseh with founding an Indian resistance movement during the War of 1812, it originated with his younger brother, Tenskwatawa.

SILVERHEELS, JAY (1912–1980). Born Harold Jay Smith on 26 May 1912, on the Six Nations Indian Reserve in Canada, Jay Silverheels, a Mohawk, was one of 10 children. His father, a farmer, fought in World War I and was the most decorated Canadian Indian to serve in the conflict. Silverheels was a gifted athlete, participating in such sports as **lacrosse**, boxing, and wrestling. He quit school at the age of 17 and became a professional lacrosse player in Toronto. He acquired the name Silverheels because he painted his lacrosse shoes silver and ran swiftly with his heels in the air, easily sidestepping his opponents. Several years before his death, he legally changed his last name to Silverheels.

Joe E. Brown, the famous comedian, helped Silverheels become an actor after seeing the handsome and graceful athlete in a lacrosse game. Silverheels performed as an extra in several "B westerns," often being shot off horses during battle scenes. During the late 1940s, he began getting better roles and appeared in such films as *Captain from Castile*, *Key Largo*, and *Broken Arrow*, the classic in which he portrayed **Geronimo**. He acted in more than 30 films and worked with such famous actors as John Wayne, James Stewart, Henry Fonda, Humphrey Bogart, Errol Flynn, Lee J. Cobb, and Tyrone Power.

Silverheels is best known for his major role as Tonto in the television series The Lone Ranger. He appeared in 221 episodes between 1949 and 1957, and in two movies based on the television series. Although Silverheels was still a victim of Hollywood stereotyping of Indian roles in television and films, his portrayal of Tonto, was one of an individual who possessed wisdom and skills that frequently saved the Lone Ranger from life-threatening situations.

In his later years, Silverheels continued to perform in television shows, films, and commercials. In the 1960s, he became more vocal about how Indians were portrayed in films and founded the Indian Actors Workshop in Hollywood, California, to help aspiring Indian thespians. He also worked on public service projects that focused on substance abuse and elderly issues. In his spare time, he raised and bred **horses** and even competed as a harness-racing driver.

In 1979, Silverheels was honored with a star on the Hollywood Walk of Fame, making him the first Native American to achieve such recognition, and in 1993, he was inducted posthumously into the Western Performers Hall of Fame at the National Cowboy and Western

Heritage Museum in Oklahoma City, Oklahoma. He died on 5 March 1980. He was the foremost Indian actor of his era.

SITTING BULL (c. 1831–1890). A Hunkpapa Lakota religious and military leader, Sitting Bull—originally called Jumping Badger— was born along the Grand River in western South Dakota in the early 1830s. He received the honorable name Sitting Bull (Tatanka Iyotanka), which was also his father's name, as a young teenager in battle counting coup for the first time against a Crow warrior. His new name symbolized a stubborn male bison resting on its powerful big legs. In other battles against Indian enemies, Sitting Bull gained further honors and became a war chief. While achieving prestige in battle, he also learned sacred ways and became known as a holy man. His participation and physical sacrifices, including the numerous self-inflicted cuts on his body that he endured in Sun Dances, reflected his spiritual commitment and further enhanced his reputation.

During the 1860s and 1870s, Sitting Bull continued to gain followers and became the principal leader of the Lakota Sioux. He did not accept **reservation** life according to the Treaty of Fort Laramie of 1868 and continued living off the reservation and hunting buffalo in the Powder River and Yellowstone valleys. One of his staunch allies was **Crazy Horse**, an Oglala Lakota leader. With the discovery of gold in the sacred Black Hills, white miners illegally poured into the region, causing further conflicts. The U.S. federal government attempted to purchase the Black Hills, but failing to do so, the United States declared that Sitting Bull and his followers had violated the 1868 treaty and demanded that they be moved to the reservation.

The result was the Battle of the Little Bighorn and the death of Lieutenant Colonel George Armstrong Custer in June 1876. It was a short-lived victory for the Sioux as the United States retaliated by sending more forces to the region, and the tribe was defeated. Sitting Bull moved into Canada, where he remained until 1881. He returned to the United States and after a brief imprisonment was sent to the Standing Rock Reservation in North Dakota. On the reservation, he farmed but still protested reservation conditions and federal policies. In 1885, he joined Buffalo Bill Cody's Wild West Show.

Sitting Bull was among the Sioux who supported the **Ghost Dance** movement at Standing Rock in 1890. It was hoped that this **revital-**

ization movement would allow the Sioux to return to the lifestyle they enjoyed before the arrival of the white man. An Indian agent ordered the Indian police to arrest Sitting Bull for his involvement in the movement, which resulted in his resisting arrest and death on 15 December 1890. This great religious and military leader was deeply mourned by his followers.

SMOHALLA (c. 1815–1895). A Wanapam Indian prophet and **shaman** in the Pacific Northwest, Smohalla led a **revitalization movement** in the 1850s, preaching that his followers should abandon white ways and return to traditional lifestyles. He believed that Indians should not become white farmers and should not consume **alcohol**; instead they should live by fishing, hunting, and root digging. His teachings became known as the Washani (Dancer's) Creed, known today as the Dreamer Religion.

Smohalla's early years are not well documented. He gained a reputation as a warrior and later started having visions and attracting others to his movement. He angered other Indians by not allowing whites to use tribal lands and refusing to go to war against whites. Smohalla and Moses, a major Indian rival, apparently engaged in a fight in which Smohalla was presumed killed but returned to life. The death and rebirth of Indian prophets is a common trait in revitalization movements and enhances the power of the prophet. It is believed that while dead or unconscious, prophets receive messages from spiritual forces and God.

Smohalla did not advocate violence in his teachings; rather, he preached that dreams would provide comfort and wisdom until the coming of God, who would restore life to the way it was before the arrival of whites to their lands. The **Ghost Dance** movement contained similar tenets. *See also* RELIGION.

SOCIETY OF AMERICAN INDIANS (SAI). In April 1911 in Columbus, Ohio, six prominent Indians, Dr. **Charles A. Eastman**, a Santee Sioux, Dr. **Carlos Montezuma**, a Yavapai, Laura Cornelius, an Oneida, Thomas Sloan, an Omaha, Charles Daganett, a Peoria, and Henry Standing Bear, a Sioux, and Dr. Fayette McKenzie, a non-Indian professor of economics and sociology at Ohio State University, met and founded the SAI, which was first called the American

Indian Association. They wanted the ideals of the Progressive Era to include Indians, and these **red progressives** and McKenzie believed that mainstream America could also benefit from Indian contributions.

On 12 October 1911, the first SAI conference was held in Columbus, Ohio. Commissioner of Indian Affairs Robert Valentine welcomed the more than 50 Native Americans in attendance. Papers were presented on such Indian issues as **education**, health, political and legal matters, and Indian occupations. At the business meeting, the Indian attendees decided that only Indians could vote and hold office in the organization but that whites could hold associate membership. They selected Washington, D.C., as their national headquarters to monitor Indian-related issues in Congress and at the **Bureau of Indian Affairs (BIA)**.

As the first major **Pan-Indian** organization, the SAI called for better relations between Indians and non-Indians, improved economic and educational opportunities for Indians, and U.S. citizenship for all Indians. In 1913, they began publishing a journal called the *Quarterly Journal of the Society of American Indians*, which renamed the *American Indian Magazine* in 1916. With the exception of 1917 and 1922, the SAI held annual conferences in Denver, Colorado, Minneapolis, Minnesota, St. Louis, Missouri, and Chicago, Illinois, between 1912 and 1923.

Factionalism, however, weakened and destroyed the society as years passed. The organization disagreed on several issues, including the abolition of the BIA, Indian representation in the SAI, and the use of **peyote**. By the early 1920s, the SAI ceased to function.

SOCIETY OF OKLAHOMA INDIANS. The formation of the Society of Oklahoma Indians was aided by a field team from the **Indian Rights Association** when a group of Osages, Creeks, and Cherokees called for a general convention of Oklahoma Indians to be held in Tulsa in February 1924. The stated purpose of the convention was to protect the civil and political rights of Oklahoma's Indian population.

The society that grew out of that convention was a diverse body with a split agenda and a leadership struggle. The speeches given by the conference attendees ranged from loss of Indian unity, **reservation** economics, Oklahoma statehood, and fraud cases with Indian plaintiffs. The one item that all in attendance agreed upon was that the new society would take up the cause of protecting the civil, social, educational, economic, and political rights of Oklahoma Indians.

The 1924 convention marked the first of four annual meetings of the society. The meetings attracted hundreds of Indians from across Oklahoma and even a few notable Indian leaders from across the nation, including **Gertrude Bonnin**. At its most effective, the society was a modest protest against perceived wrongs. The numerous resolutions passed by the group represented a broad-based agenda and many goals that lacked unified purpose. By 1927, the society was coming to an end. At that year's convention in Pawhuska, it was deadlocked in a battle over important leadership positions. By the following fall, it was nonfunctional, its leaders finding important roles in other movements that more closely fit their agendas.

STOCKBRIDGE INDIANS. The history of the Stockbridge people is one of frequent migrations and removals. Stockbridge tradition says that the tribe originally formed when a group of people moved north and then west in search of a place where the waters were never still. The earliest account of contact between the "Mahican" people and Europeans comes from Dutch fur traders in the early 17th century.

In 1734, the Mahicans welcomed Protestant missionaries. Teachers, farmers, and other settlers quickly followed the missionaries. A church and school were built, and the town of Stockbridge was incorporated. The Christianized Mahicans who called the area home became known as the Stockbridge Indians.

During the American Revolution, the Stockbridge fought on the side of the colonials, but when the war ended, they found that the new U.S. federal government did not recognize their land titles. During the next 150 years, the Stockbridge were forced to move from Massachusetts to New York and later several places in Wisconsin, where they were forced to reside with numerous Munsee Delawares. In an effort to resist removal west of the Mississippi River, the Stockbridge-Munsee agreed to move to a **reservation** in Shawno County, Wisconsin, in 1856. By 1920, as a result of the **Dawes Severalty Act**, the Stockbridge-Munsee were again landless. In 1934, the **Indian Reorganization Act (IRA)** gave the Stockbridge-Munsee the opportunity to recreate their tribal entity. The reorganized tribe acquired 15,000 acres of timber land and began establishing an official presence on the reservation.

Today, approximately 7,000 of the 14,000 members of the tribe live on the northeast Wisconsin reservation. A seven-member council organized by the IRA constitution leads the tribe. After surviving centuries of removal, the Stockbridge-Munsee people have adopted the "Many Trails" as their symbol, which signifies strength, endurance, and hope for all Mahican people.

SUN DANCE. The most important religious ceremony of the Plains Indians, the sun dance was held by each tribe once a year in early summer. The dance was an occasion for purification and strengthening and provided an opportunity to reaffirm beliefs about the universe and the supernatural. The central ritual involved male dancers who, to fulfill a vow or seek power, danced for four days without stopping for food, drink, or sleep, ending in exhaustion. Piercing and sun gazing were practiced among some tribes. *See also* RELIGION.

SURVIVAL OF AMERICAN INDIANS ASSOCIATION. Founded in 1964 by Indians in the Pacific Northwest, particularly the Nisqually and Puyallup Indians, the Survival of American Indians Association focused mainly on the protection of **fishing rights** for Native Americans in western Washington. One of its primary leaders was **Hank Adams**, an Assiniboine-Sioux. The association also supports Indian sovereignty issues.

SWEAT LODGE CEREMONY. Many Native American tribes hold sweat lodge ceremonies, which are major purification rites in their religious beliefs. Sweat lodges are generally small, dome-shaped structures made from saplings and covered with hides, blankets, or canvas. Inside the lodge, sweat baths take place by pouring water on hot stones that have been brought into the lodges. Participants believe that the hot steam improves both physical and spiritual health. Traditional songs and prayers are performed at the functions, and both men and **women** participate but usually in separate sweat bath proceedings. Sweat lodge ceremonies are also social events that bring old friends together.

The U.S. federal government forbade the sweat lodge ceremony in the 19th century, but Indians continued the practice. Sweat lodge ceremonies are still performed by Native Americans, and any Indian who is incarcerated maintains the right to hold such a function. *See also* RELIGION.

– T –

TECUMSEH (c. 1768–1813). Tecumseh was born at Old Piqua, a Shawnee village on the banks of the Mad River in Ohio. He was the fifth of nine children born to a Shawnee war chief and a Creek woman. Tecumseh's father was killed in 1774 at the Battle of Point Pleasant, and in 1779, his mother left him and his siblings and moved to Spanish territory. Tecumseh remained in Ohio, living with an older sister but remaining under the influence of his older brother, Chiksika. Chiksika vocally opposed white settlement in the Ohio River Valley, and under his brother's guidance, Tecumseh espoused the same sentiments. Tecumseh and his brother fought against American expansion in 1782 and 1783 and raided settlements south of the Ohio River in the years after the American Revolution. In 1788, Chiksika was killed in Tennessee, and Tecumseh refused to return to the Ohio Valley, thus missing the engagement against General Josiah Harmar. In 1791, Tecumseh led a group of scouts who reported on the movements of General Arthur St. Clair but did not participate in the destruction of General St. Clair's command. By 1794, Tecumseh was actively taking part in attacks against the Americans at Fort Recovery and Fallen Timbers.

After the Indian defeat at Fallen Timbers, Tecumseh and a small party of Shawnees refused to participate in the Treaty of Greenville negotiations in 1795 and withdrew first to Deer Creek in Ohio and later to the Great Miami River in western Ohio. In 1797, he again moved his followers to the Whitewater River in Indiana. He remained at his Indiana village for the next seven years until news of his younger brother reached him.

In April 1805, Tenskwatawa (the **Shawnee Prophet**), Tecumseh's brother, underwent a religious experience in which he claimed to have died and been given a vision of heaven and hell along with a doctrine of revitalization. After the Shawnee Prophet successfully predicted a solar eclipse, his influence expanded among the Ohio Valley Indians. During the summer of 1805, Tecumseh moved into his brother's village and helped him establish a larger village near modern Greenville, Ohio.

By 1808, Tecumseh was actively using his brother's religious movement to recruit allies for a political alliance that urged Indians to accept common ownership of land and avoid selling more territory to whites. He also advocated a political system that would stop village chiefs from negotiating their own agreements with the Americans. For the next three years, Tecumseh worked to build his alliance. Traveling through the Old Northwest, he urged warriors to leave their village chiefs if they were friendly to the United States and join him at Prophetstown. He also sought political support from British officials in Canada. Angry about the Treaty of Fort Wayne, Tecumseh also met with William Henry Harrison, Indiana Territory governor, and demanded that further treaties be addressed to him. In July 1811, Tecumseh traveled south to recruit warriors from the **Five Civilized Tribes**. Only the Creeks greeted him warmly.

Tecumseh returned to the ruined Prophetstown in January 1812, and attempted to assure American officials that he sought friendship; he was secretly reassembling his alliance. In July 1812, as the United States and Britain went to war, Tecumseh was in Canada, where he hoped to help the British. He led a contingent of Indian and British troops against the Americans at Brownstown and was wounded in the Battle of Monguagon near present-day Trenton, Michigan. In early August, Tecumseh again led his mixed troops against the Americans and captured Fort Detroit. He spent the winter of 1812 in Indiana, and in April 1813, led the Indian battalion that accompanied Colonel Henry Proctor's attempted siege of Fort Meigs.

By fall of 1813, after American naval victories secured the Great Lakes, Tecumseh opposed British plans to abandon Amherstburg and retreat to Niagara. Angered, Tecumseh accused the British of cowardice and commanded that they either take one last vigorous stand or turn their guns over to the Indians. The British reluctantly accepted Tecumseh's demand and agreed to take their stand near the Thames River in Ontario. The American forces advanced to the battlefield on 5 October. The British army fired three volleys and then fled from the field. Tecumseh and the Indians continued the assault, but in the fighting Tecumseh was shot and killed. After the battle, the Americans discovered Tecumseh's body and skinned it, mutilated it with knives and hatchets, and indignantly tossed it into a mass grave.

Since his demise at the Battle of the Thames, Tecumseh has become an American folk hero. He has been portrayed as the consummate "noble savage." Shrouded in myth, his story is one of resistance, not romantic myth.

TEEPEE ORDER OF AMERICA (TOA). Established in 1915 in New York City, the TOA was another example of an early **Pan-Indian** body founded by Red Fox Francis St. James, who claimed Blackfeet heritage. The TOA was not as effective as other Pan-Indian organizations, like the **Society of American Indians (SAI)**, although some SAI members also belonged to the TOA.

The TOA was initially similar in structure to the Boy Scouts of America in appealing to youth and focusing on Indian activities and ceremonies that were romantic in nature. Membership in the TOA included Indians and non-Indians from the United States, Canada, and Latin America. Blacks and European immigrants were refused association, reflecting the prejudices of the period. Although the TOA was never really effective as a movement, the body did support the granting of U.S. citizenship to Indians and questioned the effectiveness of the **Bureau of Indian Affairs**.

TERMINATION. Because of the movement toward conservatism and conformity during the late 1940s, federal Indian policy again adopted an aggressive assimilation approach to Indian affairs, abandoning many of the reform efforts of commissioner of Indian affairs **John Collier**. To ensure that Indians became part of mainstream America and to liberate them from their poverty-stricken existence, the termination policy was adopted to end the special status of Indians by terminating all federal trust relationships and responsibilities with Indian tribes. It was argued that Native Americans would then become like all other Americans and participate fully in mainstream society.

In 1953, Congress passed House Concurrent Resolution 108 that supported the policy of termination. Several tribes, including the Menominees and Klamaths in 1954, were identified as "ready" for termination, and the tribes, often under duress, signed special termination acts. The ending of federal services and other programs was devastating. For example, economic disasters and health and medical matters dramatically worsened among the terminated tribes.

By the 1960s, many Indians and non-Indians demanded the end of termination. In 1970, President Richard Nixon denounced the termination policy, and such tribes as the Menominees and Klamaths had their federal tribal status restored. It was not until 1988, however, that House Concurrent Resolution 108 was finally repealed. *See also* DEER, ADA, and MENOMINEE DRUMS.

TOTEM POLE. Pacific Northwest coast tribes carved beautiful totem poles depicting spiritual beings, ethnic identity, family and clan history, and social rank. Among the tribes that sculptured totem poles were the Bella Coolas, Haidas, Tlingits, and Tsimshians. Totem poles varied in height. Many were more than 50 feet high, and the preferred tree for carving was the red cedar. The different types of totem poles included funeral custom poles and village and house poles. Specific ceremonies and rituals were observed in carving a totem pole, and Indians frequently held a **potlatch** after the pole was completed. Indians viewed the natural destruction of totem poles as part of life's cycle.

During the 19th century, many more totem poles were carved because of improved technology available to Indians; however, by the early 20th century, totem pole making declined because of assimilation policies affecting **reservation** life and customs. A number of totem poles were illegally taken from Indians by non-Indians who collected them for museums in the first half of the 20th century. Beginning in the 1950s, Indians again started carving totem poles for traditional reasons as well as for sale as commercial art.

TRAIL OF BROKEN TREATIES. During the summer of 1972 in Denver, Colorado, Indian activists like **Hank Adams** and **Dennis Banks** met and planned the Trail of Broken Treaties caravan. The objective was to make non-Indian America aware of such Indian issues as self-determination and treaty violations by the moving of hundreds or perhaps thousands of Indians across the United States to Washington, D.C., during the presidential election in November 1972. Beginning in October, participants in the movement traveled in cars, vans, and buses to the nation's capital, stopping along the way at **reservations** and other places to attract more marchers and deliver presentations. In Minneapolis, Minnesota, the Twenty Points was written that reviewed past offenses committed by the U.S. federal government against Indians and demanded that the violations be corrected and that both federal and state governments recognize tribal sovereignty.

After their arrival in Washington, D.C., in early November, Indians and activists demonstrated at the **Bureau of Indian Affairs (BIA)**, where a confrontation ensued in which federal guards tried to keep demonstrators out of the building. The demonstrators seized the building on 2 November and held it for several days. Negotiations commenced, and the Bureau of Indian Affairs takeover was resolved on 8 November, when the occupiers agreed to leave the premises. Federal officials promised that the Twenty Points would be studied and no charges would be filed against the Indian occupants. Officials also allocated $66,000 to help Indians return to their homes. Each side blamed the other for the confrontation: The Indians believed that the federal government failed to provide them with proper accommodations upon their arrival in the city, as had been promised, while federal officials blamed Indians for extensive damages to equipment and files inside the BIA.

TRUDELL, JOHN (1946–). Growing up on the Santee Indian Reservation near Omaha, Nebraska, Trudell joined the U.S. navy in 1963 and served in Vietnam. After leaving the military, he, like many others, became involved in the civil rights movements sweeping America. Trudell's first taste of activism came at the 1969 occupation of **Alcatraz** Island off the coast of San Francisco, California, where he served as spokesman for **Indians of All Tribes**. He later joined the **American Indian Movement (AIM)** and served as national director from 1972 to 1979. In his final year as AIM director, his wife, three children, and mother-in-law were killed in a fire, and Trudell used the event to remake his career.

A meeting with Jackson Browne introduced him to the musical world, and he became a recording artist. His first album, made with Kiowa guitarist Jesse Ed Davis, was his first foray into the world of spoken-word recording. Trudell was not finished in the entertainment industry. He continued to work as an actor with roles in *Thunderheart* (1992), *On Deadly Ground* (1994), and *Smoke Signals* (1998). He has also worked as a producer of the documentary *Incident at Oglala*. Trudell continues to act and record and is active in Native American movements.

– U –

UNITED ASSOCIATION OF THE AMERICAN INDIAN (UAAI).
The UAAI was founded in 1934 by Jules Haywood, a Cherokee, and other Indian leaders in New York City. The goals of the UAAI included encouraging Indian unity, fostering respect for traditional values, and promoting awareness of Indian issues across the nation through its newsletter, *Talking Leaf*. The newsletter was the first Indian newsletter in the New York metropolitan area, and it reported on both the UAAI's social events and other news items of interest from Indian Country.

Among its successes, the UAAI raised money for a variety of causes, including aiding Mohawks who were uprooted by the construction of the St. Lawrence Seaway. The association lobbied the highest levels of government, working with the John F. Kennedy and Lyndon B. Johnson administrations to address the plight of both urban and **reservation** Indians. Today, the UAAI exists in name only, but it is fondly remembered as one of the first urban Indian organizations in the United States and Canada.

UNITED NATIVE AMERICANS. Lehman L. Brightman, claiming multitribal heritage, founded the United Native Americans in San Francisco, California, in 1968. It was one of the first **Red Power** militant organizations that responded to two controversial federal Indian policies of **termination**: 1) the ending of the special status of Indians and federal treaty obligations and 2) relocation—the moving of Indians from **reservations** to major cities for better employment opportunities. The United Native Americans condemned the **Bureau of Indian Affairs (BIA)** for not adequately protecting Indians, advocated Indian control of the BIA, and criticized the **National Congress of American Indians** for working too closely with the BIA and other federal agencies. The organization published a newsletter called *Warpath* from 1968 to 1977.

– V –

VISION QUEST. A vision quest is a ritual in which the participant, who is nearly always male, seeks communication with the spirits. Although the tradition differs from tribe to tribe, the individual prepares under the direction of one or more **shamans** or religious leaders. Ritual elements found in many of the cultures practicing vision quests include praying with the sacred pipe, fasting, and making offerings of tobacco or flesh to the spirits. A vision quest may be undertaken for numerous reasons, including a puberty ceremony to fulfill a vow, a ceremonial rite to become a healer, or as part of participation in other sacred ceremonies. During the vision quest, individuals are given sacred songs, names, objects, or ceremonies to take back to their people. After the event ends, the individual seeks out a holy man to help interpret what took place during the quest. *See also* RELIGION.

– W –

WAKONDA. The Lakota belief similar to the Iroquois **orenda** and the Algonquian **manitou**. It is a supernatural force that permeates the universe. *See also* RELIGION.

WALK FOR JUSTICE. American Indian Movement (AIM) members **Dennis Banks** and Mary Jane Wilson-Medrano organized the Walk for Justice in 1994, which began on 11 February at **Alcatraz** Island off the coast of San Francisco, California, and culminated in Washington, D.C., on 15 July. The return of the sacred Black Hills to the Sioux Nation, clemency for **Leonard Peltier**, opposition to federal efforts to settle the Navajo-Hopi land dispute, equal protection under the **law** for Native Americans, and the end of police brutality against Indians were among the major Native American issues that the Walk for Justice demanded be addressed.

WAMPUM. Wampum was a string of white and purple beads woven into belts by the Algonquians and Iroquois. The belts were used for adornment but also, and more importantly, the designs represented treaties, agreements, and records of important events. Wampum became a form of money and was used as a medium of exchange after contact with Europeans.

WAR PAINT CLUB. Established in the 1920s in Los Angeles, California, the War Paint Club sought to protect Native Americans in the film industry. The issue of having non-Indians playing Indian roles was a major complaint of the club. Not much is known on how the War Paint Club viewed other issues relating to Native Americans in film or when it ceased to function.

WARRIOR, CLYDE (1939–1968). Born near Ponca City, Oklahoma, in 1939, Warrior was raised by his grandparents, who taught him the Ponca ways and stressed ceremonial dances. He became a well-known fancy dancer and singer at Indian **powwow** events. His upbringing and participation in powwows naturally made him aware of Indian issues. Warrior later attended summer workshops and participated in the Southwest Regional Indian Youth Conference in New Mexico, where he gained more knowledge about Indian conditions. He was one of the founders of the **National Indian Youth Council (NIYC)** in 1961, and he soon became recognized as the **Red Power** prophet because of his speaking and writing skills.

Warrior demanded that Indians be more proud of their heritage and denounced white racial attitudes. He called Indians who forgot about their own people and supported programs detrimental to Indians "Uncle Tomahawks" and "Apples"—red on the outside and white on the inside. Many people in mainstream America feared his sometimes militant messages that hinted at revolution. Warrior was among those protesting violations of Pacific Coast Indians' **fishing rights** in 1964. Although he became president of the NIYC, Warrior grew more and more dissatisfied with the organization and later resigned, believing that it should become more militant in its demands. In 1968, Warrior, who suffered from **alcoholism**, died of cirrhosis of the liver.

WESTERN CONFEDERACY. *See* BRANT, JOSEPH; LITTLE TURTLE.

WHEELER-HOWARD BILL. *See* INDIAN REORGANIZATION ACT (IRA), 1934.

WHITE BUFFALO SOCIETY. Hidatsa and Mandan females held membership in the highly prestigious White Buffalo Society, which attempted to attract buffalo herds, particularly during hard times. Membership was based on age and purchase, meaning when older members left, new ones could buy into the group. During the ceremonies, society members imitated buffalo movements, performed special dances and songs, and wore specific clothing, especially a cap adorned with hawk feathers made from a white buffalo skin.

WOMEN. The role of women in Indian societies has traditionally been misunderstood by Euro-Americans. Much of the discussion concerning women during early contact and the colonial period was carried out by traders, trappers, and missionaries who talked with Indian males and developed a distorted view of Indian women. Because of the male-centered nature of Indian "ethnography," few outsiders have been able to appreciate the range of activities women performed in Indian cultures. Only in recent years has scholarly attention come to bear on the world of Indian women, focusing most frequently on material culture.

Because of the biased nature of early reporting, two stereotypes about Indian women developed. First, Euro-Americans saw women engaged in such day-to-day activities as farming, trading, and providing food for the household. These observers saw Indian women as beasts of burden, acting as nothing more than servants to their husbands, who spent the day loafing or hunting. This stereotype confirmed the Euro-American idea that Indian males exploited their women and that Indian peoples were uncivilized. Thus, Europeans had many misconceptions about Indian gender roles since Indian males did not engage in farming activities. Second, those seeking to romanticize Indian cultures wrote of the "dusky Indian princess, unbound by polite culture." For this stereotype, Indian women provided easy comfort for European invaders and often risked their lives for their white lovers, the mythic story of **Pocahontas** being the most well-known example. Thus, Indian women have been confined to two easy categories: the "squaw," exploited by her husband, or the "maiden," who existed for the sexual pleasure of any man in her life, but most especially Euro-American men.

Because of these stereotypes, the roles of Indian women have been misunderstood. In diplomacy, women played and continue to play important roles. Women like Pocahontas and Molly Brant—sister to **Joseph Brant**—during the colonial period and **Wilma Mankiller** and **Winona LaDuke** today have been successful intermediaries between rival powers. Women were also important to the social relations of the tribe, and most Indian cultures were matrilineal. However, in the United States, federal courts have ignored the matrilineal past of Indian societies and imposed patrilineal kinship definitions on tribes. In recent years, many tribal governments have adopted the imposed patrimony and allowed males to marry non-Indians and enroll their children as "Indians." At the same time, female members who marry outside the tribe are unable to register their children as tribal members.

The Supreme Court case *Santa Clara Pueblo v. Martinez* (1978) forced the United States to take a stand on who constitutes a registered member of a tribal group. In the case, Julia Martinez, a Santa Clara Pueblo, wished to leave her house to her daughters, thus fulfilling the traditional customs of the matrilineal people. The tribal council opposed her decision, noting that she was married to a Navajo man; therefore, her children were Navajo and not members of the Santa Clara Pueblo. Tribal officials stated that their position was based on the concept of Indian sovereignty and that the tribal council reserved the right to determine who was a member of the Pueblos. In response, Martinez argued that the tribal council was using an imposed and therefore colonial concept to determine tribal membership. The court sided with the tribe, underscoring the fact that matrilineal descent is rarely recognized by policymakers and those who make Indian **law**.

However, it is possible for present-day scholars to understand the role of Indian women and overcome the stereotypes that have colored our view. It is possible to gain information about the historic roles of Indian women from tribal ethnographic profiles, linguistic studies, and even aspects of material culture. All of these research avenues remain fertile ground for those seeking to understand the differing status of men and women in Indian cultures. Going beyond the categories of "maiden" and "squaw" would return Indian women to their rightful place in Indian cultures and correct centuries of misrepresentation of their roles. Across North America, Indian men and women seemed to value the contributions of the other to the tribal whole; their roles were complimentary and provided for stable community life and mutual affection.

With such varied cultural roles and norms, it would be hard to generalize the role Indian women played in their societies. Indian women are often seen as the caretakers of children and are charged with passing on cultural knowledge. However, many modern women who have earned advanced degrees must negotiate the terrain that comes from this role. Many Indian women face pressure to "work for their people," "to take from both worlds," or "to raise their children the Indian way." Indian women continue to be seen as cultural brokers. Other Indian women have become active in the larger women's rights movement in the United States. Still other Indian women argue that their primary concern is community survival and that Indian female activists have no place in the larger women's rights agenda. These complex roles and arguments cannot be easily summarized or forced into a single theme. Like women everywhere, Indian women are complex individuals who play many roles.

The actions of both modern and historic Indian women demonstrate the pervasive influence of women in Indian societies; all corners of tribal life were affected. Today, women continue to renew and revitalize Indian communities in creative and lasting ways. *See also* AQUASH, ANNE MAE PICTOU; BONNIN, GERTRUDE SIMMONS (AKA ZITKALA-SA); BRAVE BIRD, MARY (AKA MARY CROW DOG); BRONSON, RUTH MUSKRAT; DEER, ADA; FIRE THUNDER, CECILIA; HARRIS, LADONNA; PETERSON, HELEN; SACAJAWEA; SAINTE-MARIE, BUFFY.

WOMEN OF ALL RED NATIONS (WARN). Founded in 1974 by female Indian activists Lorelei Means, Madonna Thunderhawk, and Phyllis Young, WARN was dedicated to ending police brutality and granting full civil rights to all Indian people. As part of the **American Indian Movement (AIM)**, WARN realized that violence was often directed at male protesters, while female protesters were left alone and unscathed. The organization continues to advocate major issues affecting Indian women and incarcerated Native American men. *See also* WOMEN.

WOMEN'S NATIONAL INDIAN ASSOCIATION. The Women's National Indian Association was founded in 1879 in Philadelphia,

Pennsylvania, under the direction of Amelia Quinton. The association, like many of the "Friends of the Indian" groups of the era, supported the allotment policies of the time. However, the association's efforts were aimed at **education**. It petitioned Congress for more Indian schools and improved instruction. It advocated U.S. citizenship for Indians and lobbied the government to honor all treaty obligations.

The Women's National Indian Association ended its career in the early 1950s with mixed results. The association was able to increase the number of schools available to Indians, but quality instruction continued to be a problem. The association made little headway in getting the government to honor all of its treaty obligations to Indians. The organization was so closely linked with the **Dawes Severalty Act** of 1887 that when politicians reversed their decision on the efficacy of the act, the organization lost all credibility. *See also* WOMEN.

WOUNDED KNEE II. As the 1970s began, discontent with **reservation** conditions and Tribal Chairman Richard Wilson at Pine Ridge Indian Reservation in South Dakota became more intense. The impoverished reservation suffered from high unemployment and disturbing health, **education**, and other basic needs. Many Oglala Lakota accused chairman Wilson of being involved in corrupt activities and ordering violent actions against those who opposed him. **Russell Means** and the **American Indian Movement (AIM)** supported the charges against Wilson, who despised Means and AIM, and accusations and heated confrontations continued to escalate.

The **Oglala Sioux Civil Rights Organization**, an organization opposed to Wilson's administration, solicited AIM's support in its push to bring about needed changes. Some Lakota **women** believed action should be taken and suggested occupying the symbolic site of Wounded Knee, where in December 1890 federal troops tragically killed men, women, and children in their campaign to suppress the **Ghost Dance**. On 28 February 1973, Means, **Dennis Banks**, and other activists occupied the hamlet of Wounded Knee.

For the next 71 days, the nation witnessed an armed standoff between the occupiers and more than 200 Federal Bureau of Investigation (FBI) agents, U.S. marshals, **Bureau of Indian Affairs (BIA)** police, and Wilson supporters. The federal forces employed helicopters, airplanes, machine guns, armored personnel carriers, and other assault equipment. The occupiers at Wounded Knee lacked such firepower and had mostly hunting rifles. Estimates of the number of occupiers vary, but no more than about 200 people were there at any given time, and Indians frequently moved in and out of the site in spite of the perimeter established by the FBI. All told, estimates as high as 2,000 occupiers—mostly Native Americans—participated in the takeover. Firefights were commonplace, and remarkably, only two occupiers were killed. Those supporting the movement delivered food and other supplies to the occupiers.

Wounded Knee II became a major media event that the occupiers hoped would benefit their demands of getting rid of the Richard Wilson administration, reviewing treaty violations against the Sioux Nation and BIA activities, and replacing the tribal government at Pine Ridge with a traditional one. However, many believed that the standoff lasted too long, resulting in waning media coverage. Most Americans, who were later polled, expressed their support for AIM's occupation and sympathy toward the way in which Indians had been mistreated. The siege finally ended through negotiations. Federal officials agreed to investigate conditions at Pine Ridge as well as treaty issues. The occupiers were promised fair treatment concerning their participation in the takeover. Conditions at Pine Ridge continued to be confrontational, and the Wilson administration remained in power. Several of the occupiers stood trial, most notably Means and Banks, who were found not guilty because of several FBI illegal actions during the trial.

WOVOKA (c. 1856–1932). Famous as the Northern Paiute founder of the 1890 **Ghost Dance**, Wovoka's life was more than that of a prophet. Wovoka's father, Numuraivo'o, was imprisoned for his actions during the 1875 Bannock War, after which he, like many Paiutes, was shipped to the Malhuer Agency in eastern Oregon. Returning to the Walker River Indian Reservation in Nevada, he was said to be bulletproof and able to make rain. Wovoka's mother, Teeya, was described as intelligent, and contemporary accounts state that she was a great influence on her children, especially Wovoka.

According to Wovoka, he had a fever while he was gathering firewood in the Pine Grove Hills during a solar eclipse. It was here that he fell "dead" and received his great vision. In his vision, he entered heaven, where he saw all of his dead ancestors and received a personal message from God. Abstain from fighting, work with the white men, and dance the round dance were God's instructions. If Wovoka agreed, he and all Indians would receive great rewards in the next life. Wovoka was also given special powers from God: He was granted control over natural elements and made copresident of the United States. Returning to Earth, Wovoka reported his vision and little occurred.

The start of the Ghost Dance came during the 1889 and 1890 droughts that plagued his parched Nevada **reservation**. Wovoka, demonstrating his newly acquired powers, successfully predicted rain. He continued to amass followers by performing a series of miracles, including turning the Walker River to ice on a summer day, making ice fall out of a cottonwood tree, and reentering heaven in public via a trance. Once word spread of the prophet's numerous feats, it was not long until he was receiving visitors from across the nation.

The most famous visitors were the two Lakotas, Kicking Bear and Short Bull, who visited Wovoka after hearing reports of a messiah who promised Indians a new life. Their interpretation of Wovoka's message involved the destruction of whites and the resurrection of the Indian dead, along with a return of the buffalo and traditional Indian ways. Their interpretation was more in line with the teachings of **Neolin** and the **Shawnee Prophet** than with the teachings of Wovoka. The Ghost Dance messiah continued to entertain visitors and offer his message of cooperation with the whites in this world for the rewards that would come in the next life.

In the years following the arrival of the Lakotas, Wovoka found himself discredited by whites as a fraud, subjected to violence by his own Paiute people, and later crushed by news of the massacre at Wounded Knee—a direct result of Kicking Bear and Short Bull's interpretation of his message. Wovoka stopped receiving visitors and talking about his vision. For the rest of his life, the messiah supported himself by selling eagle and magpie feathers and ten-gallon Stetsons, all sacred Ghost Dance items. However, he never again offered up his message to Indian people.

Wovoka was more than the messiah of the Ghost Dance. He was also known as Jack Wilson. His name was taken from the family name of the first white settlers of the Mason Valley in Nevada, David and Abigail Wilson. As a young man, Wovoka was raised on the Wilson's ranch and developed a close relationship with their sons. In fact, it was while cutting wood with the Wilsons that he received his great vision. Thus, he was a man with two worldviews, comfortable with both Indians and whites. In the early years of the 20th century, Wovoka attempted to obtain land and was twice turned down by the U.S. federal government. He failed to receive an allotment in 1912, when the rest of the Walker River Paiutes received land. In May 1916, his claim to a five-acre plot on the Wilson ranch resulted in the Wilson's claiming that they only allowed him to use the land; he never held title to the plot.

In 1916, Wovoka also attempted to utilize the other power given to him by God: the copresidency. Reports circulated across the reservation that Wovoka was going to assist President Woodrow Wilson in World War I by freezing the Atlantic Ocean and sending an Indian army over the ice to fight the Germans. Wovoka was never far from American politics. He was active in the local temperance societies, took part in Warren G. Harding's presidential campaign, and even sent a telegram to Charles Curtis, President Herbert Hoover's Kaw Indian vice president, to congratulate him on his position and extend the hope that one day Curtis would be president of the United States. Wovoka died on 29 September 1932 from prostate cystitis. Three months later an earthquake shook the Mason Valley, something Wovoka predicted would happen upon his death. Although best remembered for his role as leader of the Ghost Dance, Wovoka was a man of conviction and sentiment and attempted to chart a new course for all Indian people.

– Z –

ZITKALA-SA. *See* BONNIN, GERTRUDE SIMMONS (AKA ZITKALA-SA).

Appendix: Indian Voices from Native American Movements

PONTIAC: *YOU MUST LIFT THE HATCHET AGAINST THEM,* 27 APRIL 1763

A Delaware Indian conceived an eager desire to learn wisdom from the Master of Life; but, being ignorant where to find him, he had recourse to fasting, dreaming, and magical incantations. By these means it was revealed to him, that, by moving forward in a straight, undeviating course, he would reach the abode of the Great Spirit. He told his purpose to no one, and having provided the equipments of a hunter—gun, powder-horn, ammunition, and a kettle for preparing his food—he set out on his errand. For some time he journeyed on in high hope and confidence. On the evening of the eighth day, he stopped by the side of a brook at the edge of a meadow, where he began to make ready his evening meal, when, looking up, he saw three well-beaten paths which entered them. He was much surprised; but his wonder increased, when, after it had grown dark, the three paths were more clearly visible than ever. Remembering the important object of his journey, he could neither rest nor sleep; and, leaving his fire, he crossed the meadow, and entered the largest of the three openings. He had advanced but a short distance into the forest, when a bright flame sprang out of the ground before him, and arrested his steps. In great amazement, he turned back, and entered the second path, where the same wonderful phenomenon again encountered him; and now, in terror and bewilderment, yet still resolved to persevere, he took the last of the three paths. On this he journeyed a whole day without interruption, when at length, emerging from the forest, he saw before him a vast mountain, of dazzling whiteness. So precipitous was the ascent that the Indian thought it hopeless to go farther, and looked around him in despair; at that moment, he saw, seated at some distance above, the figure of a beautiful woman arrayed in white, who arose as he looked upon her, and thus accosted him:

"How can you hope, encumbered as you are, to succeed in your design? Go down to the foot of the mountain, throw away your gun, your ammunition, your provisions, and your clothing; wash yourself in the stream which flows there, and you will then prepared to stand before the Master of Life."

The Indian obeyed, and again began to ascend among the rocks, while the woman, seeing him still discouraged, laughed at his faintness of heart, and told him that, if he wished for success, he must climb by the aid of one hand and one foot only. After great toil and suffering, he at length found himself at the summit. The woman had disappeared, and he was left alone. A rich and beautiful plain lay before him, and at a little distance he saw three great villages, far superior to the squalid wigwams of the Delawares. As he approached the largest, and stood hesitating whether he should enter, a man gorgeously attired stepped forth, and taking him by the hand, welcomed him to the celestial abode. He then conducted him into the presence of the Great Spirit, where the Indian stood confounded at the unspeakable splendor which surrounded him. The Great Spirit bade him be seated, and thus addressed him:

"I am the Maker of heaven and earth, the trees, lakes, rivers, and all things else. I am the Maker of mankind; and because I love you, you must do my will. The land on which you live I have made for you, and not for others. Why do you suffer the white men to dwell among you? My children, you have forgotten the customs and traditions of your forefathers. Why do you not clothe yourselves in skins, as they did, and use the bows and arrows, and the stone-pointed lances, which they used? You have bought guns, knives, kettles, and blankets, from the white men, until you can no longer do without them; and, what is worse, you have drunk the poison fire-water, which turns you into fools. Fling all these things away; live as your wise forefathers lived before you. And as for these English—these dogs dressed in red, who have come to rob you of your hunting grounds, and drive away the game—you must lift the hatchet against them. Wipe them from the face of the earth, and then you will win my favor back again, and once more be happy and prosperous. The children of your great father, the King of France, are not like the English. Never forget that they are your brethren. They are very dear to me, for they love the red men, and understand the true mode of worshipping me."

Source: Vanderwerth, W. C. *Indian Oratory: Famous Speeches by Noted Indian Chieftains.* Norman: University of Oklahoma Press, 1971, 26–28.

TECUMSEH: SPEECH TO COLONEL HENRY PROCTOR, 18 SEPTEMBER 1813

Father, listen to your children! You have them now all before you.

The war before this, our British father gave the hatchet to his red children, when our old chiefs were alive. They are now dead. In the war, our father was thrown on his back by the Americans, and our father took them by the hand without our knowledge; and we are afraid that our father will do so again this time.

Summer before last, when I came forward with my red brethren, and was ready to take up the hatchet in favor of our British father, we were told not to be in a hurry—that he had not yet determined to fight the Americans.

Listen! When war was declared, our father stood up and gave us the tomahawk and told us that he was then ready to strike the Americans— that he wanted our assistance; and that he would certainly get our lands back, which the Americans had taken from us.

Listen! You told us, at that time, to bring forward our families to this place—we did so; and you promised to take care of them, and they should want for nothing, while the men would go out and fight enemy—that we need not trouble ourselves about the enemy's garrisons— that we knew nothing about them, and that our father would attend to that part of the business. You also told your red children that you would take good care of your garrison here, which made our hearts glad.

Listen! When we were last at the Rapids it is true we gave you little assistance. It is hard to fight people who live like ground-hogs.

Father, listen! Our fleet has gone out. We know they have fought. We have heard the great guns, but we know nothing of what has happened to our father with that arm. Our ships have gone one way, and we are much astonished to see our father tying up everything and preparing to run away the other, without letting his red children know what his intentions are. You always told us to remain here and take care of our lands. It made our hearts glad to hear that was your wish. Our great father, the king, is the head, and you represent him. You always told us that you would never draw your foot off British ground; but now, father, we see you are drawing back, and we are sorry to see our father doing so without seeing the enemy. We must compare our father's conduct to a fat dog, that carries its tail upon its back, but when affrighted, it drops it between its legs and runs off.

Listen, Father! The Americans have not yet defeated us by land. Neither are we sure that they have done so by water. We therefore wish to remain here and fight our enemy, should they make their appearance. If they defeat us, we will then retreat with our father.

At the battle of the Rapids, last war, the Americans certainly defeated us, and when we retreated to our father's fort at that place the gates were shut against us. We were afraid that it would now be the case; but instead of that, we now see our British father preparing to march out of his garrison.

Father! You have got the arms and ammunition which our great father sent for his red children. If you have an idea of going away, give them to us, and you may go and welcome for us. Our lives are in the hands of the Great Spirit. We are determined to defend our lands, and if it be his will, we wish to leave our bones upon them.

Source: Richardson, John. *War of 1812.* Brockville: Canada West, 1842, 119–20.

CRAZY HORSE: *WE PREFERRED OUR OWN WAY OF LIVING,* 5 SEPTEMBER 1877

My friend, I do not blame you for this. Had I listened to you this trouble would not have happened to me. I was not hostile to the white men. Sometimes my young men would attack the Indians who were their enemies and took their ponies. They did it in return.

We had buffalo for food, and their hides for clothing and for our teepees. We preferred hunting to a life of idleness on the reservation, where we were driven against our will. At times we did not get enough to eat, and we were not allowed to leave the reservation to hunt.

We preferred our own way of living. We were no expense to the government. All we wanted was peace and to be left alone. Soldiers were sent out in the winter, who destroyed our villages.

Then "Long Hair" (Custer) came in the same way. They say we massacred him, but he would have done the same thing to us had we not defended ourselves and fought to the last. Our first impulse was to escape with our squaws and papooses, but we were so hemmed in that we had to fight.

After that I went up on the Tongue River with a few of my people and lived in peace. But the government would not let me alone. Finally, I came back to the Red Cloud Agency. Yet I was not allowed to remain quiet.

I was tired of fighting. I went to the Spotted Tail Agency and asked that chief and his agent to let me live there in peace. I came here with the agent (Lee) to talk with the Big White Chief but was not given a chance. They tried to confine me. I tried to escape, and a soldier ran his bayonet into me.

I have spoken.

Source: Vanderwerth, W. C. *Indian Oratory: Famous Speeches by Noted Indian Chieftains.* Norman: University of Oklahoma Press, 1971, 216–17.

CLYDE WARRIOR: *WE ARE NOT FREE,* FROM TESTIMONY BEFORE THE PRESIDENT'S NATIONAL ADVISORY COMMISSION ON RURAL POVERTY, 2 FEBRUARY 1967

Most members of the National Indian Youth Council can remember when we were children and spent many hours at the feet of our grandfathers listening to stories of the time when the Indians were a great people, when we were free, when we were rich, when we lived the good life. At the same time we heard stories of droughts, famines, and pestilence. It was only recently that we realized that there was surely great material deprivation in those days, but that our old people felt rich because they were free. They were rich in things of the spirit, but if there is one thing that characterizes Indian life today it is poverty of the spirit. We still have human passions and depth of feeling (which may be something rare in these days), but we are poor in spirit because we are not free—free in the most basic sense of the word. We are not allowed to make these basic human choices and decisions about our personal life and about the destiny of our communities which is the mark of free mature people.

We sit on our front porches or in our yards, and the world and our lives in it pass us by without our desires or aspirations having any effect. We are not free. We do not make choices. Our choices are made for us; we are the poor. For those of us who live on reservations these choices and decisions are made by federal administrators, bureaucrats, and their "yes men," euphemistically called tribal governments. Those of us who live in nonreservation areas have our lives controlled by local white power elites. We have many rulers. They are called social workers, "cops," school teachers, churches, etc., and now OEO employees. They call us into meetings to tell us what is good for us and how they've programmed us, or they come into our homes to instruct us and their manners are not always what one would call polite by Indian standards or perhaps by any standards. We are rarely accorded respect as fellow human beings. Our children come home from school to us with shame in their hearts and a sneer on their lips for their home and parents. We are the "poverty problem," and that is true; and perhaps it is also true that our lack of reasonable choices, our lack of freedom, our poverty of spirit is not unconnected with our material poverty.

The National Indian Youth Council realizes there is a great struggle going on in America now between those who want more "local" control of programs and those who would keep the power and the purse strings in the hands of the federal government. We are unconcerned with that struggle because we know that no one is arguing that the dispossessed, the poor, be given any control over their own destiny. The local white power elites who protest the loudest against federal control are the very ones who would keep us poor in spirit and worldly goods in order to enhance their own personal and economic station in the world. Nor have those of us on reservations fared any better under the paternalistic control of federal administrations. In fact, we shudder at the specter of what seems to be the forming alliances in Indian areas between federal administrators and local elites.

Some of us fear that this is the shape of things to come in the War on Poverty effort. Certainly, it is in those areas where such an alliance is taking place that the poverty program seems to be "working well." That is to say, it is in those areas of the country where the federal government is getting the least "static" and where federal money is being used to bolster the local power structure and local institutions. By "everybody being satisfied," I mean the people who count and the Indian or poor does not count.

Fifty years ago the federal government came into our communities and by force carried most of our children away to distant boarding schools. My father and many of my generation lived their childhoods in an almost prisonlike atmosphere. Many returned unable even to speak their own language. Some returned to become drunks. Most of them had become white haters or that most pathetic of all modern Indians—Indian haters. Very few ever became more than very confused, ambivalent, and immobilized individuals—never able to reconcile the tensions and contradictions built inside themselves by outside institutions. As you can imagine, we have little faith in such kinds of federal programs devised for our betterment nor do we see education as a panacea for all ills.

In recent days, however, some of us have been thinking that perhaps the damage done to our communities by forced assimilation and directed acculturative programs was minor compared to the situation in which our children now find themselves. There is a whole generation of Indian children who are growing up in the American school system. They still look to their relatives, my generation, and my father's to see if they are worthy people. But their judgment and definition of what is worthy is now the judgment most Americans make. Our children are learning that their people are not worthy and thus that they individually are not worthy. Even if by some stroke of good fortune, prosperity was handed to us "on a platter" that still would not soften the negative judgment our youngsters have of their people and themselves. As you know, people who feel themselves to be unworthy and feel they cannot escape this unworthiness turn to drink and crime and self-destructive acts. Unless there is some way that we as Indian individuals and communities can prove ourselves competent and worthy in the eyes of our youngsters there will be a generation of Indians grow to adulthood whose reaction to their situation will make previous social ills seem like a Sunday school picnic.

For the sake of our children, for the sake of the spiritual and material well-being of our total community we must be able to demonstrate competence to ourselves. For the sake of our psychic stability as well as our physical well-being we must be free men and exercise free choices. We must make decisions about our own destinies. We must be able to learn and profit by our own mistakes. Only then can we become competent and prosperous communities. We must be free in the most literal sense of the word—not sold or coerced into accepting programs for our own good, not of our own making or choice.

Community development must be just what the word implies, community development. It cannot be packaged programs wheeled into Indian communities by outsiders which Indians can "buy" or once again brand themselves as unprogressive if they do not "cooperate." Even the best of outside programs suffer from one very large defect—if the program falters helpful outsiders too often step in to smooth over the rough spots. At that point any program ceases to belong to the people involved and ceases to be a learning experience for them. Programs must be Indian creations, Indian choices, Indian experiences. Even the failures must be Indian experiences because only then will Indians understand why a program failed and not blame themselves for some personal inadequacy. Indians must be free in the sense that other more prosperous Americans are free. Freedom and prosperity are different sides of the same coin and there can be no freedom without complete responsibility. And I do not mean the fictional responsibility and democracy of passive consumers or programs; programs which emanate from and whose responsibility for success rests in the hands of outsiders—be they federal administrators or local white elitist groups.

Many of our young people are captivated by the lure of the American city with its excitement and promise of unlimited opportunity. But even if educated they come from powerless and inexperienced communities and many times carry with them a strong sense of unworthiness. For many of them the promise of opportunity ends in the gutter on the skid rows of Los Angeles and Chicago. They should and must be given a better chance to take advantage of the opportunities they have. They must grow up in a decent community with a strong sense of personal adequacy and competence.

America cannot afford to have whole areas and communities of people in such dire social and economic circumstances. Not only for her economic well-being, but for her moral well-being as well. America has given a great social and moral message to the world and demonstrated (perhaps not forcefully enough) that freedom and responsibility as an ethic is inseparable from and, in fact, the "cause" of the fabulous American standard of living. America has not however been diligent enough in promulgating this philosophy within her own borders. American Indians need to be given this freedom and responsibility which most American assume as their birth right. Only then will poverty and powerlessness cease to hang like the sword of Damocles over our heads stifling us. Only then can we enjoy the fruits of the American system and become participating citizens—Indian Americans rather than American Indians.

Perhaps, the National Indian Youth Council's real criticism is against a structure created by bureaucratic administrators who are caught in this American myth that all people assimilate into American society, that economics dictates assimilation and integration. From the experience of the National Indian Youth Council, and in reality, we cannot emphasize and recommend strongly enough the fact that no one integrates and disappears into American society. What ethnic groups do is not integrate into American society and economy individually, but enter into the mainstream of American society as a people, and in particular as communities of people. The solution to Indian poverty is not "government programs" but in the competence of the person and his people. The real solution to poverty is encouraging the competence of the community as a whole.

The National Indian Youth Council recommends for "openers" that to really give these people "the poor, the dispossessed, the Indians," complete freedom and responsibility is to let it become a reality not a much-heard-about dream and let the poor decide for once, what is best for themselves.

We recommend that funds or subsidy whatever it's called be provided for indigent tribes and communities so that they themselves decide what they would like to do and what they deem best for their community. Of course, we realize within the present structure this is not possible. So we further recommend that another avenue of thought be tried, such as junking the present structure and creating another, since it is typical of bureaucratic societies that when one takes upon himself to improve a situation, one immediately, unknowingly, falls into a structure of thinking that in order to improve any situation you take the existing avenues of so-called improvement and reinforce the existing condition, thereby reinforcing and strengthening the ills that are implicit in the very structure of that society.

Source: Rural Poverty: Hearings before the National Advisory Committee on Rural Poverty, Memphis, Tennessee. Washington, D.C.: Government Printing Office, 1967, 144–47.

PROCLAMATION: TO THE GREAT WHITE FATHER
AND ALL HIS PEOPLE, 20 NOVEMBER 1969

We, the Native Americans, reclaim the land known as Alcatraz Island in the name of all American Indians *by right of discovery.* We wish to be fair and honorable in our dealings with the Caucasian inhabitants of this land, and hereby offer the following treaty: We will purchase said Alcatraz Island for 24 dollars ($24) in glass beads and red cloth, a precedent set by the white man's purchase of a similar island about 300 years ago. We know that $24 in trade goods for these 16 acres is more than was paid when Manhattan Island was sold, but we know that land values have risen over the years. Our offer of $1.24 per acre is greater than the 47¢ per acre the white men are now paying the California Indians for their land. We will give to the inhabitants of this land a portion of that land for their own, to be held in trust by the American Indian Government—for as long as the sun shall rise and the rivers go down to the sea—to be administered by the Bureau of Caucasian Affairs (BCA). We will further guide the inhabitants in the proper way of living. We will offer them our religion, our education, our lifeways, in order to help them achieve our level of civilization and thus raise them and all their white brothers up from their savage and unhappy state. We offer this treaty in good faith and wish to be fair and honorable in our dealings with all white men.

We feel that this so-called Alcatraz Island is more than suitable as an Indian Reservation, as determined by the white man's own standards. By this we mean that this place resembles most Indian reservations, in that:

1. It is isolated from modern facilities, and without adequate means of transportation.
2. It has no fresh running water.
3. The sanitation facilities are inadequate.
4. There are no oil or mineral rights.

5. There is no industry and so unemployment is very great.
6. There are no health care facilities.
7. The soil is rocky and nonproductive, and the land does not support game.
8. There are no educational facilities.
9. The population has always been held as prisoners and kept dependent upon others.

Further, it would be fitting and symbolic that ships from all over the world, entering the Golden Gate, would first see Indian land, and thus be reminded of the true history of this nation. This tiny island would be a symbol of the great lands once ruled by free and noble Indians.

Source: Indians of All Tribes *Alcatraz File.* Los Angeles: University of California at Los Angeles, American Indian Studies Center Library.

A SUMMARY OF THE TWENTY POINTS, 31 OCTOBER 1972

1. Restoration of Constitutional Treaty-Making Authority: This would force federal recognition of each Indian nation's sovereignty.
2. Establishment of a Treaty Commission to Make New Treaties: Reestablishes all existing treaties, affirms a national commitment to the future of Indian people, and ensures that all Indians are governed by treaty relations without exception.
3. An Address to the American People and Joint Sessions of Congress: This would allow us to state our political and cultural cases to the whole nation on television.
4. Commission to Review Treaty Commitments and Violations: Treaty-based lawsuits had cost Indian people more than $40 million in the last decade alone, yet Indian people remain virtual prisoners in the nation's courtrooms, being forced constantly to define our rights. There is less need for more attorney assistance than for an institution of protections that reduce violations and minimize the possibilities for attacks on Indian rights.
5. Resubmission of Unratified Treaties to the Senate: Many nations, especially those in California, have made treaties that were never ratified. Treaty status should be formalized for every nation.

6. All Indians to Be Governed by Treaty Relations: Covers any exceptions to points 1, 2, and 5.
7. Mandatory Relief against Treaty Violations: Federal courts to automatically issue injunctions against non-Indians who violate treaties, eliminating costly legal delays.
8. Judicial Recognition of Indian Right to Interpret Treaties: A new law requiring the U.S. Supreme Court to hear Indian appeals arising from treaty violations.
9. Creation of Congressional Joint Committee on Reconstruction of Indian Relations: Reconfigurement of all committees dealing with Indian affairs into a single entity.
10. Land Reform and Restoration of a 110-Million-Acre Native Land Base: Termination of all Indian land leases, reversion of all non-Indian titles to land on reservations, consolidation of all reservation natural resources under local Indian control.
11. Restoration of Rights to Indians Terminated by Enrollment and Revocation of Prohibition against "Dual Benefits": An end to minimum standards of "tribal blood" for citizenship in any Indian nation, which serves to keep people with mixed Indian ancestors from claiming either heritage.
12. Repeal of State Laws Enacted under Public Law 280: Eliminates all state powers over Indians, thereby ending disputes over jurisdiction and sovereignty.
13. Resume Federal Protective Jurisdiction over Offenses against Indians: Since state and local courts have rarely been able to convict non-Indians of crimes against Indians, Indian grand juries should have the power to indict violators, who will then be tried in federal courts.
14. Abolition of the Bureau of Indian Affairs: The BIA is so much a prisoner of its past that it can never be expected to meet the needs of Indians. Better to start over with an organization designed to meet requirements of new treaties.
15. Creation of an Office of Federal Indian Relations and Community Reconstruction: With 1,000 employees or fewer, this agency would report directly to the president and preserve equality between Indian nations and the federal government.
16. Priorities and Purpose of the Proposed New Office: The previous agency would address the breakdown in the constitutionally pre-

scribed relationship between the United States and the Indian nations.

17. Indian Commerce and Tax Immunities: Eliminate constant struggles between Indian nations and the states over taxation by removing states' authority for taxation on reservations.

18. Protection of Indian Religious Freedom and Cultural Integrity: Legal protection must be extended to Indian religious expression and existing statutes do not do this.

19. National Referendums, Local Options, and Forms of Indian Organizations: An appeal to restrict the number of Indian organizations and to consolidate leadership at every level.

20. Health, Housing, Employment, Economic Development, and Education: Increased funding, better management, and local control.

Source: Means, Russell, with Marvin J. Wolf. *Where White Men Fear to Tread: The Autobiography of Russell Means.* New York: St. Martin's Press, 1995, 228–30.

Bibliography

CONTENTS

I. INTRODUCTION

The bibliography for a work of this nature could potentially fill its own volume. Works concerning Native Americans began to appear as soon as Europeans landed in the New World. What follows is a selection of what have been considered the best or most useful works on the history, anthropology, law, customs, and other aspects of Indian life. While the list is in no way exhaustive, the authors believe that these works are those that need to be consulted to begin further investigation into any of the various topics of American Indian life and culture.

Much of the early written history of American Indians evolved out of James Fenimore Cooper's "Leatherstocking Tales," a series of novels that presented Indians as "noble savages." Others interested in the history of Native America had their own agendas that colored their work. Early practitioners saw Indians as an obstacle to civilization, an ever-retreating group just one step ahead of destruction. The famous essay, "The Significance of the Frontier in American History," written by Fredrick Jackson Turner in 1893, solidified among historians the popular idea that Indians were on the brink of vanishing from the nation.

Still others treated Indians as "savages" in their work, presenting them as barbarous creatures of nature akin to wild animals—most frequently wolves. These early historical conceptions of Indians were nearly always the province of white writers, and as such, modern readers should view the history of authors like Francis Parkman with some skepticism.

More modern historical writing has sought to overcome the stereotyping of its predecessors. However, more recent scholars have entered into another debate that will forever haunt Indian history. Such white scholars engaged in Indian history as Francis Paul Prucha, William Hagan, Robert Utley, Colin G. Calloway, and others have established themselves as some of the top experts in the field. Despite their careers, the works of non-Indian authors have come under scrutiny in recent years by those who call these scholars "outsiders" and "pretenders" who exploit Indian people for their own benefit. Since the 1960s, a number of Indian scholars have begun creating academic and narrative history. Such historians as D'Arcy McNickle, Vine Deloria Jr., Donald L. Fixico, and R. David Edmunds present Indian history through the eyes of the insider— one comfortable with the culture they are studying.

This Indian versus non-Indian history debate is purely academic, and the general reader should give little credence to it. Rather, general readers would be best served by beginning their foray into the waters of Indian history with a close read of a few wonderful textbooks written by both Indians and non-Indians. The works of Angie Debo, Arrell Morgan Gibson, Colin G. Calloway, and R. David Edmunds provide an excellent starting point for those seeking to understand the history of Indian America and its various movements.

Important insights and critical evaluations can be found in all of the works listed below, and general readers are advised to proceed almost without direction. Perhaps the best way to come to terms with the variety of literature available on Native Americans is to dive right into the water and allow the various authors to teach them to swim. For those engaged in professional history, it was often one book—perhaps *Bury My Heart at Wounded Knee: An Indian History of the American West*, by Dee Brown, or *Custer Died for Your Sins: An Indian Manifesto*, by Vine Deloria Jr.—that sent us into the pool of Indian history. It was not until later in our careers, when we entered universities and colleges, that we were given the direction necessary to become academic historians. General readers should proceed without caution and jump right in—the water is fine.

The more refined scholar may explore this bibliography and see nothing but what was not included. The lack of inclusion of certain works is not meant as any slight by the authors of this volume. Those scholars engaged in Indian history, art, anthropology, law, and other disciplines know the rigors of compiling a bibliography such as this. Scholars just beginning their careers in Indian history should make fast friends with the staffs at some of the major libraries and collections around the nation. The D'Arcy McNickle Center at the Newberry Library, the Huntington Library, the National Archives and Records Administration, the Western History Collection at the University of Oklahoma, and the Beinecke Library at Yale University all hold material valuable to scholars. There are so many other collections, archives, libraries, and museums that could be listed.

During the 1990s, the Internet became a new source for important issues in the field, and a number of websites have devoted themselves entirely to American Indian issues. This bibliography includes a list of some very important Internet sites, with a warning that URL addresses frequently change. Should an address fail, a search using any one of the many search engines will reveal millions of sites.

Finally, the authors would like to direct those interested in American Indian topics to consult academic journals devoted to Native American history, culture, law, anthropology, and so forth. In addition to this dictionary, a number of guides, encyclopedias, and overviews of the field demonstrate that as a field of scholarly inquiring, American Indian peoples and their movements are being regularly discussed and critiqued. It would be well to think that the days of easy racial categories and stereotypes will be corrected by a close examination of this reference and others like it that attempt to inform readers about the various issues that affect American Indians.

II. GENERAL REFERENCE WORKS

Bonvillain, Nancy. *Native Cultures and Histories of Native North America.* Upper Saddle River, N.J.: Prentice Hall, 2001.

Brown, Dee. *Bury My Heart at Wounded Knee: An Indian History of the American West.* New York: Bantam Books, 1970.

Calloway, Colin G. *First Peoples: A Documentary Survey of American Indian History.* 2nd ed. Boston: Bedford St. Martins, 2004.

Champagne, Duane, ed. *Chronology of Native North America History: From Pre-Columbian Times to the Present.* Detroit, MI: Gale Research, 1994.

——, ed. *Native America: Portrait of the Peoples.* Detroit, MI: Visible Ink Press, 1994.

——, ed., *The Native North American Almanac.* Detroit, MI: Gale Research, 1994.

Davis, Mary B., ed. *Native America in the Twentieth Century: An Encyclopedia.* New York: Garland, 1994.

Deloria, Philip J., and Neal Salisbury. *A Companion to American Indian History.* Malden, MA: Blackwell, 2002.

Dickason, Olivia Patricia. *Canada's First Nations: A History of Founding Peoples from Earliest Times.* Norman: University of Oklahoma Press, 1992.

Edmunds, R. David, Frederick Hoxie, and Neal Salisbury. *The People: A History of Native America.* Boston: Houghton Mifflin, 2005.

Gibson, Arrell Morgan. *The American Indian: Prehistory to Present.* Lexington, MA: D. C. Heath and Company, 1980.

Hirschfelder, Arlene, and Paulette Molin. *The Encyclopedia of Native American Religions.* New York: Facts on File, 1992.

Hoxie, Frederick, ed. *Encyclopedia of North American Indians: Native American History, Culture, and Life from Paleo-Indians to the Present.* Boston: Houghton Mifflin, 1996.

Hurtado, Albert, and Peter Iverson. *Major Problems in American Indian History.* 2nd ed. Boston: Houghton Mifflin, 2001.

Josephy, Alvin, Jr. *The Native Americans: An Illustrated History.* Atlanta, GA: Turner Publishing, 1992.

Klein, Barry T. *Reference Encyclopedia of the American Indian.* 7th ed. West Nyack, N.Y.: Todd Publications, 1995.

La Potin, Armand S. *Native American Voluntary Organizations.* New York: Greenwood Press, 1987.

Lobo, Susan, and Steve Talbot. *Native American Voices: A Reader.* 2nd ed. New York: Longman, 2001.

Mancall, Peter, and James H. Merrell, eds. *American Encounters: Natives and Newcomers from European Contact to Indian Removal, 1500–1850.* New York: Routledge, 2000.

Maynard, Jill, ed. *Through Indian Eyes: The Untold Story of Native American Peoples.* Pleasantville, N.Y.: Reader's Digest Association, 1996.

McNickle, D'Arcy. *They Came Here First: The Epic of the American Indian.* New York: Harper & Row, 1949.

Nabokov, Peter, ed. *Native American Testimony: A Chronicle of Indian-White Relations from Prophecy to the Present, 1492–1992.* New York: Viking Penguin, 1991.

Nichols, Roger L. *Indians in the United States and Canada: A Comparative History.* Lincoln: University of Nebraska Press, 1998.

Olson, James S. *Encyclopedia of American Indian Civil Rights.* New York: Greenwood Press, 1997.

———. *Historical Dictionary of the Spanish Empire, 1402–1975.* New York: Greenwood Press, 1992.

Perdue, Theda. *Sifters: Native American Women's Lives.* New York: Oxford University Press, 2001.

Pritzker, Barry M. *A Native American Encyclopedia: History, Culture, and Peoples.* New York: Oxford University Press, 2000.

Prucha, Francis Paul. *Atlas of American Indian Affairs.* Lincoln: University of Nebraska Press, 1990.

———. *The Great Father: The United States Government and the American Indians.* 2 vols. Lincoln: University of Nebraska Press, 1984.

Ray, Arthur J. *I Have Lived Here since the World Began: An Illustrated History of Canada's Native People.* Toronto: Lester Publishing/Key Porter Books, 1996.

Shoemaker, Nancy, ed. *American Indians.* Malden, MA: Blackwell, 2001.

Sturtevant, William C., ed. *Handbook of North American Indians.* Washington, D.C.: Smithsonian Institution Press, 1978.

Trafzer, Clifford E. *As Long as the Grass Shall Grow and Rivers Flow: A History of Native Americans.* Fort Worth, TX: Harcourt Brace, 2000.

Trigger, Bruce, and Wilcomb E. Washburn, eds. *North America.* Vol. 1 of *The Cambridge History of the Native Peoples of the Americas.* New York: Cambridge University Press, 1996.

Vanderwerth, W. C. *Indian Oratory: Famous Speeches by Noted Indian Chieftains.* Norman: University of Oklahoma Press, 1971.

Waldman, Carl. *Atlas of the North American Indian.* Rev ed. New York: Checkmark, 2000.

Watkins, Joe. *Indigenous Archaeology: American Indian Values and Scientific Practice.* Walnut Creek, CA: Alta Mira Press, 2000.

Weeks, Philip. *"They Made Us Many Promises": The American Indian Experience, 1524–Present.* 2nd ed. Wheeling, IL: Harlan, 2002.

Wesson, Cameron B. *Historical Dictionary of Early North America.* Metuchen, N.J.: Scarecrow Press, 2005.

Wilson, James. *The Earth Shall Weep: A History of Native America.* New York: Grove Press, 1998.

Woodhead, Henry, ed. *The American Indians.* Alexandria, VA: Time-Life Books, 1992–1996.

III. AMERICA BEFORE THE EUROPEANS

Ames, Kenneth M., and Herbert D. G. Maschner. *Peoples of the Northwest Coast: The Archaeology and Prehistory.* London: Thames & Hudson, 1999.

Cordell, Linda S. *Ancient Pueblo Peoples.* Washington, D.C.: Smithsonian Institution Press, 1994.

Dillehay, Thomas. *The Settlement of the Americas: A New Prehistory.* New York: Basic Books, 2000.

Fagan, Brian. *Ancient North America: The Archaeology of a Continent.* 3rd ed. London: Thames & Hudson, 2000.

———. *The Great Journey: The Peopling of Ancient America.* London: Thames & Hudson, 1987.

Fiedel, Stuart. *Prehistory of the Americas.* New York: Cambridge University Press, 1987.

Haynes, Gary. *The Early Settlement of North America: The Clovis Era.* New York: Cambridge University Press, 2002.

Jennings, Jesse. *Prehistory of North America.* Mountain View, CA: Mayfield, 1989.

———, ed. *Ancient North Americans.* San Francisco: W. H. Freeman, 1983.

Josephy, Alvin M., Jr. *America in 1492.* New York: Alfred A. Knopf, 1992.

Kennedy, Roger. *Hidden Cities: The Discovery and Loss of Ancient North American Civilization.* New York: Penguin, 1994.

Kopper, Philip. *The Smithsonian Book of North American Indians: Before the Coming of the Europeans.* Washington, D.C.: Smithsonian Institution Press, 1986.

Madsen, D. B. *Entering America: Northeast Asia and Beringia before the Last Glacial Maximum.* Salt Lake City: University of Utah Press, 2004.

Plog, Stephen. *Ancient Peoples of the American Southwest.* London: Thames & Hudson, 1997.

Roper, Donna C., and Elizabeth P. Pauls, eds. *Plains Earthlodges: Ethnographic and Archaeological Perspectives.* Tuscaloosa: University of Alabama Press, 2005.

Shaffer, Lynda Norene. *Native America before 1492: The Moundbuilding Centers of the Eastern Woodlands.* Armonk, N.Y.: M. E. Sharpe, 1992.

Stuart, David. *Anasazi America.* Albuquerque: University of New Mexico Press, 2000.

Thomas, David H. *Exploring Native North America.* New York: Oxford University Press, 2000.

Young, Biloine Whiting, and Melvin Fowler. *Cahokia: The Great Native American Metropolis.* Urbana: University of Illinois Press, 2000.

IV. CONTACT AND COLONIAL PERIOD

Bourne, Russell. *The Red King's Rebellion: Racial Politics in New England, 1675–1678.* New York: Oxford University Press, 1990.

Bouvier, Virginia M. *Women and the Conquest of California, 1542–1840.* Tucson: University of Arizona Press, 2001.

Calloway, Colin G. *On Vast Wintercount: The Native American West before Lewis and Clark.* Lincoln: University of Nebraska Press, 2003.

Cave, Alfred. *The Pequot War.* Amherst: University of Massachusetts Press, 1996.

Cronon, William. *Changes in the Land: Indians, Colonists, and the Ecology of New England.* New York: Hill & Wang, 1983.

Crosby, Alfred. *The Columbian Exchange: Biological and Cultural Consequences of 1492.* Westport, CT: Greenwood Press, 1972.

Delage, Denys. *Bitter Feast: Amerindians and Europeans in Northeastern North America.* Vancouver: University of British Columbia Press, 1993.

Drake, James D. *King Philip's War: Civil War in New England.* Amherst: University of Massachusetts Press, 1999.

Gallay, Alan. *The Indian Slave Trade: The Rise of the English Empire in the American South, 1677–1717.* New Haven, CT: Yale University Press, 2002.

Gleach, Frederic W. *Powhatan's World and Colonial Virginia: A Conflict of Cultures.* Lincoln: University of Nebraska Press, 1997.

Henig, David. *Numbers from Nowhere: The American Indian Contact Population Debate.* Norman: University of Oklahoma Press, 1998.

Hudson, Charles. *Knights of New Spain, Warriors of the Sun: Hernando De Soto and the South's Ancient Chiefdoms.* Athens: University of Georgia Press, 1997.

Ingersoll, Thomas N. *To Intermix with Our White Brothers: Indian Mixed Bloods in the United States from Earliest Times to the Indian Removals.* Albuquerque: University of New Mexico Press, 2005.

Jennings, Francis. *The Invasion of America: Indians, Colonialism, and the Cant of Conquest.* New York: W. W. Norton, 1976.

Knaut, Andrew. *The Pueblo Revolt: Conquest and Resistance in Seventeenth Century New Mexico.* Norman: University of Oklahoma Press, 1995.

Kupperman, Karen Ordahl. *Indians and English: Facing Off in Early America.* Ithaca, N.Y.: Cornell University Press, 2000.

Lepore, Jill. *The Name of War: King Philip's War and the Origins of American Identity.* New York: Alfred A. Knopf, 1998.

Mancall, Peter, and James H. Merrell, eds. *American Encounters: European Contact to Indian Removal.* New York: Routledge, 2000.

Milanich, Jared T. *Florida Indians and the Invasion of Europe.* Gainesville: University of Florida Press, 1995.

O'Brien, Greg. *Choctaws in a Revolutionary Age, 1750–1830.* Lincoln: University of Nebraska Press, 2002.

Richter, Daniel K. *Facing East from Indian Country: A Native History of Early America.* Cambridge, MA: Harvard University Press, 2000.

Rountree, Helen C. *Pocahontas's People: The Powhatan Indians of Virginia through Four Centuries.* Norman: University of Oklahoma Press, 1990.

Salisbury, Neal. *Manitou and Providence: Indians, Europeans, and the Making of New England, 1500–1643.* New York: Oxford University Press, 1982.

Steele, Ian K. *Warpaths: Invasions of North America.* New York: Oxford University Press, 1994.

Thornton, Russell. *American Indian Holocaust and Survival: A Population History since 1492.* Norman: University of Oklahoma Press, 1987.

Weber, David J. *The Spanish Frontier in North America.* New Haven, CT: Yale University Press, 1992.

White, Richard. *The Middle Ground: Indians, Empires, and Republics in the Upper Great Lakes, 1650–1815.* New York: Cambridge University Press, 1991.

V. THE 18TH CENTURY

Anderson, Fred. *Crucible of War: The Seven Years' War and the Fate of Empire in British North America.* New York: Alfred A. Knopf, 2000.

Axtell, James. *The Invasion Within: The Contest of Cultures in Colonial North America.* New York: Oxford University Press, 1985.

——. *Natives and Newcomers: The Cultural Origins of North America.* New York: Oxford University Press, 2001.

Calloway, Colin G. *The American Revolution in Indian Country: Crisis and Diversity in Native American Communities.* New York: Cambridge University Press, 1995.

——. *New Worlds for All: Indians, Europeans, and the Remaking of Early America.* Baltimore: Johns Hopkins University Press, 1997.

——. *The World Turned Upside Down: Indian Voices from Early America.* Boston: Bedford Books, 1994.

Clayton, Andrew, and Frederika Teute, eds. *Contact Points: American Frontiers from the Mohawk Valley to the Mississippi, 1750–1830.* Chapel Hill: University of North Carolina Press, 1998.

Dowd, Gregory Evans. *A Spirited Resistance: The North American Indian Struggle for Unity, 1745–1815.* Baltimore: Johns Hopkins University Press, 1992.

——. *War under Heaven: Pontiac, the Indian Nations, and the British Empire.* Baltimore: Johns Hopkins University Press, 2002.

Hinderaker, Eric. *Elusive Empires: Constructing Colonialism in the Ohio Valley, 1673–1800.* New York: Cambridge University Press, 1997.

Mancall, Peter. *Deadly Medicine: Indians and Alcohol in Early America.* Ithaca, N.Y.: Cornell University Press, 1995.

Mandell, Daniel R. *Behind the Frontier: Indians in Eighteenth-Century Eastern Massachusetts.* Lincoln: University of Nebraska Press, 1996.

Merrell, James. *Into the American Woods: Negotiators on the Pennsylvania Frontier.* New York: W. W. Norton, 1999.

Merritt, Jane T. *At the Crossroads: Indians and Empires on a Mid-Atlantic Frontier, 1700–1763.* Chapel Hill: University of North Carolina Press, 2003.

O'Brien, Jean. *Dispossession by Degrees: Indian Land and Identity in Natick, Massachusetts, 1650–1790.* New York: Cambridge University Press, 1997.

Perdue, Theda. *Cherokee Women: Gender and Culture Change, 1700–1835.* Lincoln: University of Nebraska Press, 1998.

Richter, Daniel K. *Ordeal of the Longhouse: The Peoples of the Iroquois League in the Era of European Colonization.* Chapel Hill: University of North Carolina Press, 1992.

Usner, Daniel H. *Indians, Settlers, and Slaves in a Frontier Exchange Economy: The Lower Mississippi Valley before 1783.* Chapel Hill: University of North Carolina Press, 1992.

Wood, Peter, Gregory Waselkov, and M. Thomas Hatley, eds. *Powhatan's Mantle: Indians in the Colonial Southeast.* Lincoln: University of Nebraska Press, 1989.

VI. THE 19TH CENTURY

Akers, Donna L. *Living in the Land of Death: The Choctaw Nation, 1830–1860.* East Lansing: Michigan State University Press, 2004.

Anderson, Gary. *Little Crow: Spokesman for the Sioux.* St. Paul: Minnesota Historical Society Press, 1986.

Ball, Eve. *Indeh: An Apache Odyssey.* Norman: University of Oklahoma Press, 1980.

Barrett, S. M. *Geronimo: His Own Story.* New York: Penguin, 1996.

Calloway, Colin G. *Our Hearts Fell on the Ground: Plains Indians Views of How the West Was Lost.* Boston: Bedford Books, 1996.

Edmunds, R. David. *The Shawnee Prophet.* Lincoln: University of Nebraska Press, 1983.

Fowler, Don D. *A Laboratory for Anthropology: Science and Romanticism in the American Southwest, 1846–1930.* Albuquerque: University of New Mexico Press, 2000.

Greene, Jerome, ed. *Lakota and Cheyenne Indian Views of the Great Sioux War, 1876–1877.* Norman: University of Oklahoma Press, 1994.

Horsman, Reginald. *Expansion and American Indian Policy, 1783–1812*. Norman: University of Oklahoma Press, 1992.

Hoxie, Frederick. *Parading through History: The Making of the Crow Nation in America, 1805–1935*. New York: Cambridge University Press, 1995.

Hurt, R. Douglas. *The Indian Frontier, 1763–1846*. Albuquerque: University of New Mexico Press, 2002.

Isenberg, Andrew C. *The Destruction of the Bison*. New York: Cambridge University Press, 2000.

Jackson, Donald, ed. *Black Hawk: An Autobiography*. Urbana: University of Illinois Press, 1964.

Kehoe, Alice Beck. *The Ghost Dance: Ethnohistory and Revitalization*. 2nd ed. Long Grove, IL: Waveland Press, 2006.

La Vere, David. *Contrary Neighbors: Southern Plains and Removed Indians in Indian Territory*. Norman: University of Oklahoma Press, 2000.

Martin, Joel. *Sacred Revolt: The Muskogee's Struggle for a New World*. Boston: Beacon Press, 1991.

McLoughlin, William G. *Cherokee Renascence in the New Republic*. Princeton, N.J.: Princeton University Press, 1986.

Mooney, James. "The Ghost Dance Religion and the Sioux Outbreak of 1890," *14th Annual Report of the Bureau of American Ethnology*, 1892–1893, part 2. Washington, D.C.: Government Printing Office, 1896.

Moore, John H. *The Cheyenne*. Cambridge, MA: Blackwell, 1996.

Nabokov, Peter. *Two Leggings: The Making of a Crow Warrior*. Lincoln: University of Nebraska Press, 1982.

O'Connell, Barry, ed. *On Our Own Ground: The Complete Writings of William Apess, Pequot*. Amherst: University of Massachusetts Press, 1992.

Perdue, Theda, and Michael Green, eds. *The Cherokee Removal: A Brief History with Documents*. Boston: Bedford Books, 1995.

Robinson, Charles M., III. *A Good Year to Die: The Story of the Great Sioux War*. New York: Random House, 1995.

Ronda, James P. *Lewis and Clark among the Indians*. Lincoln: University of Nebraska Press, 1984.

Sheehan, Bernard. *Seeds of Extinction: Jeffersonian Philanthropy and the American Indian*. Chapel Hill: University of North Carolina Press, 1973.

Stands In Timber, John, and Margot Liberty. *Cheyenne Memories*. Lincoln: University of Nebraska Press, 1972.

Sugden, John. *Blue Jacket: Warrior of the Shawnees*. Lincoln: University of Nebraska Press, 2000.

———. *Tecumseh: A Life*. New York: Henry Holt, 1998.

Utley, Robert. *The Indian Frontier of the American West, 1846–1890*. Albuquerque: University of New Mexico Press, 1984.

——. *The Lance and the Shield: The Life and Times of Sitting Bull.* New York: Henry Holt, 1993.

——. *The Last Days of the Sioux Nation.* New Haven, CT: Yale University Press, 1963.

Wallace, Anthony F. C. *The Death and Rebirth of the Seneca.* New York: Alfred A. Knopf, 1969.

——. *Jefferson and the Indians: The Tragic Fate of the First Americans.* Cambridge, MA: Harvard University Press, 1999.

——. *The Long and Bitter Trail: Andrew Jackson and the Indians.* New York: Hill & Wang, 1993.

West, Elliott. *The Contested Plains: Indians, Goldseekers, and the Rush to Colorado.* Lawrence: University Press of Kansas, 1998.

VII. THE 20TH CENTURY AND BEYOND

Adams, David Wallace. *Education for Extinction: American Indians and the Boarding School Experience, 1875–1928.* Lawrence: University Press of Kansas, 1995.

Ambler, Marjane. *Breaking the Iron Bonds: Indian Control of Energy Development.* Lawrence: University Press of Kansas, 1990.

Archuleta, Margaret, Brenda Child, and K. Tsiannina Lomawaima, eds. *Away from Home: American Indian Boarding School Experiences, 1879–2000.* Phoenix, AZ: The Heard Museum, 2000.

Banks, Dennis, and Richard Erdoes. *Ojibwa Warrior: Dennis Banks and the Rise of the American Indian Movement.* Norman: University of Oklahoma Press, 2004.

Bernstein, Alison. *American Indians and World War II: Toward a New Era in Indian Affairs.* Norman: University of Oklahoma Press, 1990.

Bordewich, Fergus M. *Killing the White Man's Indian: Reinventing Native Americans at the End of the Twentieth Century.* New York: Doubleday, 1996.

Brave Bird, Mary, and Richard Erdoes. *Ohitika Woman.* New York: Grove Press, 1993.

Castile, George P. *Taking Charge: Native American Self-Determination and Federal Indian Policy, 1975–1993.* Tucson: University of Arizona Press, 2006.

——. *To Show Heart: Native American Self-Determination and Federal Indian Policy, 1960–1975.* Tucson: University of Arizona Press, 1998.

Chamberlain, Kathleen P. *Under Sacred Ground: A History of Navajo Oil, 1922–1982.* Albuquerque: University of New Mexico Press, 2000.

Child, Brenda J. *Boarding School Seasons: American Indian Families, 1900–1940*. Lincoln: University of Nebraska Press, 1998.

Cohen, Fay G. *Treaties on Trial: The Continuing Controversy over Northwest Indian Fishing Rights*. Seattle: University of Washington Press, 1986.

Cornell, Stephen. *The Return of the Native: American Indian Political Resurgence*. New York: Oxford University Press, 1988.

Crow Dog, Mary, and Richard Erdoes. *Lakota Woman*. New York: Harper-Collins, 1990.

Deloria, Vine, Jr. *Custer Died for Your Sins: An Indian Manifesto*. New York: Macmillan, 1969.

Deloria, Vine, Jr., and Clifford Lytle. *The Nations Within: The Past and Future of American Indian Sovereignty*. New York: Pantheon, 1984.

Eastman, Charles. *From the Deep Woods to Civilization: Chapters in the Biography of an Indian*. Lincoln: University of Nebraska Press, 1977.

Edmunds, R. David, ed. *The New Warriors: The Past and Future of American Indian Sovereignty*. Lincoln: University of Nebraska Press, 2001.

Eichstaedt, Peter H. *If You Poison Us: Uranium and Native Americans*. Santa Fe, N.M.: Red Crane Books, 1994.

Ellis, Clyde. *A Dancing People: Powwow Culture on the Southern Plains*. Lawrence: University Press of Kansas, 2003.

Fixico, Donald L. *The Invasion of Indian Country in the Twentieth Century: American Capitalism and Tribal Natural Resources*. Niwot: University of Colorado Press, 1998.

——. *Termination and Relocation: Federal Indian Policy, 1945–1960*. Albuquerque: University of New Mexico Press, 1986.

——. *The Urban Indian Experience in America*. Albuquerque: University of New Mexico Press, 2000.

Harring, Sidney. *Crow Dog's Case: American Indian Sovereignty, Tribal Law, and United States Law in the Nineteenth Century*. New York: Cambridge University Press, 1994.

Hoxie, Frederick E. *The Final Promise: The Campaign to Assimilate the Indians, 1888–1920*. Lincoln: University of Nebraska Press, 1984.

——, ed. *Talking Back to Civilization: Indian Voices from the Progressive Era*. Boston: Bedford Books, 2001.

Iverson, Peter. *Carlos Montezuma and the Changing World of American Indians*. Albuquerque: University of New Mexico Press, 1982.

——. *Dine: A History of the Navajos*. Albuquerque: University of New Mexico Press, 2002.

——. *"We Are Still Here": American Indians in the Twentieth Century*. Wheeling, IL: Harlan Davidson, 1998.

——, ed. *"For Our Navajo People": Dine Letters, Speeches, and Petitions, 1900–1960*. Albuquerque: University of New Mexico Press, 2002.

Jaimes, M. Annette, ed. *The State of Native America: Genocide, Colonization, and Resistance*. Boston: South End Press, 1992.

Josephy, Alvin M., Jr. *Now That the Buffalo Are Gone: A Study of Today's American Indians*. Norman: University of Oklahoma Press, 1984.

King, C. Richard, and Charles Fruehling Springwood, eds. *Team Spirits: The Native American Mascot Controversy*. Lincoln: University of Nebraska Press, 2001.

LaDuke, Winona. *All Our Relations: Native Struggles for Land and Life*. Cambridge, MA: South End Press, 1994.

Lawrence, Bonita. *"Real" Indians and Others: Mixed-Blood Urban Native People and Indigenous Nationhood*. Lincoln: University of Nebraska Press, 2004.

Lomawaima, K. Tsianina. *They Called It Prairie Light: The Story of the Chiloco Indian School*. Lincoln: University of Nebraska Press, 1994.

Mason, W. Dale. *Indian Gaming: Tribal Sovereignty and American Politics*. Norman: University of Oklahoma Press, 2000.

McDonnell, Janet A. *The Dispossession of the American Indian, 1887–1934*. Bloomington: Indiana University Press, 1991.

Means, Russell, with Marvin J. Wolf. *Where White Men Fear to Tread: The Autobiography of Russell Means*. New York: St. Martin's Press, 1995.

Meyer, Melissa L. *The White Earth Tragedy: Ethnicity and Dispossession at a Minnesota Anishinaabe Reservation, 1889–1920*. Lincoln: University of Nebraska Press, 1994.

Moses, L. G. *Wild West Shows and the Image of American Indians, 1883–1933*. Albuquerque: University of New Mexico Press, 1996.

Moses, L. G., and Raymond Wilson, eds. *Indian Lives: Essays on Nineteenth and Twentieth-Century Native American Leaders*. Albuquerque: University of New Mexico Press, 1985.

Nagel, Joanne. *American Indian Ethnic Renewal: Red Power and the Resurgence of Identity and Culture*. New York: Oxford University Press, 1996.

Olson, James S., and Raymond Wilson. *Native Americans in the Twentieth Century*. Urbana: University of Illinois Press, 1984.

Parman, Donald L. *Indians and the American West in the Twentieth Century*. Bloomington: Indiana University Press, 1994.

Philip, Kenneth R., ed. *Indian Self-Rule: First Hand Accounts of Indian-White Relations from Roosevelt to Reagan*. Salt Lake City, UT: Howe Brothers, 1986.

Pratt, Richard Henry. *Battlefield and Classroom: Four Decades with the American Indian, 1867–1904*. Edited by Robert M. Utley. New Haven, CT: Yale University Press, 1964.

Rawls, James J. *Chief Red Fox Is Dead: A History of Native Americans since 1945*. Fort Worth, TX: Harcourt Brace, 1996.

Smith, Paul Chaat, and Robert Allen Warrior. *Like a Hurricane: The Indian Movement from Alcatraz to Wounded Knee*. New York: New Press, 1996.

Smith, Sherry. *Reimagining Indians: Native Americans through Anglo Eyes, 1880–1940*. New York: Oxford University Press, 2000.

Standing Bear, Luther. *My People the Sioux*. Boston: Houghton Mifflin, 1928.

Townsend, Kenneth William. *World War II and the American Indian*. Albuquerque: University of New Mexico Press, 2000.

Utter, Jack. *American Indians: Answers to Today's Questions*. Norman: University of Oklahoma Press, 2001.

Wilkins, David E. *American Indian Politics and the American Political System*. Lanham, MD: Rowman & Littlefield, 2002.

———. *American Indian Sovereignty and the Supreme Court: The Masking of Justice*. Austin: University of Texas Press, 1997.

Wilkins, David E., and K. Tsianina Lomawaima. *Uneven Ground: American Indian Sovereignty and Federal Law*. Norman: University of Oklahoma Press, 2001.

Wilson, Raymond. *Ohiyesa: Charles Eastman, Santee Sioux*. Urbana-Champaign: University of Illinois Press, 1999.

VIII. ELECTRONIC MEDIA

Bureau of Indian Affairs
http://www.doi.gov/bureau-indian-affairs.html

Circumpolar and Aboriginal North America Resources
http://natsiq.nunanet.com/~nic/WWWVL-ANA.html

Cradleboard Teaching Project
http://www.cradleboard.org/mainmenu.html

EnviroTech Online
http://www.envirotech.org/cgi-bin/freedb/uslawws.pl

Fourth World Documentation Project
http://www.halcyon.com/FWDP/fwdp.html

Index of Native American Resources on the Internet
http://hanksville.phast.umass.edu/misc/Naresources.html

Indian Country Today Online
http://www.indiancountry.com

Indian Health Service
http://www.tucson.ihs.gov

Native American Anthology: Internet Resources
http://www.wsu.edu:8080/~dee/NAINRES.HTM

Native American Documents Project
http://coyote.csusm.edu/projects/nadp

Native American Resources on the Internet
http://www.tucson.ihs.gov/PublicInfo/AmerIndian/index.asp

Native Americans and the Environment
http://conbio.rice.edu/nae

Native Web
http://www.nativeweb.org

Oliver, Phil. *The American Indian.* CD-ROM. Carmel: Guild Press of Indiana,
1998.

Smithsonian: Native American History and Culture
http://www.si.edu/resource/faq/nmai/start.htm

About the Authors

Todd Leahy (Ph.D., Oklahoma State University) is assistant professor of history at Fort Hays State University in Hays, Kansas. He teaches courses on Colonial America and the Early National period, emphasizing American Indians. Among his publications are "My First Days at the Carlisle Indian School: The Charles Gansworth Manuscript," in *Pennsylvania History*, and "Beef Instead of Bayonets: The Failure of Cattle Ranching on the Kiowa-Comanche-Apache Reservation," in *The Chronicles of Oklahoma*. His forthcoming book *They Called It Madness: The Canton Asylum for Insane Indians, 1899–1934*, has been accepted for publication by the University of Nebraska Press and will appear on the big screen as "Hiawatha Diary," produced by Still Spring Productions.

Raymond Wilson (Ph.D., University of New Mexico) is chair and professor of history at Fort Hays State University in Hays, Kansas. He teaches courses on Indian history, the American West, and U.S. military history. Among his publications are *Ohiyesa: Charles Eastman, Santee Sioux* (1983), *Native Americans in the Twentieth Century* (1984), *Indian Lives: Essays on Nineteenth- and Twentieth-Century Native American Leaders* (1985), and *Kansas Land* (1988). He is writing a book on two Indian physicians, Dr. Charles A. Eastman and Dr. Carlos Montezuma, which compares and contrasts their careers as advocates of Indian reform policies.